Going Along to Get Along

I0131249

Diplomatic Studies

Series Editor

Jan Melissen
(*Leiden University and University of Antwerp*)

VOLUME 22

The titles published in this series are listed at *brill.com/dist*

Going Along to Get Along

Diplomatic Pressure and Interstate Socialization at the United Nations

By

Naif Al-Mulla

BRILL

LEIDEN | BOSTON

Originally published in hardback in 2024.

Cover illustration: *Hallway of Flags in the United Nations Building in New York City*. Diplomatic Security Service from Washington, D.C., United States of America (2019). Public domain. Wikimedia Commons.

The Library of Congress Cataloging-in-Publication Data is available online at https://catalog.loc.gov

Typeface for the Latin, Greek, and Cyrillic scripts: "Brill." See and download: brill.com/brill-typeface.

ISSN 1872-8863
ISBN 978-90-04-75675-5 (paperback, 2025)
ISBN 978-90-04-71146-4 (hardback)
ISBN 978-90-04-71193-8 (e-book)
DOI 10.1163/9789004711938

Copyright 2025 by Naif Al-Mulla. Published by Koninklijke Brill BV, Leiden, The Netherlands.
Koninklijke Brill BV incorporates the imprints Brill, Brill Nijhoff, Brill Schöningh, Brill Fink, Brill mentis, Brill Wageningen Academic, Vandenhoeck & Ruprecht, Böhlau and V&R unipress.
Koninklijke Brill BV reserves the right to protect this publication against unauthorized use. Requests for re-use and/or translations must be addressed to Koninklijke Brill BV via brill.com or copyright.com.
info@brill.com for more information.

This book is printed on acid-free paper and produced in a sustainable manner.

For my family, with love and gratitude

∵

My analysis has led me to conclude that the United Nations is an important body worthy of our best attention. What happens there matters in some ways that are not often understood. What happens in the United Nations shapes matters in the long run rather than in the short run. What happens in the United Nations shapes attitudes in cumulative ways. The specifics are less important than the cumulative impact. The United Nations shapes agendas and focuses world attention and assumptions about what is and is not possible in what is euphemistically called the community of nations.

To the proposition that the United Nations is an important body, I would add that I believe that in the long-range ways the patterns of alliance that develop inside the United Nations and the rhetoric that is used there are influential all over the world. They influence interactions and agendas in bodies as remote as the Organization of African Unity, the Organization of American States, and ASEAN (the Association of South East Asian Nations). They influence questions on the foreign policy agendas of nations as remote as Burundi and as major as the Soviet Union.

Ambassador Jeane Kirkpatrick 2007, 97

∴

Contents

Acknowledgments

Completion of this work was made possible with the support of the Department of Politics and International Relations at the University of Cambridge.

I am incredibly grateful to Professor Jason Sharman, who supervised my doctoral research with exceptional guidance and invaluable feedback. His mentorship profoundly enriched my Ph.D. journey and played an indispensable role in bringing this project to fruition. Jason's ability to challenge me, his constant support, and his indelible contributions to my intellectual growth have been immeasurable. I cannot thank Jason enough for his dedication, insight, and the most admirable example he set.

I also appreciate Professors Aaron Rapport and Ayse Zarakol's constructive criticism of and advice on my work. Professor Mette Eilstrup-Sangiovanni offered critical comments on the earlier phases of my research. Professors Duncan Bell and Darren Weinberg were pivotal influences on my research methods. My gratitude extends to Professors Marc Weller, Pieter van Houten, and Philippe Bourbeau for supporting me as an MPhil student at the Department and encouraging me to pursue my research ideas further. During my *viva voce*, Professors Giovanni Mantilla and Margarita Petrova provided valuable feedback and constructive criticism, which I sincerely appreciate. Their insights made the exercise truly memorable, and I am humbled to have been part of it. It has been a great honor to learn from each of these esteemed scholars.

I am also thankful to my reviewers for their thoughtful feedback, which contributed to this work. I express my abundant gratitude to Brill for its fantastic support. I acknowledge Simona Casadio, Associate Editor; Irene Jager, Production Editor; Jason Prevost, Acquisitions Editor; and Professor Jan Melissen, Series Editor. My gratitude extends to David Prout for his meticulous and attentive work on the Index, making this work more navigable.

Girton College provided a stimulating academic environment at Cambridge. Special thanks go to Professor Elizabeth Kendall, Mistress of Girton College, for her strong encouragement, Professor Susan Smith, her predecessor, and Graduate Tutor and Director of Studies Professor Hilary Marlow, for fostering a vibrant and supportive academic community.

I sincerely thank the University, College, and Faculty Libraries and their dedicated staff, whose resources and assistance contributed greatly to my research. I commend the Dag Hammarskjöld Library at the United Nations for providing convenient access to a diverse array of indispensable resources that enhanced this work.

I also thank Professor Alan Tidwell from Georgetown's School of Foreign Service in Washington, D.C., for supporting me and believing in my potential at Cambridge. Alan inspired me to pursue my academic interests further.

I am deeply grateful to my family and friends for their unwavering support during my time at Cambridge. Their presence in my life has been a constant source of strength and inspiration, and I am immensely thankful for their kindness and positivity throughout my academic journey. Your love and encouragement have made a significant difference, and I sincerely appreciate you. All this is to say that completing this work was hardly a solitary journey, thanks to those ever around me.

While the support and guidance I received were essential, the views and conclusions presented in this work are solely my own.

Figures and Tables

Figures

Tables

Introduction

On December 6th, 2017, President Donald Trump announced that the U.S. would recognize Jerusalem as Israel's capital and move its embassy from Tel Aviv to Jerusalem. Many countries reacted with alarm. At the U.N. General Assembly, a coalition of states brought forth a resolution to mobilize diplomatic opposition to the move and discourage others from following suit. The U.S. response was dramatic. U.N. Permanent Representative Nikki Haley vowed to take names, suggested that the President take the vote personally, and warned that the U.S. would withhold hundreds of millions—if not billions—of dollars in foreign aid assistance to those who voiced opposition.

"All of these nations that take our money and then they vote against us at the Security Council, or they vote against us, potentially, at the Assembly, they take hundreds of millions of dollars and even billions of dollars, and then they vote against us," the President asserted (Trump in Landler 20.12.2017). "Well, we're watching those votes. Let 'em vote against us, we'll save a lot." "We're not going to be taken advantage of any longer."

In the end, the U.S. achieved partial success. Some member states, which received substantial American foreign aid that year, uncharacteristically did not show up for the vote. Others, most dependent on American foreign aid as a percentage of GDP, joined the U.S. to vote no on the resolution as they typically do on related issues. Still, many states did not take well to the Trump Administration's efforts. The vast majority—including significant recipients of American foreign aid—went ahead to support the motion to condemn the U.S. move and made it a point to reaffirm respect for the international "consensus" on Jerusalem.

"The United States will be putting a great deal of pressure on its allies, but … I think it's going to succeed only in isolating itself," Canada's former Permanent Representative Paul Heinbecker commented. "That's generally the kind of provocation that gets people to tell you to go to hell. And I suspect it will be in this case especially since the person who's taking names is a president whose reputation internationally puts the United States' standing at the lowest ebb it's ever been" (Heinbecker in Dyer 2017).

For Canada, the Trump Administration's pressure came at an awkward moment. Prime Minister Justin Trudeau's government had been seeking election to the U.N. Security Council, requiring 129 positive votes from other countries. According to Heinbecker, joining ranks with the U.S. risked alienating some 50 Muslim-majority nations, making it unlikely to gain the votes needed to win a seat at the Security Council. The previous Steven Harper government

© NAIF AL-MULLA, 2025 | DOI:10.1163/9789004711938_002

was widely believed to have blown its shot at the Council over its support for Israeli Prime Minister Benjamin Netanyahu.

This vignette begs the question: why would leading American officials—especially the Trump Administration, which later touted a brash America First foreign policy agenda at the U.N.—care about whether other states supported their stance on Jerusalem? Why did the Administration care so much to link that political support to substantial material aid to other states rather than decide to terminate the aid assistance altogether at the first sign of dissent? And why were so few states like Canada receptive to the material threats? This may seem like an isolated episode—characteristic, perhaps, of the Trump Administration's more unconventional statecraft—but it is not. Previous presidential administrations have made similar material threats on crucial foreign policy issues, only in a less public manner. "The idea that you can use foreign assistance as a lever to influence the behavior of countries is not a new one," as one State Department official put it (Landler 20.12.2017). And there is growing evidence of other powerful states having done the same.

The point is that states care deeply about how other states see them on foreign policy issues. Even the most powerful states go to great lengths to avoid the appearance of international isolation, regardless of whether that isolation makes a noticeable material difference to the eventual outcome. "The only sin at the UN is being isolated," as one former permanent representative observed (Pouliot 1 2016, 22). This concern with isolation suggests that the (interstate) social context on an issue can shape foreign policy positions and, by extension, common outcomes.

This book submits that diplomatic, social pressure exerts a decisive influence on global governance. Importantly, states can strategically mobilize diplomatic pressure to achieve foreign policy objectives. I question how states can initiate a socialization process, consolidating a political consensus on global, multilateral issues over time. By consensus, I mean an overwhelming *public*—and not necessarily private or internalized—agreement among states on a topic. In other words, I ask how a groundswell of interstate public opinion can congeal on common problems in international relations. I also theorize how certain factors can condition socialization over time. Consolidating an interstate consensus on an issue can entail a universal sense of community, where states make much about how others perceive them on that issue and adjust their foreign policy positions, accordingly, going along to get along.

My book takes issue with that social notion of community and demonstrates its powerful implications for global governance. I propose a novel social constructivist argument on interstate socialization using the United Nations—especially the General Assembly—as the focal point for that socialization.

I weigh my argument in three case studies: racial discrimination in South Africa from 1946 to 1961, the United States embargo on Cuba from 1991 to 2016, and the ban on nuclear weapons from 1946 to 1961.

Why should we care about global, multilateral diplomacy? Much of international politics converge around global, multilateral focal points—the most central of which are the U.N.'s intergovernmental bodies like the General Assembly and Security Council. For better or worse, these bodies are often how governments mobilize to govern critical common challenges, ranging from human rights and disarmament questions to general norms of interstate relations and the environment. The significance of these proceedings lies in the lengths to which states contend over the issues and attempt to shift outcomes to their advantage. The fact that the contestation exists is more important than whether there is anything inherently "right" or "wrong" about what states address or how they end up addressing them.

1   The Argument and Contribution

How can states initiate a socialization process that crystalizes a political consensus on global, multilateral issues over time? What can condition the success or failure of that socialization? I present a novel constructivist argument on socialization in international relations. Aside from my original empirical focus, which addresses crucial diplomatic—and not necessarily legal—outcomes since World War Two, I do so by drawing into focus the "multi-partisan" *social* construction of global, multilateral diplomacy at the U.N. I contemplate how interstate coalitions can mobilize diplomatic (social) pressure as part of a persistent campaign to gain an audience's acceptance of a cause.

My argument is that a "core" coalition of states can create a spotlight of diplomatic pressure that draws into focus an issue. That diplomatic pressure sets in motion a process of collective legitimization, which assumes a life of its own and creates common expectations that make support for a particular position legitimate. Over time, these expectations can incline other states—particularly those opposing or otherwise "on the fence"—towards joining in on a common position, leading to a convergence in expectations. Interstate socialization occurs because public—though not necessarily private—viewpoints converge around a more legitimate, socially sustainable stance on the issue. The outcome reflects a social compromise in which socialization subjects eschew *public* association with the illegitimate or socially unsustainable position. Socialization subjects do not necessarily take to heart and change their private views.

I also submit that an agent's perceived integrity on an issue can make socialization efforts more (or less) influential. Socialization efforts are more likely to fail when proponents lack that integrity—and are therefore seen as hypocritical—because the target states do not see a political downside to maintaining the status quo. On the other hand, socialization efforts are more likely to succeed when proponents enjoy a sense of integrity on an issue— and are therefore seen to be trustworthy advocates of the cause—because the target audience perceives a credible political cost to maintaining the status quo. By integrity, I mean a social constructivist (and not a rationalist) take on reputation, which relates to how much or little a potential socialization subject regards a socialization agent as a trustworthy advocate of a cause.

This highly generalizable theoretical refinement is critical to understanding the conditions under which socialization efforts can work (or fail to work) in international relations. Social constructivists now have a wealth of theoretical knowledge on how states can respond to diplomatic (social) pressure. Yet we still lack theoretical insight—save for passing reference to this or that contributor to socialization—on how states can deploy that pressure effectively or ineffectively. We need more insight into how certain theoretical conditioning factors can interact with existing social constructivist theory to produce socialization. My book manuscript provides a model.

To weigh the theoretical model, my book considers three issue areas as case studies: racial discrimination in South Africa from 1946 to 1961, the United States embargo on Cuba from 1991 to 2016, and the ban on nuclear weapons from 1946 to 1961. The first two case studies demonstrate empirical support for my theoretical argument, provided the contribution of certain empirical factors specific to the case studies. These two case study chapters advance my theoretical discussion about examples of states moved by the core coalitions' diplomatic efforts.

The third case study considers the ban on nuclear weapons as an area where socialization does *not* occur. The point of studying a nonpositive case study is to add nuance to my theoretical argument and empirical tests by considering the conditions under which socialization will and will not occur.

I select these three issue areas as case studies for methodological and theoretical reasons. Methodologically, the three cases meet five necessary scope conditions, which impose qualitative requirements for the type of issue areas that this book can address. The first condition is that we must examine issues with a consistent recurring character. This condition addresses an empirical limitation: issues that do not come up for consideration repeatedly lack periodic updates on state positions that some resolutions provide. These recurring issues or resolutions need not necessarily extend across a fixed period. Nor do they need to encompass subject areas considered under the same resolution title verbatim or even as points of discussion inside the United Nations context. This condition only ensures a constant record of states' positions on the same issues over time. The criteria, therefore, addresses a theoretical assumption: periodic evidence of state positions on similar, if not identical, issues is essential to weigh a perspective on interstate socialization.

The second scope condition is that a clear and concise issue must be apparent within the applicable resolutions. This condition addresses the need to evaluate how state positions converge (or fail to converge) on an issue over time, which requires a constant issue area that serves as a focal point for interstate consideration and, in turn, helps concentrate on and perhaps even accentuate the surrounding interaction. We can then understand how this interaction can affect states' subsequent positions on a particular issue. To some extent, this condition also controls for alterations in a focal point of discussion that may or may not enter the conversation among states. This second condition recognizes the importance of the precise wording of a resolution that states may or may not respond to. However, it ensures that the resolution's language does not undergo significant changes such that its substantive point assumes a new direction. This allows peripheral variance in language to factor into (or fail to factor into) the conversation, though not to the extent that it changes the focal point of proceedings. The second scope condition, therefore, relates to a resolution's specific focus, which must address a consistent point throughout its consideration with some underlying consistency.

The remaining three scope conditions are universal state participation, decision-making by majority vote, and publicity. I refer to Giovanni Mantilla for these three conditions, which can act as "enablers and sharpeners" for diplomatic pressure (Mantilla 2018, 329). See this book's Appendix for further commentary.

Theoretically, the two positive case studies present relatively "hard" cases for social constructivists but should have been relatively "easy" cases for theoretical approaches emphasizing material power. The former two positive studies address interstate socialization proceeding against the wishes of the more materially capable states or states closely aligned with them. In the first case, a core coalition of states helped build an almost unanimous consensus against apartheid from 1946 to 1961 despite staunch opposition from the more materially capable states, including each of the world's former colonial powers. Similarly, in the second case study, a core coalition of states helped build an almost unanimous consensus against the Cuba embargo from 1991 to 2016

despite staunch opposition from the United States, which made explicit material threats toward third states to refrain from supporting a common position
against the embargo. This is to say that both positive case studies showcase
the limits of a materialist focus on diplomacy at the United Nations, as we
shall see.

CHAPTER 1

Global, Multilateral Diplomacy at the United Nations

> The prevailing image portrays the United Nations as an arena mirroring the exogenous forces of international politics. This image is wrong only in the sense that it is incomplete. There is much more to be learned about the U.N.'s role in the world community, but significant progress seems unlikely until we recognize the implications of narrowly framed research questions and redefine our conceptual vantage points accordingly
>
> DIXON 1981, 59

∴

0   Chapter Outline

This chapter takes stock of what international relations scholars have said about the empirical patterns of interaction that characterize diplomacy at the General Assembly. The main empirical research focus has been on interstate bloc politics: political or otherwise allegiance formations that take shape across issue areas. Much of the empirical literature assumes that certain allegiance formations are the main feature of diplomacy in a global, multilateral context. To advance this critique, I first encapsulate what I mean by bloc politics at the United Nations. Next, I provide an overview of how this empirical research emphasis finds expression in the literature across its historical trajectory. That trajectory corresponds, although is not limited to three main clusters, which draw attention to the following interstate bloc formations: (i) East versus West, (ii) North versus South, and (iii) the United States versus the rest of the world. A fourth empirical research cluster relates to a more specific focus on the cohesion of member states of certain intergovernmental organizations. These clusters are my way of identifying themes in the literature and are not absolute generalizations.

I finally draw out implications from the literature for this book. Empirical research focusing on interstate bloc politics is wrong because it is incomplete

© NAIF AL-MULLA, 2025 | DOI:10.1163/9789004711938_003

(Dixon 1981). Despite its fecundity, the prevailing research focus in the field comes at the expense of an overall perspective on interstate socialization— which can follow from diplomatic pressure that transcends bloc politics. Hence, states can also see themselves as belonging to a more universal diplomatic community that shapes how they relate to each other and joint issues. This is important because states often make much about how the diplomatic community sees them on the issues—especially when isolated—and adjust their foreign policy positions, accordingly, often going along to get along.

1   Bloc Politics in a Nutshell

Much of what has been said about the empirical patterns of interaction that characterize diplomacy at the General Assembly has been drawn toward accounts of bloc politics. The main idea is that political and/or otherwise alliance formations take shape among states to various degrees, often regardless of the issue area. Hence, there has been substantial descriptive analysis of notions of "camps," "caucuses," "cleavages," "clubs," and the like (e.g. Alker 1964; Ball 1951; Bueno de Mesquita 1975). Thomas Hovet's *Bloc Voting at the United Nations* is among the earliest and most extensive accounts and encapsulates the broad research focus. For Hovet, bloc politics predominate intestate politics at the General Assembly (Hovet 1960, 29). He defines a "bloc" as a "group of states, which meets regularly in caucus ... and the members of which are bound by the caucus decision" (Hovet 1960, 30). Hovet also distinguishes a bloc from regional groups, interest groups, and caucusing groups—each of which relates to the cohesiveness or formal nature of a particular political or otherwise allegiance formation (Hovet 1960, 29–46). The work proceeds to make an empirical case for various such formations and suggests how they form. For Hovet, for example, a state's membership in a particular bloc can develop out of necessity. It provides "an opportunity to create a combined voting power which can be a critical factor in negotiating with other groups" (Hovet 1960, 114). States thereby keep in step with a particular alliance formation to hedge against or counteract others.

2   Themes

The first empirical theme centers around a concern for an East vs. West interstate pattern of bloc politics (e.g. Alker 1964; Gareau 1970; Rai 1972). Some scholars, among other things, draw attention to forming "Soviet" and

"Western" blocs that counteract each other across issue areas. Hayward Alker's *Dimensions of Conflict in the General Assembly* is an early example. The work makes the case that East-West cleavages "dominate most issues before the United Nations, with the exception of budgetary concerns" (Alker 1964, 647). It avers that the cleavage constitutes some sixty-four percent of all "explainable" interstate alignments and underscores how it takes shape across various issues (Alker 1964, 647; 657; 650). The work also goes on to suggest a "two-way process of interdependence," whereby specific trade, foreign aid, and military relationships—that is, with either the United States or the Soviet Union—serve as a bellwether of where states stand in relation to the two blocs (Alker 1964, 654–655). Alker contends, for example, that Soviet foreign aid was at the time "strongly related to East-West voting alignments in the United Nations" (Alker 1964, 656). And the author points to "buying votes" and "rewarding friendship" as potential reasons for the outcome (Alker 1964, 655). Hence, the work can speak to one central empirical research cluster that draws attention to an interstate, East-West bloc formation. A comparable, more recent variation of this empirical focus comes from Martin Mosler and Niklas Potrafake, who examine the "voting behavior of Western-allied countries in line with the United States over the period 1949 until 2019" (Mosler and Potrafake 2020, 481).

Another central research cluster comes from an empirical emphasis on a North-South, developing-developed world interstate cleavage at the General Assembly. This cluster suggests interstate, bloc politics are not necessarily limited to a Cold War context. Instead, some scholars point to the growing collective strength of "Third World" states—especially in throughout decolonization—as pushing the development of new alliance formations (e.g. Iida 1988; Kim and Russett 1996; Seabra and Sanches 2018). As Soo Yeon Kim and Bruce Russett write, "the East-West division no longer prevails in General Assembly deliberations; a North-South cleavage has superseded cold war alignments, giving rise to state preferences defined along developmental lines" (Kim and Russett 1996, 629). The idea is that this alignment, as Pedro Seabra and Rodrigues Sanches write, is "deeply rooted in a strong sense of common solidarity over global governance, economic and development issues ... often against Northern-led conceptualizations of the international order" (Seabra and Sanches 2018, 586).

Keisuke Iida's *Third World Solidarity: The Group of 77 in the UN General Assembly* exemplifies this research focus. In a more explicit neorealist tradition, that work emphasizes the distribution of material capabilities among units as a "binding constraint on the foreign policy of nation-states" (Iida 1988, 379). That material constraint, for Keisuke Iida, leads to the following perspective:

> Nation-states, which are most concerned with self-preservation, are
> expected to ally with the weaker side to prevent the stronger side from
> dominating them. While it is slightly different from alliance behavior
> because it is not concerned with self-preservation, a similar logic may be
> extended to solidarity. Economically weak states are threatened by strong
> states' economic domination. They try to cooperate with other weak
> states to protect themselves from domination. Thus, the weaker they are,
> the more united they will be.
>
> IIDA 1988, 379

Iida makes two more specific points. On one hand, "when Third World states
feel that they are losing power, they step up their efforts to coordinate their
policy positions so that they will increase their bargaining power" (Iida 1988,
394). On the other hand, "when their power is growing, they have less need for
presenting a unified front" (Iida 1988, 394). In whichever case, Keisuke Iida's
work speaks to the broader research emphasis on bloc politics. States keep
rank or maintain "solidarity" with a particular alliance formation to hedge
against or, by some measure, counteract others, culminating with an empirical
emphasis on a North-South, developing-developed world interstate cleavage.

A third empirical research cluster suggests a cleavage involving the United
States and the rest of the world. The empirical focus is on the reconfiguration
of material power relations in international relations following the Cold War,
particularly in the context of resistance to the United States (e.g. Datta 2009;
Schaefer and Kim 2013a; 2013b; 2018; Voeten 2004). As Monti Datta suggests,
the basic idea is to explore "the impact of anti-Americanism within the United
Nations, the General Assembly of which serves as the collective voice of its
nearly 200 member-states" (Datta 2009, 4). "States seek to balance against
the unipolar might of the United States—not in the traditional sense of using
military buildups, war-fighting alliances, or transfers to military opponents—
but through 'soft balancing', in which states leverage international institutions, economic statecraft, and diplomatic arrangements to counterbalance
U.S. hegemony" (Datta 2009, 5).

Erik Voeten's *Resisting the Lonely Superpower: Responses of States in the
United Nations to U.S. Dominance* is a noteworthy example. That work underscores a "unilateralist turn" in American foreign policy, with the United States
opposing multilateral engagement with the rest of the world altogether. It
also highlights what appears to be an interstate preference gap continuum,
with the United States on one end and the rest of the world on the other. The
work charges that "widespread foreign backing for the U.S. position on issues
of global concern has become somewhat of a rarity over the course of the

post-Cold War period" (Voeten 2004, 729). "The preference gap between the United States and the rest of the world widened considerably and at a constant rate between 1991 and 2001" (Voeten 2004, 747). Voeten adds,

> The increase in the gap is not a phenomenon limited to states from particular parts of the world, and there is not much evidence that some states have chosen to bandwagon with the United States. It appears that U.S. hegemony has elicited almost universal resistance.
>
> VOETEN 2004, 747

Voeten largely attributes this preference gap to "structural phenomena," less affected by temporal variations in American foreign policy (Voeten 2004, 747). The point is that this work is similar to those referenced above in that it emphasizes the existence of a bloc-like cleavage between states, which takes shape across issue areas.

The previous paragraphs suggest three empirical research clusters for international relations literature on the General Assembly. What remains is a final cluster that has to do with a more specific empirical focus on the alignment of other blocs or groups of states. This research cluster includes a focus on the cohesion of member states of certain intergovernmental organizations such as BRICS (e.g. Dijkhuizen and Onderco 2019; Ferdinand 2014a; Hooijmaaijers and Keukeleire 2014), the European Union (e.g. Burmester and Jankowski 2014a; 2018; Luif 2003; Jin and Hosli 2013) and ASEAN (Burmester and Jankowski 2014b; Ferdinand 2014b). One key focus is how member states of intergovernmental organizations like these "speak with one voice" at the General Assembly. An example is Bas Hooijmaaijers and Stephan Keukeleire's work, which analyzes the "degree of voting cohesion among the BRICS in the General Assembly in general and in its various main committees in the period 2006–2014" (Hooijmaaijers and Keukeleire 2016, 389). The BRICS, the authors suggest, "found each other in their commitment to counter, according to them, the "unjust" Western-dominated multilateral world in which they are in general underrepresented" (Hooijmaaijers and Keukeleire 2016, 393).

Karen Smith and Katie Laatikainen's recent work offers a more comprehensive study of "group politics" in the UN system. The study investigates political groups that identify as such, including formal regional or more widely-based organizations, less formal groups, and the various "Friends of" initiatives in the UN setting (Smith and Laatikainen 2020, 4). Notably, Smith and Laatikainen distance themselves from research on bloc politics, "which is too redolent of Cold War politics and implies that groups are quite rigid in terms of membership, discipline and positions" (Smith and Laatikainen 2020, 5). "Group discipline varies widely, the composition of groups can be quite fluid, and groups positions can be open to change through negotiation" (Smith and Laatikainen 2020, 5). The work goes on to investigate the influence that group dynamics can have on multilateral politics at the UN.

3   A Call for More Perspective

We have now seen that much of what has been said about global, multilateral diplomacy has been drawn toward accounts of bloc or group politics. The main idea has been that political and otherwise allegiance formations take shape among states to various degrees, often regardless of the issue area in question. This empirical research focuses on interstate bloc politics is incomplete. It emphasizes bloc formations as the main feature of diplomacy in a global, multilateral context at the expense of an overall perspective on socialization. Prevailing research thus overlooks the potential for interstate socialization to occur following diplomatic pressure that transcends the time's political or otherwise bloc formations. We are left not expecting such socialization to occur, let alone shape how states relate to the issues. This shortcoming is especially puzzling when common ground expands among states on those issues over time. Conflicts of interest—such as those defined by political or otherwise allegiance formations—may prove inherent to states arriving at that common ground. Nevertheless, focusing on those cleavages overlooks the extent to which exogenous social effects can operate and exert overall pressure upon states as members of a more universal international community.

International relations research on global, multilateral diplomacy at the United Nations needs to pay attention to how states can find common causes of the issues in a manner that cuts across the bloc or group formations one may associate them with. This can entail a broader sense of diplomatic community, influencing how states relate to each other and position themselves on common issues. States often make much about how the diplomatic community sees them on the issues—especially when isolated—and change foreign policy positions, accordingly, often going along to get along. Moreover, states go to great lengths to contend with each other to win over the community's support for specific issues in a manner that cuts across bloc politics.

This latter point on interstate socialization has some immediate traction in the literature on the General Assembly. For example, Steven Holloway and Rodney Tomlinson emphasize that the end of the Cold War—and the subsequent emergence of the new world order—has not only been about resisting the lonely superpower. The two authors draw attention to a marked turning point in interstate relations, whereby certain bloc formations unraveled to make way for what some referred to as an overarching "spirit of accommodation" (Holloway and Tomlinson 1995, 252). That spirit of accommodation entails a "positive transformation ... in substituting a policy of cooperation for that of confrontation"; it amounted to newfound concerns for "wide consensus," "shared common interests," "family of nations," and the like (A/46/PV.1). The two authors then demonstrate the extent to which some concern for that spirit of accommodation finds expression across issue areas. Holloway and Tomlinson thus entertain the possibility of interstate socialization at the General Assembly. Other international relations scholars seem to have, in some part, moved in that direction. David Bearce and Stacy Bondanella have spoken to this perspective, emphasizing overall interstate "interest convergence" in connection with the work of international organizations more broadly (Bearce and Bondanella 2007). Diana Panke and Samuel Brazys have more recently also, in some part, touched upon it via a notion of international "pull" factors, which in their most applicable sense refer to efforts to avoid interstate isolation (Panke 2014; Panke and Brazys 2017a).

Much of the literature above is incomplete because of its general emphasis on quantitative methods, which compartmentalizes how states see common issues into more water-tight "yes," "no," and "abstain" vote categories. This focus is unfortunate since some then use these categories to definitively mark where member states stand in relation to each other on those issues. However, inferences drawn from those methods have limited value. They oversimplify how states relate to the issues by overlooking how delegations interpret and express their positions, including in direct conversations with other delegations. Fastidious attention to and thorough analysis of these exchanges reveals that more is at stake, including intersubjective expectations that start with the common choice to converge around the given focal point of discussion in the first place. Suppose this common "convergence" is any indication. Intersubjective expectations would then be central to how states see the issues, even for those states that seem to oppose each other, as the juxtaposition of "yes" and "no" votes would indicate. As such, those latter states would share more in common than categorical distinctions allow, inviting commentary on the social construction of interstate relations. In short, the positions states express in conversation are more meaningful than—and can extend well beyond the confines of—select vote categories at the United Nations.

CHAPTER 2

Diplomatic Pressure in Global, Multilateral Diplomacy

> The vigorous effort that states customarily make to prevent the passage of formal denunciations of their positions or policies indicates that they have respect for the significance, if not for the validity, of adverse judgments by international organs. While states may act in violation of General Assembly resolutions, they evidently prefer not to do so, or to appear not to do so, on the ground that collective approbation is an important asset and collective disapprobation a significant liability in international relations. ... This is simply to say that statesmen [stateswomen, and statespersons] take collective legitimacy seriously as a factor in international politics; the opinions and attitudes of other states, manifested through the parliamentary mechanism of the United Nations, must be taken into account in the conduct of foreign policy.
>
> CLAUDE 1966, 374–375

∵

0   Chapter Outline

We have been interested in how states can initiate a socialization process that builds a consensus on an issue over time. This book draws upon proceedings at the United Nations—especially the General Assembly—as the locus for that interstate socialization in a global, multilateral context. I now posit a novel social constructivist argument for how a core coalition of states can build a consensus on a select issue at the United Nations. By consensus, I mean an overwhelming public—and not necessarily private or internalized—level of agreement on an issue. This notion of consensus closely tracks but is distinct from procedural notions of consensus in diplomacy that require unanimity (Mantilla 15.10.2021, 2).

I bring to bear a plethora of social constructivist scholarship—such as Ian Hurd's argument on the strategic manipulation of the norms of liberal

© NAIF AL-MULLA, 2025 | DOI:10.1163/9789004711938_004

internationalism—to advance and add theoretical granularity to the argument. Although this book is less concerned with immersing the reader in existing scholarship and will be less comprehensive in its references to relevant literature, it is an attempt to encourage the reader to think about how governments can exploit diplomacy to achieve foreign policy objectives.

I argue that a core coalition of states can create a spotlight of diplomatic pressure that draws into focus an issue. That diplomatic pressure sets in motion a process of collective legitimization, which assumes a life of its own and creates common expectations that make support for a particular position "legitimate." Over time, these expectations can incline other states—particularly those opposing or otherwise "on the fence"—towards joining in on a common position, leading to a convergence in expectations. Interstate socialization occurs because public—and not necessarily private—viewpoints converge around a common, more legitimate, or "socially sustainable" stance on the issue.

The chapter has five main components, which unpack the book's overall argument. The first component conceptualizes my focus on a "core" interstate coalition as agents of socialization. Such coalitions exist by a shared initial extent of support for a position on an issue. The second component comments on the proactive diplomatic efforts a core coalition of states can undertake to mobilize interstate support for a cause. The main idea is that core states can do so by strategically manipulating normative rhetoric, which can bring diplomatic pressure to bear on a target audience. The third component considers how these diplomatic efforts can initiate socialization. I assert that mobilizing diplomatic pressure gives rise to a process of collective legitimization, which can, in turn, incline a target interstate audience towards support for a cause.

The chapter then discusses "conditioning factors," which combine with my theoretical argument to contribute to interstate socialization (Tocci 2008a; 2008b; 6.11.2018). I posit that socialization efforts can be more successful when a state agent enjoys a sense of integrity on the issue. By contrast, socialization efforts are less influential when the target audience sees the socialization agents as hypocritical.

I finally consider limitations and caveats to my theoretical argument. These relate to the extent to which a process of collective legitimization captures what happens in the "real world," and how strong an influence it can wield in international relations.

1   The Core Coalition

My focus on a core coalition is a theoretical construct that does not necessarily require a coalition's official formation. I take core coalitions to exist by
a shared, initial extent of support for a stance on an issue. This is to say that
a core interstate coalition takes shape by its initial convergence around support for a cause. This initial support can lead those states to fashion themselves as proactive representatives of the cause and conjure up expectations
that, at some level, appeal to those of the interstate community at large. A core
coalition assumes this totemic role *ipso facto*, not necessarily thanks to some
broader, explicit endorsement of their moral leadership on the issue. What
matters is that the coalition nevertheless projects the views as such. This can
put the coalition—particularly its more fired-up "spokespersons"—in a position to mobilize diplomatic pressure to support the position.

Nicole Deitelhoff and Linda Wallbott make a similar point. Concerning the
Alliance of Small Island States in climate negotiations, for example, the two
emphasize that:

> delegates of AOSIS regarded themselves not just as partners or negotiat-
> ing bodies, but also as the 'moral voice' and 'the moral authority in nego-
> tiations' in the negotiations. The AOSIS presented itself as an advocate
> of global public goods which was trying to push things forward in the
> long-term interests of the developed countries, future generations, and
> the 'fate of the world'.
>
> DEITELHOFF AND WALLBOTT 2012, 358

For further reference, numerous social constructivist scholars have emphasized
the significance of coalitions—namely, among like-minded states as well as
non-governmental organizations—in socialization processes (e.g. Deitelhoff
2009, 58; Price 1998, 623–627; Rosert 2019, 1109–1110). More recently, Giovanni
Mantilla has emphasized the "protagonism" of interstate coalitions in developing specific rules of international humanitarian law (Mantilla 2018; 2019; 2020a;
2020b). Karen Smith and Katie Laatikainen focus on interstate "groups": states
that (formally or informally) self-identify as members of formal or less formal
political groups and not necessarily coalitions of states that share in support of
a particular cause—and can be socially influential—regardless of those asso-
ciations (Smith and Laatikainen 2020). Ian Hurd focuses on the influence of a
single state, a departure from the emphasis on interstate coalitions as agents of
socialization (Hurd 2005; 2008).

The formation of a core coalition is *not* necessarily contingent upon a like-minded, wholehearted commitment to upholding a norm as some social constructivist scholars suggest (e.g. Finnemore and Sikkink 1998, 896; Price 1998, 615; Rosert 2019, 1108–1110). From a social constructivist perspective, there are numerous theoretical reasons why the coalition can consist of some states and not others. One reason can relate to certain status and leadership aspirations (Mantilla 2020a; 2020b; Petrova 2016; 2019). Giovanni Mantilla, for example, comments that post-war international diplomacy led by states from the developing world "had clear and competitive status-seeking goals pursued through skillful coalition-making and vociferous public rhetoric" (Mantilla 2020b, 21). "Decolonization ... was an international social and diplomatic struggle, as much as a set of 'domestic' wars of self-determination" (Mantilla 2020a, 23).

The most relevant reason for a core coalition's formation relates to pre-existing interstate relationships at a particular historical juncture. For example, a sense of "friendship" can make some states more supportive (or sympathetic) towards each other, where at least one raises a public complaint about a foreign policy issue. This is intuitive: two or more "friends" are more likely to understand—and thereby support—each other's point of view than two or more "enemies." In other words, two or more friends seem likelier to backstop each other in crisis than two or more rivals or enemies. This point addresses Alexander Wendt's social theory of international politics, which makes a distinction between "enemies," "rivals," and "friends" as critical determinants for how states interact with each other at particular points in time (Wendt 1992, 396–397; 1999, 246–308). For Wendt, these political cultures are not necessarily uniform across the interstate system; multiple interstate role relationships can exist simultaneously such that "states act differently toward enemies than they do toward friends" (Wendt 1992, 397). What political cultures prevail between states can, in the first place, shape how they relate to the issues, especially if those issues are specific to—or even "attack"—a specific state. This implies a socio-strategic element to the composition of a core coalition, which can but may not necessarily form based on a response to the "normatively undesirable condition" *per se* that some scholars contemplate (Rosert 2019, 1108).

A brief empirical example helps demonstrate the point. Several years ago, the United Kingdom brought a complaint to the United Nations about the use of chemical weapons in Salisbury (s/pv.8203; s/2018/218; s/pv.8224). According to the UK Government, the move was part of an attempt to organize a response from the international community (UK Government, 13.3.2018; 26.3.2018). The United Kingdom castigated the attack, investigated the incident, and suggested that Russia was "highly likely" to have been responsible (s/2018/218, 2). The initial extent of support for that position came from some twenty other states, including those that view the United Kingdom as part of an airtight "friendship" (Dewan, Veselinovic, and Jordan 2018). They include the United States, which shared this observation with the Security Council:

> We are here today to discuss the use of a chemical weapon by one Council member on the territory of another Council member. Let me make one thing clear from the very beginning—the United States stands in absolute solidarity with Great Britain … No two nations enjoy a stronger bond than that between the United States and the United Kingdom. Ours is truly a special relationship. When our friends in Great Britain face a challenge, the United States will always be there for them.
>
> s/PV.8203, 4

Australia, Canada, Germany, and France shared similar sentiments (s/PV.8203; s/PV.8224; Nair and Heffer 2018). By contrast, other states—those that did not see themselves as part of such a friendship—took a more reticent position on the United Kingdom's complaint. They include China, which was terse in its call for a "comprehensive, objective and impartial investigation based on the facts and in accordance with the relevant rules" (s/PV.8203, 7–8). It also included the likes of Bolivia, Kazakhstan, and Iran.

This is to say that how states view each other—whether as friends, enemies, rivals, or otherwise—can also help "construct" how they view specific issues in the first instance. In the present example, the United Kingdom's initial, most enthusiastic supporters were those it calls "friends." They constitute a core coalition by their initial, common position to bring the Russian Federation to book for the attack in Salisbury.

2   The Core Coalition and Rhetorical Action

My argument speaks to Thomas Risse's point about "rhetorical action," which is distinct from mutual socialization (Risse 2000, 9–10). The idea is that state agents do *not* engage in "truth-seeking with the aim of reaching a mutual understanding based on a reasoned consensus" (Risse 2000, 1–2). Agents are largely inflexible and unprepared to change their positions. They do not necessarily view each other as equals and strategically manipulate normative rhetoric to win over a broader audience to support a cause (Risse 2000, 9–10). Another notable rendition of the concept comes from Frank Schimmelfennig, who explicitly refers to rhetorical action as "the strategic use of norm-based arguments" to back up selfish goals and delegitimize opponents (Schimmelfennig 2001, 48).

Similarly, Margarita Petrova presents a case for "strategic arguing" (Petrova 2016). A more recent albeit implicit presentation of the concept comes from Giovanni Mantilla's analysis of "frontal diplomatic struggle," which involves "clear and competitive status-seeking goals pursued through skillful coalition-making and vociferous public rhetoric" (Mantilla 2020a, 4, 21). The underlying theoretical observation is that political actors can "rarely take tangible steps or advance policy positions without justifying those stances and behavior—in short, without framing":

> Politics may entail coercion or distribution, but at the same time it involves the struggle over meanings. Meanings, however, cannot be imposed unilaterally or through the exercise of material power alone. They are, by their very nature, intersubjective (Laffey and Weldes, 1997), and the effort to forge shared meanings implicates some audience in the process.
>
> KREBS AND JACKSON 2007, 45

How can socialization agents engage in rhetorical action that can cumulatively build a consensus on an issue over time? I point to three basic steps from the previous chapter's literature review. The first step relates to the practical measures agents can take to "create" an issue. These measures entail that state agents expose an undesirable condition to the public to leverage its influence on the target audience (e.g. Finnemore and Sikkink 1998, 897; Schimmelfennig 2001, 64; Rosert 2019, 1108–1109). At the United Nations, issue creation typically entails "information politics" following an agent's opposition to the status quo (Rosert 2019, 1108–1109). Common strategies include publicly expressing a complaint informally via remarks to the media and formally via intervention in a political body. Information politics can also entail that a member state circulates a note verbale, requests that a topic be included in the agenda of a regular meeting session, presents a draft resolution for other delegations to consider, cosponsor, and eventually take action on. These efforts can structure the conversation that ensues around the agent's viewpoint and away from their opponent's (Petrova 2016, 389). Information politics requires that socialization agents specify, categorize, and emotionalize an issue to be effective (Rosert 2019, 1108–1109). Specifying an issue means "defining what the current and the desired situations are and pointing out the discrepancy between the two," as well as "identifying the scope and the causes of the problem and those actors responsible for developing and implementing the solutions" (Rosert 2019,

1109). Categorizing means "sorting the problem into a broader category of problems" (Rosert 2019, 1109). My empirical case study chapters allude to these two points on information politics by way of introduction.

Emotionalizing an issue means "pointing out the features of a problem that are expected to invoke the audience's feelings, for example, threats to moral values or bodily harm" (Rosert 2019, 1109). It more broadly speaks to the literature on normative "framing," "grafting," and "nesting" (e.g. Price 1998; Finnemore and Sikkink 1998; Deitelhoff 2009), as well as to literature on the strategic manipulation of international norms (e.g. Schimmelfennig 2001; 2003; Hurd 2005; 2008; Petrova 2016). This strategy is central to my theoretical argument. It relates to the second step in a proactive socialization effort: "rhetorical action," which entails that an agent manipulates the "norms of liberal internationalism" to pressure an audience into supporting a cause (Hurd 2005; 2008). Socialization agents do *not* have the unlimited latitude to "fabricate" rhetoric. The general idea is that socialization agents must *appear* to exclude public appeals to private interests to be effective (Elster 2015, 403). Jon Elster writes,

> In a public debate, a speaker who said, "We should do this because it is good for me" would not persuade anyone, and would, moreover, be subject to informal sanctions and ostracism that would make her less effective in the future. Even those who are motivated solely by interest are constrained by the public setting to present their policy proposals as motivated by more impartial values.
>
> ELSTER 2015, 403–404

Similarly, socialization agents must also draw upon their environment's "normative repertoires" to be effective (Schimmelfennig 2003, 196). Ronald Krebs and Patrick Jackson observe,

> ... speakers may not say just anything they would like in the public arena: rhetoric is not infinitely elastic but is structured ... they are *not* free to deploy utterly alien formulations in the course of contestation: such arguments would fall, almost literally, on deaf ears. The available space for rhetorical contestation is, therefore, locally bounded, and the parties to a contentious episode cannot introduce entirely novel arguments. They must configure their appeals utilizing rhetorical tools drawn from a chest that is, in the short term, effectively fixed (Swidler, 1986).
>
> KREBS AND JACKSON 2007, 45

At the United Nations, one specific way a coalition of states can engage in rhetorical action is via appeals to some "stamp of political approval or disapproval" concerning a cause (Claude 1966, 372). Agents can do this by situating an issue within some previously agreed upon interstate normative frameworks, such as the norms present in the Charter and the more universal propositions contained within resolutions of various political bodies at the United Nations. The aim is not to push the wholesale development of a new international norm but rather to claim ownership over "normative terrain," interjecting the cause within normative parameters such that the two become seen as the same (Price 1998, 629). This can make the cause seem less strident (or "outrageous") than it would otherwise be, and thereby, more possible that the target audience countenance the issue in comparable normative terms (Price 1998, 629; Deitelhoff 2009, 44–45). Importantly, manipulating a normative frame can introduce a more palpable sense of legitimacy into the conversation because it strikes a chord with what other states have recognized as such. This projection of legitimacy is critical since third states cannot "see" it save through "an assessment of whether the audience acknowledges it" (Finnemore 2009, 61–62; Hurd 2008, 31). If successful, rhetorical manipulation can thus tap into the diplomatic pressure that sustains these normative frameworks.

Socialization agents can amplify this diplomatic pressure by "cuing." This is the third step in my argument. Rodney Goodman and Derek Jinks refer to cuing as a strategy that involves an agent prompting a target audience to "think harder" about the merits of a counter-attitudinal message (Goodman and Jinks 2013, 25). It is based on the assumption that introducing new information can prompt subjects to examine, defend, and even change their beliefs (Johnston 2001, 496; Goodman and Jinks 2013, 25). Goodman and Jinks adduce numerous studies to substantiate the claim. However, cuing can have normative as well as socio-strategic connotations. A socialization agent can also present new "information" to make the status quo appear increasingly at odds with common notions of legitimacy. Hence, continuous informational cues can give the impression that more and more is at stake within the interstate social context of the time. Ian Hurd suggests a similar idea: Libya trumpeted new violations of the sanctions regime as evidence that the American and British position was increasingly "out of step with the [international] community" (Hurd 2005, 513; 2008, 154). Libya also made it a point to publicize its efforts as a "good international citizen" to substantiate it further (Hurd 2005, 512; Hurd 2008, 153). At each indication, Libya's rhetorical purpose was to make it seem as though it was increasingly supported by and in support of the "'mainstream' of international opinion" (Hurd 2005, 512; Hurd 2008, 153). Presenting these rhetorical "cues" continuously questioned the status quo and prompted the target audience to consider its interstate social ramifications.

As Hurd suggests, it is important to emphasize that rhetorical action can be mendacious but influential (Hurd 2005, 499). Similarly, "it does not matter whether actors believe what they say, whether they are motivated by crass material interests or sincere commitment" as Ronald Krebs and Patrick Jackson argue (Krebs and Jackson 2007, 42). What matters is how the target audience responds to—or even tolerates—specific normative claims and the extent to which "mere rhetoric" can have the power to move governments into acceptance of otherwise undesirable foreign policy positions (Hurd 2008, 164). Thus, rhetoric can affect "political outcomes even when all actors are cynical operators with little interest in genuine deliberation" (Krebs and Jackson 2007, 42).

3   The Core Coalition and Interstate Socialization

So far, we have conceptualized the point about a core coalition of states as agents of socialization. I then suggested practical measures socialization agents can take to "create" an issue and the normative rhetoric they can manipulate to eke out more interstate support for the cause. In this subsection, I assert that these diplomatic efforts can exert diplomatic, social pressure upon the target interstate audience. This diplomatic pressure gives rise to a process of collective legitimization, which can, in turn, incline a target interstate audience towards support for a cause. For reference, diplomatic pressure refers to a "form of attempted, nonmaterial influence by some (source) actors upon other (target) actors, designed or tending to force the target's hand (conduct) to accord with a social expectation," as Giovanni Mantilla writes (Mantilla 2020b, 19).

My concern with diplomatic pressure is especially relevant to a specific empirical focus on diplomacy at the United Nations. Consider the following observation. In a seminar at the University of Cambridge, John Baird—Canada's Minister of Foreign Affairs from 2011 to 2015—spoke to the nature of diplomacy in that context. In Baird's view, "pressure to go along to get along is so real in the United Nations. The pressure is so significant. There aren't enough countries that base decisions on the force of conviction" (Baird 11.1.2018). Baird went on to caution against "moral relativism," suggesting that "speaking truth to power" ought to be—but is often not—how states relate to common issues (Baird 11.1.2018). I agree. How the states in question see the issues in a global, multilateral context can be heavily influenced (or "constituted") by the interstate social context of the time.

Nevertheless, the foreign minister could also emphasize that diplomatic pressure is not an "inevitable" feature of diplomacy. Pressure to go along to get along is an interstate social construct; state agents can proactively construct and reinforce that environment to incline others toward support for a cause. That third states like Canada complain of feeling pressured to comport with a more common interstate position suggests evidence of those general social effects, which seem more pronounced in an institutional context such as the United Nations. The more striking concern is that third states—like Canada, in this illustration—adjust to perhaps otherwise undesirable foreign policy positions to deflect opprobrium.

The operation of diplomatic pressure in global, multilateral diplomacy is contingent upon the assumption that:

> human beings are social or "community beings." As community members, they seek social approval and respect from the other community members. In other words, they want to be recognized as legitimate. Conversely, they are sensitive to social disapproval and disrespect. They are concerned with their image and reputation in the community and do not want to be regarded as unreliable or illegitimate. If community member P is able to demonstrate that member O violates the community standard of legitimacy to which he subscribed, O will be induced to conform with the standard.
>
> SCHIMMELFENNIG 2003, 218

More specifically, diplomatic pressure operates on the assumption that a state subject cares about its self-identity as a member of the international community and sees a need for collective approval by state counterparts at the United Nations (Claude 1966, 370; Hurd 2008, 164). Inis Claude was among the first international relations scholars to stress the significance of collective approval at the United Nations.

> While statesmen [stateswomen, and states persons] have their own ways of justifying their foreign policies to themselves and their peoples, independently of external judgments, they are well aware that such unilateral determinations do not suffice. They are keenly conscious of the need for approval by as large and impressive a body of other states as possible, for multilateral endorsement of their positions- in short, for collective legitimization. Moreover, it is a political judgment by their fellow practitioners of international politics that they primarily seek, not a legal judgment rendered by an international judicial organ.

> ... This is simply to say that statement [stateswomen, and states per-
> sons] take collective legitimacy seriously as a factor in international pol-
> itics; the opinions and the attitudes of other states, manifested through
> the parliamentary mechanism of the United Nations, must be taken into
> account in the conduct of foreign policy.
>
> CLAUDE 1966, 370–375

Numerous international relations scholars have echoed the point (e.g.
Finnemore and Sikkink 1998, 903; Schimmelfennig 2001, 49; Hurd 2005, 501;
2008, 138). Frank Schimmelfennig has made the case that "in an 'institutional environment' ... political actors are concerned about their reputation
as members and about the legitimacy of their preferences and behavior"
(Schimmelfennig 2001, 49). Recently, Giovanni Mantilla has asserted that
"social pressure operates upon state diplomats because it taps onto key status
anxieties at particular historical moments" (Mantilla 2020b, 11).

My point is that states subscribe to common norms by their membership in
the United Nations as *member* states. These norms (or "symbols" more broadly)
reflect a sense of community and can inculcate a "currency of power because
enough individuals believe that others believe in them" (Hurd 2002, 37). Thus,
associating or disassociating with the community's common norms can have
"powerful" interstate social ramifications.

More importantly, manipulating shared norms via rhetorical action can
exert diplomatic pressure on third states—especially those otherwise "on the
fence"—that inclines them to support an issue. As Giovanni Mantilla writes,
diplomatic pressure stems from the "revelation of a broken social expectation"
(Mantilla 2020b, 19). The revelation of a broken common expectation can
entail significant social consequences—such as casting certain discourses and
behaviors as "illegitimate"—that bespatter a subject's integrity vis-à-vis other
states (Mantilla 2020b, 20). Moreover, diplomatic pressure can accumulate and
become more conspicuous as other states with lower subjective thresholds (or
"tipping points") for a policy change join in opposition to the status quo. These
latter states can include those who may have been more sympathetic to the
cause from the outset and those who support it for other reasons.

Ian Hurd makes a similar point, suggesting that Libya's strategic manipulation of international norms gave certain states the legitimate "tools" (or
arguments) that "emboldened" them to change course on the international
sanctions regime (Hurd 2008, 163). These initial changes came from states with
solid reasons to oppose the regime from the start but refrained from doing so,
given the potential damage to their relationships with the pro-sanctions states
(Hurd 2008, 163). As such, Libya's cumulative efforts, in the end, increased the

diplomatic pressure on the pro-sanctions states to abandon the regime. This is to say that a socialization agent's efforts can amplify social anxieties over time, increasing pressure on an audience to comport with a specific common expectation. Margarita Petrova suggests that social pressure of this nature can have powerful effects when about 50 percent of all states change positions, amplifying social anxieties about remaining an outlier (Petrova 2019, 591).

In response to these social anxieties, many states will seek to avoid at least the appearance of challenging or being insouciant to the given common expectation. "States indifferent to or adversely affected by the norm are more likely to accept it gradually to avoid being left behind than to rush in cascade-like" (Petrova 2019, 591). This can entail that a state reaffirms the value in the common expectation, even where that same state is suspected of having implicitly or explicitly undermined it (Weinberg 30.1.18; 5.2.18). Prior public commitment to the expectation "locks in" a state subject in the process of argumentative exchanges and scrutiny from other state interlocutors; a subject cannot argue against the already accepted expectation without losing face (Petrova 2016, 387).

Socialization does not necessarily culminate in "internalization," meaning that norms "achieve a 'taken-for-granted' quality that makes conformance with the norm almost automatic" (Finnemore and Sikkink 1998, 904). Nor is it necessary that state subjects "adopt new positions because they are sincerely convinced about their merits" (Petrova 2016, 387). Demonstrating these latter two points can prove elusive—or "methodologically intractable," as Krebs and Jackson assert—because it requires "unmediated access to people's minds" (Krebs and Jackson 2007, 40; Petrova 2016, 388). The critical point is that diplomatic pressure can give rise to socio-strategic and socially mediated normative concerns in the public embrace of an otherwise undesirable position. In practice, this means that global, multilateral agreements can take shape regardless of whether parties have been genuinely convinced by—or perhaps even despite—their merits.

Interstate socialization thus takes place in the sense that public—and not necessarily private—viewpoints converge around a common, more legitimate (or "socially sustainable") stance on the issue (Krebs and Jackson 2007, 47; Petrova 2016, 387). The outcome reflects a social compromise rather than a "reasoned consensus" or a fundamental preference readjustment (Mantilla 2020b, 27–28; Petrova 2016, 388). Socialization subjects do not necessarily take to heart and change their internal views on the issue; at a minimum, they eschew public association with what has become an "illegitimate" or socially unsustainable position (Schimmelfennig 2001, 65). Socialization subjects may very well acquiesce publicly to the position even as they maintain opposing views privately (Mantilla 2020b, 12). This means that a socialization agent's argument:

> 'wins' not because its grounds are 'valid' in the sense of satisfying the demands of universal reason or because it accords with the audience's prior normative commitments or material interests, but because its grounds are socially sustainable—because the audience deems certain rhetorical deployments acceptable and others impermissible.
>
> KREBS AND JACKSON 2007, 47

Note that this assertion does not hinge on a distinction between theoretical logic consequences and logic of appropriateness. The mobilization of diplomatic (social) pressure can exert a continuum of non-material and non-coercive effects that start with more content-neutral, relational concerns for a need to conform and extend to more content-based, normative concerns for the issue's substance. The former effects have more to do with preserving a certain relationship with or "role" within a community than with a sense of conviction to the issue (Checkel 2005; Goodman and Jinks 2013; Johnston 2005). The latter social effects overlap with and extend further than the former. Pressure to conform remains relevant—with ostracism (or isolation) as its social sanction—but to the further extent that the state subject in question develops a sense of attachment to the issue in circulation. Whereas the former effects are more content-neutral, the latter effects churn up a more content-based perspective supporting the issue as "legitimate." The associated social "sanction" then relates to disapprobation, with ostracism *and* a sense of shame for failure to uphold what resounds as "legitimate" within the community. In sum, diplomatic pressure can exert effects—especially "powerful social opprobrium pressures," as Giovanni Mantilla puts it—that nurture socio-strategic and socially mediated normative concerns in accepting an undesirable position (Mantilla 2018, 319). Hence, socio-strategic and normative concerns complement each other (Hurd 2005, 497; 2008, 137–138; Hurd 2009, 13–14).

4   What Can Make the Theoretical Argument Work?

We now look at theoretical "conditioning factors" that contribute to socialization. I borrow the term from Professor Nathalie Tocci (Tocci 2008a; 2008b; 6.11.2018). Numerous scholars point to the importance of an issue's material stakes, specific content, and the intensity/duration of its consideration. My empirical research has not found empirical evidence in favor of or against these theoretical propositions.

Thus, my proposition relates to a separate, empirically relevant factor: a socialization agent's *perceived* integrity on an issue. By integrity, I mean a social constructivist (and not a rationalist) rendition of "reputation," which relates to the extent to which a socialization subject regards a socialization agent as a trustworthy advocate of a cause (Mantilla 15.10.2021, 3). I stress that my use of the concept is intersubjective. It asks to what degree a potential socialization subject views a socialization agent as meaning what they say—namely, "talking the talk" *and* "walking the walk"—on the specific issue. Otherwise put, integrity entails that a target audience perceives an agent's rhetorical action as consistent: namely, that the agent's arguments and actions are seen to match, that the agent's arguments used in different times and different contexts are seen to match, and that the agent's views are seen to match internally (Schimmelfennig 2003, 221).

The crucial point is that an agent's perceived integrity on an issue can make socialization efforts more (or less) influential. On the one hand, socialization efforts are more likely to fail when proponents lack that integrity—and are therefore seen as hypocritical—because the target states do not see a credible political cost or downside to maintaining the issue's status quo. Recall that the crux of those efforts is to manipulate rhetoric to mobilize public opposition to those who appear to have "broken social expectations" (Mantilla 2020b, 19). Socialization agents cannot effectively mobilize such opposition if the target audience perceives them as having broken those expectations. In that case, socialization efforts are most likely to fail regardless of the social expectations. "A participant who is seen as choosing norms à la carte, and discarding them whenever they work against him, will undermine himself [herself, or themself] in the long run" (Elster 1992 in Schimmelfennig 2003, 221). Furthermore, when an agent "fails to remain faithful to her 'initial projection' ... she causes a 'disruptive event' likely to discredit her image and to lead to a breakdown of the interaction" (Goffman 1959: 12; Schimmelfennig 2003, 197). "Some of the assumptions upon which the responses of the participants had been predicated become untenable, and the participants find themselves lodged in an interaction for which the situation has been wrongly defined and is now no longer defined" (Goffman 1956, 6).

On the other hand, socialization efforts are more likely to succeed when proponents enjoy a sense of integrity on an issue—and are therefore seen to be trustworthy advocates of the cause—because the target audience perceives a political cost to maintaining the status quo. The underlying assumption is that a socialization agent's heft vis-à-vis the target states emanates from an implicit or explicit "credible threat" to win over a third-state audience, which can deprive target states of the option of not responding to or even ignoring its efforts, and in turn, accentuate social pressure upon states that do not support the cause (Krebs and Jackson 2007, 47). Crucially, socialization agents only need to be seen as trustworthy advocates of the specific cause—and not the norm or social expectations, more generally—for the threat to be credible.

Why an agent is seen as trustworthy on an issue is less important than the perception or "social" fact that it indeed is. For those interested, I suggest a socialization agent's first-hand exposure to the status quo to conceptualize perceived integrity. A complaint that at least one state derives from its imme-diate national circumstances can seem more trustworthy than a complaint drawn from another's immediate national context. The presence of at least one such state in a core coalition of states coalition can substantiate the sincerity of the cause and thereby lend more credence to an appeal to change the status quo. The critical point is that the more third states see that state—individually or in coalition with other states—as specifically and adversely affected by the status quo, the more credence the cause can appear to have.

Ian Hurd omits this possibility in his commentary on Libya, which may have been more influential not because it enjoyed moral stature for its adherence to select "norms of liberal internationalism" or because its use of those norms was sincere but because the target states did not doubt its determination to oppose the status quo. Yet, my theoretical refinement is critical to understanding the conditions under which socialization efforts can work (or fail to work) in inter-national relations. Social constructivists now have a cornucopia of theoretical knowledge on how states can respond to diplomatic pressure. Nevertheless, we still lack theoretical insight—save for passing reference to this or that contrib-utor to socialization—on how state agents can deploy that pressure effectively or ineffectively. We need more insight into how certain theoretical condition-ing factors can interact with existing social constructivist theory to produce socialization.

For reference, my theoretical refinement builds upon constructivist litera-ture on international relations (e.g. Checkel 2005, 813; Finnemore and Sikkink 1998, 901; Johnston 2001, 497). Ian Johnston, for example, emphasizes that "information from sources that are liked is more convincing than from sources that are disliked. Liking will increase with more exposure, contact, and famil-iarity" (Johnston 2001, 901). Alexandra Gheciu similarly argues that NATO influ-enced states' acceptance of specific international codes of conduct "by virtue of the authority enjoyed *qua* the key security institution of the Western com-munity" (Gheciu 2005, 980). Martha Finnemore and Kathryn Sikkink apply the point to state agents, drawing attention to the influence "critical states" can have on others (Finnemore and Sikkink 1998, 901). Nicole Deitelhoff and Linda Wallbott contend that the "success of coalitions might be a result of pure numbers, for example, a maximized pooling of bargaining resources, but of their perceived legitimacy in the negotiation process" (Deitelhoff and Wallbott 2012, 349). More recently, Margarita Petrova asserts that "who delivers the message may be more important than the message's content" (Petrova 2016, 388–389).

5   Theoretical Limitations and Caveats

I suggest at least two theoretical limitations to this chapter's argument. First, the chapter's theoretical assertion about a process of collective legitimization is an ideal type that does not occur in pure form (Risse 2000, 3). The theoretical discussion above, therefore, is not an absolute account of what takes place. The social world is complex, with an "indefinitely large number of things about which observations can be made and an indefinitely large set of observations to make about them" (Schegloff 1999, 578). What matters is the extent to which the above theory captures that complexity. My second theoretical limitation relates to how a solid social structure operates in my theoretical argument. Social structure refers to the diplomatic pressure that a core coalition of states brings to bear on an issue (and ultimately culminates in collective legitimization). The strength or weakness of that pressure refers to how it operates "over and above" interstate relations and shapes how it positions itself on the issues. In my view, diplomatic pressure is not determinative; it is, at most, socially influential. My theoretical focus on diplomatic pressure is a preliminary interpretation of circumstances, which may, in the end, lead to analysis paralysis or prove "too complex to theorize" in specific contexts (Bennett and Checkel 2012, 6). More importantly, my theoretical perspective is not that diplomatic pressure exerts as consequential an influence on states as the structure in neorealist theory (which contemplates relatively homogeneous outcomes). Hence, I do not anticipate diplomatic pressure influencing all states equally or even at all. Thus, I allow for more heterogeneous effects.

A second theoretical limitation is that my argument hinges on how much a state subject places a premium on its standing on a particular issue. However, specific states may care more (or less) about the "consequences of public embarrassment to their self-image, status, and reputation" (Mantilla 2020b, 177). As Giovanni Mantilla writes, the former states are more "socially vulnerable" because they wish to be seen as "'good' standing as members of the international community, particularly among social competition" (Mantilla 2020b, 177). On the other hand, diplomatic pressure cannot affect states with little concern for how they are seen vis-à-vis other states on a particular issue. This second point alludes to states that maintain a certain position despite the prevailing interstate social repercussions. A state that does not care about those repercussions—particularly regarding maintaining an intersubjective sense of legitimacy—is less likely to come around for that reason. Ambassador Nikki Haley's recent observation demonstrates the point: "We are proud to buck the mob when it comes to the principles we believe in" (Haley 3.11.18).

The extent to which a state values its legitimacy in the international community matters (Mantilla 2018, 331). If a state commonly adopts a "renegade attitude" towards international norms—for example, by boasting about its status as an outcast on an issue—it is less likely to be moved by diplomatic pressure and more likely to remain outside the ambit of what resounds as "legitimate" at a particular point in time (Mantilla 2018, 331). Thus, a state subject's renegade attitude towards the international community on an issue can enervate diplomatic pressure. Similarly, the absence of an audience whose general approval is sought by the state subject can also render diplomatic pressure inefficacious (Petrova 14.10.2021, 3). Ian Hurd makes a similar point (Hurd 2008, 166).

Diplomatic pressure can also weigh down on state subjects but not lead them towards support for a policy change due to other priorities. This outcome speaks to states inclined to support the given position but acquiesce to an alternative position given material inducement. Prime Minister Imran Khan's recent observation about attributing state responsibility for the Jamal Khashoggi assassination demonstrates the point: "We are desperate for money" (Khan in Sengupta 2018). "Unless we get loans from friendly countries … we'll have real, real problems" (Khan in Sengupta 2018). This is to say that diplomatic pressure cannot operate in as decisive a manner as certain material resource inducement. In sum, I propose that state subjects can be affected by common elements of social structure but have a unique threshold (or "tipping point") with its effects.

Several caveats concern this chapter. There are at least three. The first relates to the point that a core coalition acts as the interstate socializing agent: why does pressing others into acceptance of a position require a *coalition* of states rather than a single state? There are two points to consider in response to this question: theoretical and empirical. The theoretical point is that I do not dismiss the influence that a "one-state wrecking crew" can have in initiating socialization, as the previous subsection on success factors suggests. I allow the theoretical possibility that a single state *can* do most of the legwork and exert such influence, including in concert with those who share some initial support for the given cause.

The empirical point is that states that look to facilitate a socialization pro-cess often seem to not stand alone, in complete isolation from others. Even for the "rogue" (or "maverick") state, complete isolation on some issues seems rare from a social constructivist perspective. Hence, even Ian Hurd's analysis of Libya's strategic manipulation of liberal institutionalism is open to a theo-retical perspective on how a coalition of states can act as socializing agents. Hurd comments, for example, that the likes of Libya from 1992 to 2003 and Iraq from 1990 to 2003 stood in opposition to an international community that was "largely"—but not exclusively—decided in its opposition to them (Hurd 2008, 139). The two states could have acted as ring leaders alongside other states—if not at least alongside each other—to end the sanctions regime. Although Hurd's work overlooks that significant possibility, what matters most is the influence of strategic rhetorical manipulation on other states.

A second caveat comes from a perspective on mutual interstate socializa-tion, meaning that socialization occurs among states that simultaneously socialize and become socialized. Thomas Risse, for example, makes a case for argumentation, deliberation, and persuasion as a process by which "human actors engage in truth-seeking with the aim of reaching a mutual understand-ing based on a reasoned consensus" (Risse 2000, 1–2). This perspective speaks most to a negotiation setting in that the actors are prepared to change their position to reach the above-reasoned consensus. It has less to do with contexts that involve rhetorical action (or "loudspeaker diplomacy"), where at least one agent is not, and instead keeps up some persistent effort to win over a broader audience in support of its position (Risse 2000, 9–10). That latter context best relates to what my chapter contemplates because it implies some interstate campaign to muster support for a cause where the agents see themselves as "hidebound" or *unwilling* or unable to make concessions. The socialization that can ensue is then not simultaneous, per Risse's main point. It is more on par with Ian Hurd's commentary on Libya, where the agents exploit diplomatic discourse more cynically (Hurd 2005, 499). This becomes clear upon examin-ing how those agents' positions remain invariable despite decided opposition.

In addition to the above two caveats, one could also question: who precisely are the state actors? Are they executives, foreign offices, individual state rep-resentatives, specific stakeholders, and the above? I have two points to make. One is that this section's primary concern is the social construction of inter-state interaction in a global, multilateral context. It contemplates how those state units relate to each other rather than how they come into being. Hence, the book assumes that states exist as unitary actors, as Alexander Wendt does in his social theory of international politics (Wendt 1999, 193–245). This leads to my second point. By state, I mean governments, which include the diplomats who represent the government in an official capacity, like heads of state (and heads of government), ministers (or secretaries), special envoys, ambassadors, and less senior diplomats. Whatever the specific government official, what matters is that the common position or "company line" she expresses marks that of the state in question.

On this latter point, some may still question my emphasis on states as the units of analysis. This is because individual state representatives—not some unitary concept of a state—set the direction of national foreign policy. Since these individuals are acting, we need to focus on their role in how the states they represent assume an array of national positions. Margarita Petrova suggests a further challenge: "if the 'state' has been socialized, one will have to show how its practices have been constrained despite the individual preferences of those representing it later on" (Petrova 14.10.2021, 2). This general line of criticism in the literature can also come from Ian Johnston, who contends that social constructivism demands that individuals serve as the units for socialization (Johnston 2001, 507).

These caveats can offer insight into the current research investigation on at least two accounts. First, state representatives, wherever stationed, can prove effective in pushing the adoption of a particular foreign policy position among their "back bench" or colleagues at headquarters—perhaps, for example, by transmitting to them the effects of the diplomatic pressure outside in the external international environment. These effects can then influence decision-makers higher up in the food chain, much as one would expect them to influence the states. Second, individual state representatives themselves can enjoy a certain extent of autonomy from headquarters—as much work on principal-agent theory expects—and can thereby be the ones to affect and be affected by outcomes (Pollack 2007, 59). According to this latter account, state representatives are both agents and/or subjects of socialization and, therefore, require more research attention.

These two caveats are separate from the theoretical focus on states as the units of analysis in this section. That individual representatives serve as the agents and subjects of international socialization to affirm their position at the "cutting edge" of their respective state's foreign policy; the individuals would still seem to remain subject to the broader diplomatic pressure "out there," beyond the cutting edge. Thus, the representatives would still have to contend with an international social environment as the presumed "states" would have to do. Therefore, an emphasis on individuals in the research procedure seems to be a more fine-grained perspective on interstate interaction on specific issues.

Yet even if these individuals were the ones to drive the bargain, their participation in an international context seems only to gain currency if attributable to that of the respective state in question. This makes intuitive sense. What Donald Trump and Nikki Haley have had to say about the final status of Jerusalem before taking on their respective governmental roles seems hardly to have generated much international attention. However, as representatives of the United States of America, the matter had been quite different. This suggests that individuals, if not representatives for their respective states, have more limited diplomatic influence alone.

I also emphasize that my theoretical argument requires only that the individuals who comprise a state—at a specific "bounded" point in time—acquiesce to otherwise undesirable foreign policy positions (Krebs and Jackson 2007, 41). My argument does not necessarily need to culminate with internalization, which may demand that future government officials adhere to the foreign policy positions that previous ones grudgingly accepted. Future officials, for example, may assume a more "renegade" attitude towards the international community on the issue in question. However, this does not detract from a focus on states. A change in attitude of that nature would still presuppose the continued presence of diplomatic pressure sustained by other states whose individual representatives may very well have also changed. Hence, my focus on states remains relevant.

Nevertheless, I am still reluctant to characterize socialization as lasting "in the sense of forestalling normative contestation over the long run," as Ronald Krebs and Patrick Jackson contend (Krebs and Jackson 2007, 41). "Norms are inherently subject to challenge, and that the rhetorical arrangements sustaining norms are never fully stabilized and are at best *relatively* stable" (Krebs and Jackson 2007, 41). For reference, Ian Hurd makes a similar point (Hurd 2002, 45–47; 2005, 502; 2008, 137–138; 2014, 8–9).

6   Theoretical Critiques

What remains is a consideration of the main theoretical counterpoint to my argument. This comes from materialist accounts of socialization, which emphasize how agents deploy specific material—rather than ideational—resources to initiate socialization. Research on material coercion and interstate socialization dates back to at least the English School's concern with the expansion of European International Society (e.g. Bull 1977; Bull and Watson 1984; Buzan 2001). According to those accounts, acceptance of a certain "standard of civilization"—like norms on cooperation in international relations—served as the price of admission to that society. Some states achieved this via material coercion—including resorting to a threat or use of physical violence—throughout the age of imperialism (Bull and Watson 1984, 118; Suzuki 2005, 142–146). John Ikenberry and Charles Kupchan, and Jeffrey Lantis provide similar materialist accounts (Ikenberry and Kaplan 1990; Lantis 2016). For Ikenberry and Kupchan, socialization can occur when hegemons manipulate material incentives to coerce smaller states to change policies (Ikenberry and Kaplan 1990, 290). A comparable, more recent perspective comes from Jeffrey Lantis, who characterizes norms as "interdependent with great power norm stewardship, subject to bounded manipulation and refinement by actors that have sufficient material power" (Lantis 2016, 387).

Further relevant ideas relate to accounts on material side-payments or "gift exchanges," which states provide or receive as compensation for adopting certain policy positions in connection with some multilateral context (Lundborg 1998). Some have drawn attention to positive and negative incentives related to World Bank projects, IMF loans, foreign aid, and other material resource inducements (Adhikari 2019a; 2019b; Dreher and Strum 2012; Woo and Chung 2017). Other scholars consider the extent to which a state's foreign aid can influence the support it gains from other states on issues at the General Assembly. The main focus has been on China (Abudula 2018; Xun and Shuai 2018) and the United States (e.g. Carter and Stone 2015; Dreher, Nunnenkamp and Thiele 2008; Woo and Chung 2017). A more recent focus on the United States includes Anastassia Obydenkova and Vinícius Rodrigues Viera's work, which considers the extent to which American-sponsored regional development banks influence the views of developing states (Obydenkova and Viera 2020). The authors suggest that "the higher the material capabilities of a borrowing state that takes loans, the less likely it is to align with the United States at the UN General Assembly (UNGA)" (Obydenkova and Viera 2020, 130).

I acknowledge that material resource manipulation can also elicit support for specific issues, especially in a global, multilateral context. More broadly, I also recognize that material, interstate relationships can influence where that support comes from. In my view, though, what ensues is not necessarily an "epiphenomenal" reflection of those same material resources. I say this because those who resort to material resource manipulation, at last, seek to produce the *appearance* of interstate support on a common issue. Thus, Carter and Stone, for example, emphasize that "US policy is not buying votes to ensure or block the passage of resolutions; rather, the United States is buying votes to appear less isolated and to purchase legitimacy on key foreign policy initiatives" (Carter and Stone 2015, 2). This makes sense. There would seem no need to buy out counterparts, meet out side payments, trade horses, and the like if not to achieve some social objective. The use of side payments is embedded within a diplomatic, social context, owing its form to the common interstate expectations that sustain it. This implies that manipulating those material resources is a more finite and costly end-of-pipe measure to build a groundswell of global support for an issue. Even for the most materially capable, such support would be out of reach absent the necessary *non-material* support from other states. This returns the research focus to the overall social environment that prevails among states and consequently has some resort to more concealed, *a*social measures to countervail its influence.

For reference, social constructivist (and realist-constructivist) scholars have their own responses to the material resource critique. Nicole Deitelhoff, for example, highlights a socialization process that occurs inexplicably in terms of material resource inducement. Deitelhoff contemplates "normative conditions conducive to persuasion," which involve strategies "initiated by alliances between middle powers and non-state actors who lack sufficient leverage compared to the major powers" (Deitelhoff 2009, 35). Ian Hurd addresses the material resource critique, referencing Richard Haas' policy brief on "sanctions fatigue," which entails that "sanctions regimes have a natural tendency to erode and that the costs of maintaining an enforcing coalition increase" (Hurd 2008, 163). Hurd contends that "rising costs to maintaining the sanctions regime were indeed decisive in pushing the pro-sanctions states toward a compromise. But the nature of and change in these costs cannot be explained except with reference to Libya's manipulations of international norms" (Hurd 2008, 163). Finally, Giovanni Mantilla's work "runs against the expectations of prominent realist and critical scholarship," arguing that materially weaker states can have a meaningful influence on international rule-making processes against the wishes of more materially powerful states (Mantilla 2020a, 8). Mantilla suggests numerous empirical cases in which "major powers faced negative odds in multilateral settings and remained engaged without deploying exit options, coercive threats, or linkage strategies" (Mantilla 2020a, 10). Accepting a new position is a "grudging, socially pressured move" (Mantilla 2020b, 171).

Each of these perspectives is valuable. Although materialist accounts of socialization provide a useful counterpoint, social constructivists like me will agree that they are not the most persuasive way to understand the workings of global, multilateral diplomacy. This will become more apparent as we delve deep into our first empirical case study in the next chapter.

Apartheid (1946–1961)

Enquires indicated that if we abstained, we would find ourselves
alone. There would be serious and world-wide misrepresentations,
and Australia would incur a solitary hostility among African and
Asian nations. The choice was therefore between my own own
personal position, which became one of humiliation, and in fact
exposed me to considerable ridicule, and the general repute of my
country. Under these circumstances, we decided that, with reservations orally indicated by our representative, we would vote with the
United Kingdom.

> Prime Minister Robert Menzies 1961 in PREM 11/3598, 9

∴

0   Chapter Outline

Recall that this book advances a social constructivist perspective on interstate socialization. It draws upon diplomatic history at the United Nations—
especially the General Assembly—as the vortex for interstate socialization in
a global, multilateral context. I question how states can initiate a socialization process that cumulatively builds a consensus on an issue over time. By
consensus, I mean an overwhelming public—and not necessarily private or
internalized—extent of agreement among states on a topic. I argue that a core
coalition of states can create a spotlight of diplomatic pressure that draws into
focus an issue. That diplomatic pressure sets in motion a process of collective
legitimization, which assumes a life of its own and creates common expectations that make support for a particular position "legitimate." Over time, these
expectations can incline other states—particularly those opposing or otherwise "on the fence"—towards joining in on a common position, leading to a
convergence in expectations. Interstate socialization occurs because public—
though not necessarily private—viewpoints converge around a common,
more "legitimate" or socially sustainable stance on the issue. Socialization
subjects do not necessarily take to heart and change their internal views. At

© NAIF AL-MULLA, 2025 | DOI:10.1163/9789004711938_005

a minimum, they publicly repudiate what has become an "illegitimate" or socially unsustainable position.

I qualify this argument with the assertion that an agent's perceived integrity on an issue can make socialization efforts more (or less) influential. Socialization efforts are more likely to fail when proponents lack that integrity—and are therefore seen to be hypocritical—because the target states do not see a political drawback to maintaining the status quo. On the other hand, socialization efforts are more likely to succeed when proponents enjoy a sense of integrity on an issue—and are therefore seen to be trustworthy advocates of the cause—because the target audience perceives a credible political cost to maintaining the status quo. By integrity, I mean a social constructivist (and not a rationalist) version of "reputation," which refers to the extent to which a socialization subject regards a socialization agent as a trustworthy advocate of a cause.

We now test this argument on my first empirical case study: "apartheid," or racial discrimination in South Africa. This case study can span a half-century of proceedings in the General Assembly from the mid-1940s to the mid-1990s. I cannot weigh my theoretical point concerning all those proceedings. Instead, I focus on a specific period, from 1946 to 1961. I focus on this tract of time for the following empirical reason. 1946 was the first session of the General Assembly, during which member states first considered racial discrimination in South Africa. 1961, on the other end, was the year that member states reached an almost unanimous consensus on the issue.

The chapter proceeds as follows. The introduction suggests a compendious empirical background for this case study. This acclimates the reader to the empirical context, including how the Government of India, alongside other core states, created a global, multilateral "issue" out of the status quo in South Africa. My commentary alludes to Chapter Two's analysis of "information politics," particularly regarding the requirement that socialization agents specify and categorize an issue (Rosert 2019). The introduction also considers international relations literature on South Africa. The most relevant theoretical work is Audie Klotz's *Norms in International Relations: The Struggle Against Apartheid*. Although the work applies to a different period—from the mid-1960s onwards—the section distances itself from Kltoz's work in its theoretical emphasis on the diffusion of a global norm on racial equality. The reason is that one can already make the case for a universal *interstate* acceptance of that norm by the First Session of the General Assembly in 1946.

Following the introduction, we proceed to the chapter's three main parts. Each of these parts corresponds to the three-step means of analysis in the data and methods chapter. Part One makes a case for a "core" coalition of states—namely, a support base—on racial discrimination in South Africa. The leading proponents of the position were the Soviet Union (and states associated with the Eastern Bloc) and states that later formed the Non-Aligned Movement. India and the latter were among the coalition's most vocal proponents. I identify these core states from proceedings on South Africa in 1946 at the United Nations. Those states took a clear, unequivocal stance on the issue in that year and each subsequent year until 1961. I also identify these states given their more vocal support for the position throughout those years. My task is to theorize the views that those states express. I closely examine the discursive practices (or "rhetorical action") that the socializing agents use to pressure others into supporting the cause. As we shall see, agents manipulate common norms to galvanize interstate support against racism in South Africa. This point does not necessarily mean the agents stand on some moral high ground. It allows the theoretical suggestion that the agents engage in rhetorical action for more cynical reasons.

Part Two considers how the core coalition of states' efforts influenced other states' positions regarding racial discrimination in South Africa. It pays attention to how those latter positions change, particularly to states that did not favor a clear, unequivocal stance in previous years. I comment on the United Kingdom, Australia, and Canada, respectively, as examples. I use these three states as illustrative country cases for empirical reasons. The first reason is that Australia, Canada, and the United Kingdom were among the states on the fence. In other words, these three states had not taken an unequivocal and unambiguous stance against apartheid throughout all but the final year of study. I also refer to Australia, Canada, and the United Kingdom because these countries' cases present abundant empirical evidence to examine. As we shall see, each of these examples provides access to a rich and rare set of primary materials.

My empirical argument is that close observation of how these positions change suggests evidence for an interstate socialization process set in motion by the core coalition of states. This is to say that my theoretical argument's observable implication—following Ian Hurd's 2005 and 2008 works—comes from how state representatives express changes in national positions on apartheid. Hence, how state representatives articulate ideas against the status quo makes the difference; it makes some states potential socialization subjects and others not. The observable implication does not come from the fact that "everyone condemned South Africa." For good measure, my observable implication also comes from a collation of supplementary primary source work that lends more direct support to the interpretation. This latter strand of evidence also helps contemplate the influence of certain empirical conditioning factors that contributed to the eventual interstate consensus against apartheid by April 1961 (Tocci 2008). In this chapter, the most crucial empirical conditioning factors are the emergence of newly independent states from Africa and Asia, South Africa's unwillingness to make concessions, and South Africa's departure from the Commonwealth.

In Part Three, we finally cross-check my inferences against alternative perspectives. These alternative perspectives come from international relations critiques addressed in the previous Chapter. The most relevant point is material resource inducement, which can be a theoretical antagonist to the present social constructivist account. Other alternative perspectives come from historical accounts of the current empirical circumstances, including South Africa's insistence on maintaining apartheid policies.

1   Introduction

Racial discrimination in the Union of South Africa first came onto the agenda at the United Nations in 1946 during the First Session of the General Assembly. The issue did not gain the platform thanks to some universal interstate concern for racial discrimination, as can now seem to be the case from the commemoration of Nelson Mandela International Day (A/RES/64/13). Nor did the issue become and remain an "issue" worth interstate attention thanks to a global abhorrence of apartheid, as the more recent interstate unanimity on the matter can suggest (e.g. A/RES/44/244; A/RES/48/233; A/RES/44/27). The issue was, from the outset, disputatious. It became a subject of global, multilateral concern owed to the Government of India's specific complaint about racial discrimination in the Union of South Africa (A/68; A/68/Add.1). Absent India's (and later Pakistan's) diplomatic efforts, it is unclear—at least, until the late 1950s—how else racial discrimination in South Africa would have come onto the agenda. Thus, in 1946, there was no inevitable trajectory on the agenda item's eventual lifespan. It was from the onset high maintenance, requiring significant interstate support to remain in the global, interstate "spotlight." Absent that support, the issue lost its airtime, as at the Second Session of the General Assembly in 1947.

The substance of India's complaint pointed to racial discrimination in aspects of socio-economic and political life in the Union of South Africa (A/68; A/68/Add.1; A/C.1&6/SR.1–6, 52–131). It toured the relevant albeit by then long-standing pieces of national legislation, which culminated with the Asiatic Land Tenure and Indian Representation Act (or "Ghetto Act") in 1946. For India, the most recent measures gave "permanent recognition to the principle of segregation," which was the subject of its protest since the late eighteen hundreds (A/68, 30–31). That protest took various forms and came up in imperial conferences, roundtable meetings, correspondence, and various attempts at negotiation, compromise, and agreement (e.g. A/68; A/68/Add.1; A/167). As early as 1875, for example, the then Secretary of State for India was adamant that formerly indentured persons become "free men in all respects with privileges no whit inferior to those of any class of Her Majesty's subjects resident in the colonies" (A/SPC/SR.7, 24). The Government of India maintained that position over the years but saw that it was not one to which the authorities in South Africa—both before and after it became a union of former colonies in 1910—had been amenable (A/68; A/68/Add.1; A/577; A/PV.50; A/1794). Accordingly, by 1946, the Union of South South Africa defended the practice of racial segregation (A/167). "Necessary measures [were] introduced from time to time to meet the needs of the day, and which are mainly concerned to relieve the tensions caused by the residential juxtaposition of different races, with clashing creeds and cultural dissimilarities" (A/167, 1).

India saw its turn towards the United Nations as a last resort. At the General Assembly, its delegation sought to organize an international response to the status quo and leverage its diplomatic pressure on third states, as my theoretical argument chapter suggests. In Ambassador Vijayalakshmi Pandit's words,

> over many years my government irrespective of its constitution and character, has appealed complained, protested sought compromises and agreements and finally has been forced into retaliation and to bring this matter before the bar of world opinion. The Union Government has taken no step, and even during the proceedings in this Assembly, despite the suggestion we have thrown out, has not given the slightest indication that it contemplates even the temporary suspension of even the latest installment of its offending legislation.
>
> A/PV.50, 1016–1017

The "bar of world opinion" took shape in response to a draft resolution named after India's complaint in 1946: "Treatment of People of Indian Origin in the Union of South Africa" (e.g. A/RES/44(I); A/RES/265(III); A/RES/395(V)). The resolution addressed a specific issue over some thirteen years, from 1946 to 1959. As the title suggests, it invited other member states to evaluate life for people of Indian origin in South Africa. It also called on India and South Africa to talk things out, including via a good offices mediation initiative (A/205; A/1548). Aside from that, the resolution left the rest open for other states to consider, which they did both in connection with that resolution and another

on the Future Status of Southwest Africa (Namibia) (e.g. A/RES/65(I); A/RES/
141(II); A/RES/227(III)). In 1952, India and other states threw another, more
explicit resolution into the conversation: "The Question of Race Conflict …
in the Union of South Africa" (e.g. A/2183; A/2610; A/3722). That resolution
spoke to more recent circumstances at the time: the introduction of a policy of
"apartheid" by Prime Minister Daniel Malan's National Party in 1948. The resolution was more explicit on racial discrimination but, for consecutive sessions,
put in writing what had been in conversation from the outset, as we shall later
see. The applicable period for that latter agenda item is from 1952 to 1961.

Empirical case studies on the Union of South Africa have been the subject of disparate research efforts in the international relations research tradition. The most theoretically relevant is Audie Klotz's *Norms in International
Relations: The Struggle Against Apartheid* (1995). From a social constructivist
perspective, the work asks how the diffusion of an international norm on racial
equality by the mid-1960s led to interstate sanctions policies by the mid-1980s
(Klotz 1995, 6). It makes the case that the increasing strength of a global norm
on racial equality provides a systemic explanation for adopting military and
economic sanctions against the Union of South Africa. The work argues, for
example, that the United States' eventual adoption of sanctions against South
Africa came in response to global pressures for racial equality (Klotz 1995, 93–
111). The United States "responded to rather than initiated … global pressures
for racial equality" (Klotz 1995, 93). "Racial equality became a prerequisite for
attaining material goals. The norm redefined U.S. interests" (Klotz 1995, 111).
Notwithstanding Klotz's empirical concern with material sanctions, which
speaks to a time frame we cannot cover, the work remains the closest theoretical counterpart to this chapter. It provides a social constructivist account
on how common expectations shaped the adoption of material sanctions
against the Union of South Africa, and in a manner inconsistent with rationalist accounts of international relations.

Theoretically, I distance myself from Klotz's analysis on one key
point: the assertion that a common interstate position on racial equality had
been strengthening from the mid-1960s onwards. The reason is that the First
Session of the General Assembly (1946–1947) established an already strong,
virtually unanimous interstate norm on racial equality. In Resolution 103(I), for
example, member states expressed virtually unanimous common cause in an
Egyptian proposal to call for "an immanent end to … racial persecutions and
discrimination," and thus to "take the most prompt and energetic steps to that
end" (A/RES/103(I)). France, like other member states, was unequivocal and
unambiguous:

> I belong to a country which is particularly proud of the fact that its laws
> have never recognized any inequality of treatment on racial grounds.
> I may add that our way of life and our national thought are, and always
> have been, radically opposed to any such conception.
>   The French delegation will therefore vote wholeheartedly for the pro-
> posal of the representative of Egypt.
>
> A/PV.48, 975

Throughout the year's plenary meetings, numerous delegations also reaffirmed credence in the same ideas via articles one, thirteen, fifty-five, and fifty-
six of the Charter (e.g. A/PV.6; A/PV.7; A/PV.8; A/PV.9). They also further set
out those ideas with work on what culminated in the Universal Declaration
of Human Rights (A/PV.183). This is to say that racial equality *per se* was an
uncontroversial interstate expectation by the time the United Nations came
into existence.

This also seems more so if one takes a step back to consider what member states at the time made of experiences in World War Two, which for most
were part and parcel with notions of racial discrimination. In consideration of
Resolution 103(I), Poland was among those to draw out the point:

> The Polish nation was for six years under nazi occupation, and knows
> what racial discrimination means. Six million of our citizens perished
> during that occupation; more than three million of these were Jews. We
> welcome, therefore, the spirit of the resolution.
>
> A/PV.47, 959

A norm on racial equality may have flourished (or strengthened) in the years
to come, as Klotz argues, and as a series of other unanimous resolutions can
indicate (e.g. A/RES/1536(XV); A/RES/1780(XVII); A/RES/18/1904). However,
those resolutions, which others have succeeded until today, hardly seem to
have drawn upon a more hard-pressed intersubjective backdrop than what
came from World War Two. By the First Session of the General Assembly, some
interstate expectation of racial equality was already strong. As one delegation
put it, the issue was a "burning question" on the global interstate agenda (A/
PV.47, 959).

Some member states may not have initially supported the expectation at
the time regarding South Africa. But it does not follow that those states did
not "take to heart" or were ambivalent towards an interstate norm on racial
equality. On the contrary, some states were more inclined to stand alongside
South Africa in its "stiff fight" with India and were, therefore, more willing to at

least remain in a "shell of reserve" on the substantive matter (*Times*, 25.3.1960 in Dubow 2011, 1111; *Times of India*, 10.3.1948). From a social constructivist perspective, the reason speaks back to Alexander Wendt's point about "friendship." The main idea was that certain friendships can make some states more supportive towards others in relation to some common issue, especially if that issue concerns or "attacks" the specific state. That political sense of friendship seems prevalent in the present case study. For example, several delegations on India's complaint were proud to point out the close socio-economic, political, and military relationships with South Africa—including in connection with a position against fascism in World War Two and communism in the nascent Cold War (e.g. A/AC.53/SR.32, 172; A/AC.61/SR.11, 54; A/SPC/SR.87, 17; A/SPC/SR.86, 8–9; A/SPC/SR.123, 173). It is intuitive to suppose that a sense of friendship, in turn, made some states—at least in 1946—more sympathetic towards South Africa's position than India's. Hence, an interstate norm on racial equality *per se* was present from the outset but was nevertheless not a byword for a common intergovernmental position on South Africa, given other priorities. As the next section postulates, that synonymousness took the proactive efforts of a coalition of states to construct.

2   Part One

2.1   *The Core Coalition*
India was central to creating the global, multilateral issue out of racial discrimination in South Africa and opening up the possibility for its prolonged treatment at the United Nations. India, however, was not alone in the endeavor. A core coalition of states coalesced around shared, unequivocal opposition to racial discrimination in the country in 1946 and each subsequent year until 1961. This section examines that coalition of states—particularly its more outspoken members—as the first step in its research procedure. Per my theoretical argument, I make a case for rhetorical action: the core coalition strategically manipulated common norms to mobilize more interstate opposition to the status quo in South Africa.

As set out in my argument chapter, a core coalition of states can achieve this by appealing to some "stamp of political approval or disapproval" concerning a particular situation. This means that the core states attempt to situate or "frame" an issue within some already accepted *interstate* normative framework such that the two become seen as one and the same. The coalition's efforts in the present case study can speak to this theoretical point. Some states consistently held out the status quo in South Africa as a normative question—in particular, one that resonates with a wider, interstate moral abhorrence to racial discrimination (e.g. A/PV.50, 1019; A/PV.51, 1029, 1038–1040; A/C.1/SR.107; A/PV.120, 1146; A/PV.360, 329–330). In 1946, the Indian delegation's perspective encapsulates the point:

> The bitter memories of racial doctrines in the practice of States and Governments are still fresh in the minds of all of us. Their evil and tragic consequences are part of the problems with which we are called upon to deal.
>
> A/PV.37, 732

Six weeks later, at the plenary meetings, the Indian delegation made a further point:

> We appreciate fully the difficulties and embarrassment of many countries on different questions, but on this question, there has been little basic difference of opinion, and abstention in this instance can only indicate to the world a lack of concern in a vital human problem. I ask you not to abstain. Let us have the courage of our convictions and vote for the Charter.
>
> A/PV.50, 1018

As the commentary suggests, the Indian delegation pushed for a notion of appropriateness that could come across as more agreeable to third states. The status quo was not just abhorrent to India or its coalition counterparts; it was abhorrent in reference to some broader intersubjective, interstate consensus on racism. The "bitter memories of racial doctrines" were held out to have been "still fresh in the minds of all," and were, by extension, resonant with a normative stance against racial discrimination in specific relation to South Africa. Hence, India also claimed "little basic difference of opinion" on the issue. India and other states were more explicit in their appeal to some "stamp of political approval or disapproval." Its delegation pointed, for example, to the recent adoption of Resolution 103(I) as evidence of "couching the unanimous will to wipe out all sorts of discrimination, whether due to race, religion or creed" (A/PV.51, 1037).

In sum, a core coalition of states attempted to project a sense of legitimacy into a position against the status quo in South Africa by manipulating its resonance (or "frame") within a common norm on racial equality. It also amplified that intersubjective resonance by "cuing," namely by prompting other delegations to see the dissonance between the status quo and interstate expectations

on racial discrimination. A coalition of states did this by making that dissonance appear as though it was from the outset becoming starker and starker,
such that its interstate repercussions were becoming more and more "abhorrent" (A/PV.315, 532; A/PV. 401, 336; A/577, 4; Nehru in Trumbull 1949, 19). In
1946, the Soviet Union was among those to hammer on the point:

> Over a period of many decades, in South Africa as well as in the South
> African Union, and in the separate South African Republics even before
> the creation of the Union, discrimination was systematically fostered
> and continues to be fostered; furthermore, it is increasing year by year,
> becoming more and more acute and assuming a more and more provoc-
> ative and acute character.
>
> A/PV.52, 1041

India's delegation pushed even further to insist that "the case ... contained in
its racialism the seeds of the next war" (Pandit in *NY Times* 1.12.1946). For example, one can refute the social construction of this position by suggesting that
racial discrimination in South Africa was appalling in its own terms. One could
also contend that the status quo was deteriorating at the time, referencing the
kind of national legislation being put into force. That legislation could relate
to the later outline of a policy of "apartheid" by Daniel Malan's National Party
in 1948. Yet it is hardly axiomatic that those last apartheid policies were any
more "abhorrent" than those that preceded them by 1948. There are at least
three reasons why.

First, South Africa's position did not alone spell out some inherent abhorrence of racial discrimination at the time. As South Africa's delegation emphasized in October 1946, "the Government was determined to maintain its
Christian civilizing mission in South Africa and would not allow the work of
centuries to be undone" (A/167, 15). "The Indian Memorandum ... [contains]
no recognition of the economic, social and educational advantage which the
Indians in South Africa have enjoyed, which have placed them far in advance
of their kind in India" (A/167, 1). "The presence of a large Indian population in
South Africa is the physical proof of their satisfaction with the conditions of
Natal" (A/167, 3–4). One can make the same point about Prime Minister Malan's
vision for apartheid. In the National Party's own words, apartheid sought the
"welfare of South Africa, and to promote the well-being and happiness of its
citizens, both white and non-white" (National Party 1947). It was to "safeguard
the future of every race in the country," and regard "any policy of oppression
or exploitation of the non-whites by the whites as ... unacceptable" (National
Party 1947). This remained the position of later prime ministers Johannes

Strijdom and Hendrik Verwoerd. As Hendrik Verwoerd put it in August 1960, "the policy of separate development is not based on the desire to suppress any non-white group. Conversely, it is seen as a solution by which Whites would not dominate any of the colored peoples" (Verwoerd 1960 in Menzies 1968, 203).

Second, on the deterioration point, the policies of apartheid were not a departure from what had been by 1946, a familiar experience in the area. In 1952, the United Nations Commission on the Racial Situation in the Union of South Africa reached that conclusion in its extensive study. The Commission emphasized, for example, that "the racial problem in the Union of South Africa … is no new thing in the life of the nation and did not begin when the Nationalist Party conceived and began to apply the so-called *apartheid* doctrine" (A/2505, 115). "Apartheid" was then only a repackaged, local substitute term for racial "segregation" that meant to "breathe new life into an old concept" (A/2505, 53). Apartheid was only a "recent development of an old situation" (A/2505, 58). This point is also consistent with the National Party's policy outline, which emphasized that apartheid was a "concept historically derived from the experience of the established white population of the country" (National Party 1947). Thus, for these two reasons, one *can* suggest that a coalition of states from the outset projected the atmospherics of a deteriorating situation in South Africa. That projection tapped into—and in turn accentuated—a pre-existing, collective sense of hatred to racism.

A corollary to the core coalition's rhetorical action was normative assertions against apartheid meant to supersede procedural claims against the United Nations' competence. The specific line of argument was that the normative ramifications of racial discrimination in South Africa were so abhorrent that they warranted unequivocal interstate condemnation, despite the norms on non-intervention that some delegations insisted on (e.g. A/PV.50, 1019; A/PV.51, 1039–1040; A/PV.360, 329; A/PV.52, 1042). As India's Ambassador Pandit argued,

> The issue brought before you is by no means a narrow or local one. Nor can we accept any contention that a gross and continuing outrage of this kind against the fundamental principles of the Charter can be claimed by anyone, and least of all by a Member State, to be a matter of no concern to this Assembly of the world's peoples.
>
> A/PV.37, 732

A more explicit formulation of the position came from the Kingdom of Iraq's delegation:

> This is not a question of internal affairs ... It is a much bigger issue, a
> human question in which Asiatic is against the Westerner, colored against
> white—vast international implications extending far beyond the shores
> of Cape Town. Unless the people of Korea, Indo-China, and elsewhere in
> Asia feel the United Nations stands for brotherhood among men, all our
> work here will be in vain.
>
> JAMALI in *The New York Times*, 15.11.1950

This is to say that a core coalition of states asserted that the issue's normative ramifications were so ignominious—or, as India's delegation put it, "grave
and momentous"—that they demanded immediate interstate attention and,
by extension, unequivocal denunciation (A/C.1&6/SR.1–6, 26). The issue was,
therefore, "by no means a narrow or local," as India's delegation put it in 1946
(A/PV.37, 732). It presented a problem that was of "deep international concern,"
"supreme importance to all our countries," "affected all nations and all the peoples of the word," and so on (A/C.1&6/SR.1–6, 23; A/PV.120, 1146; A/PV.212, 430;
A/PV.213, 432).

The abhorrence of racial discrimination meant to supersede and vitiate certain delegations' procedural position against the United Nations' competence
on the issue. A common reference for this procedural position was Article Two,
Section Seven of the Charter, which asserts that "nothing contained in the present Charter shall authorize the United Nations to intervene in matters which
are essentially within the domestic jurisdiction of any state." Accordingly,
some delegations held that apartheid was not a global, multilateral concern
(e.g. A/PV.50, 1010–1012, 1031; A/PV.51, 1032). The following intervention by the
French delegation provides an example of the viewpoint:

> When the Ad Hoc Political Committee of the General Assembly consid-
> ered our agenda item entitled "The question of race conflict in South
> Africa resulting from the policies of *apartheid* of the Government of the
> Union of South Africa," the French delegation stated its view that that
> question fell essentially within the domestic jurisdiction of the Union of
> South Africa ...
>
> The policy practiced by the government of any Member State towards
> its own nationals, within its own frontiers, is an intrinsic part of the sov-
> ereign rights reserved for the jurisdiction of each State and jealously
> safeguarded against even the best intentioned incursions by the orga-
> nized collectivity of the other members of the international community.
> By committing one violation of those rights, no matter how important
> the particular case may be, the United Nations collectively commits a

breach of the Charter and at the same time endangers the security of each Member.

A/PV.401, 335

Notice that this intervention is at most tepid about opposition to the status quo but does not challenge head-on the common norm on racism that the core coalition of states put into question. As the Polish delegation observed in 1946, "it is difficult of course for many delegations to say: 'We are in support of racial discrimination; we are in support of the oppression of the Indians in the Union of South Africa'" (A/PV.120, 1162). Thus, the latter position allows normative sentiment to reverberate year after year and opens the door to rhetorical "self-entrapment" at the United Nations. I say self-entrapment because the proponents of the latter arguments drew from near-identical norms in other contexts but would not support them concerning South Africa. An example includes the United Kingdom and its later position on decolonization some twelve years later, as we shall discuss in the next section.

3   Part Two

We have paid close attention to the more proactive members of a core coalition of states that took shape by a shared initial position against racial discrimination in the Union of South Africa in 1946. We can now consider the extent to which those efforts pressured other states to take similar positions, with particular attention to how third-state positions change over the next decade and a half. As we shall see, the core coalition's diplomatic efforts set in motion a process of collective legitimization, which in turn inclined third states into adopting an unequivocal and unambiguous stance against apartheid in 1961.

I qualify this argument with the assertion that the core coalition's perceived integrity on apartheid made their efforts more influential. India, among other coalition members, was seen as a "growing problem," determined to "keep the pot boiling," as the American delegation put it in 1952 (O'Malley 2020, 212–213). India's Prime Minister would "never let the matter rest ... at every opportunity that presented itself, he would wage war on apartheid and the country which practiced it," as Australia's Robert Menzies observed in 1961 (Menzies 1968, 214). Thanks to this perceived integrity, as we shall see, target states were undoubtedly concerned about the political costs of maintaining their long-standing positions on apartheid. This supports the interpretation that socialization efforts are more likely to succeed when proponents are seen as trustworthy—rather than hypocritical—advocates of a cause. The United Kingdom, Australia, and Canada serve as illustrative country cases.

3.1   *The United Kingdom*

The United Kingdom is one example of a state that seems to have been influenced by India and other states' cumulative efforts since the First Session of the General Assembly in 1946. The most relevant facts are as follows. In April 1961, the United Kingdom took an unequivocal and unambiguous position against apartheid after fifteen years of reservation. At the Special Political Committee, its delegation made the following point:

> Apartheid confronts us with the circumstances which are, so far as I know, unique in the annals of this Organization. We see the deliberate adoption, retention and development of a policy specifically based on total racial discrimination. This is further distinguished by the circumstance that it is discrimination amongst and against the permanent inhabitants of the country itself. Such a policy, which is a deliberate exaltation of discriminatory principles, stands alone in its category.
>
> Smithers in DE LINT 1976, 17

At the later plenary meetings, the United Kingdom's delegation made the further point:

> The United Kingdom delegation, upon further consideration, decided to vote in favor of the draft resolution ... We consider that this is essentially an aspect of apartheid which is now no longer of purely domestic concern, for reasons we have explained elsewhere in the United Nations.
>
> A/PV.981, 261

Throughout that same session, the United Kingdom's delegation further clarified its position with votes favoring the then-two resolutions on South Africa. Those resolutions recalled all prior resolutions on the issue and, in one case, took an explicit position against racial discrimination in the country (A/RES/ 1663(XVI); A/RES/1662(XVI)). The Commonwealth Relations Office observed that the position was "a new departure of policy" from a long-standing position in South Africa (PREM 11/3598). Otherwise, the United Kingdom's stance was a move "off the fence," as a 1961 news piece from *The Guardian* put it (*The Guardian*, 6.4.1961).

The first observation one must make about the position is what it does not in its own terms suggest: a concern for—or "discovery" of—the policies of apartheid in South Africa. If that were the case, one would expect some previous interstate proceedings to demonstrate as much. Apartheid had been an explicit policy for some fifteen years and drew from explicit segregation laws that had beset the country for many more years before. This leads to the question of whether there had been some change in the domestic circumstances to encourage the above position. In some part, this was the United Kingdom's view, as its time-specific reference to "now" can suggest. The perspective has some traction, as the one-year-old Sharpeville incident can suggest. On those terms, one would need to expect that the incident was so abhorrent that it alone countenanced condemnation in the above manner. One would also need to expect comparable incidents—those involving mass casualties at the hands of the local authorities—were also abhorrent enough to warrant condemnation comparably. That condemnation would entail some manifest opposition to similar incidents since 1946, the first of which was the Witwatersrand Strike (Dubow 2008, 67–68). Yet, no such opposition to those incidents exists at the United Nations, as the United Kingdom's previous engagement with interstate proceedings in South Africa indicates. In fact, throughout those years—and considering those circumstances—the United Kingdom was so far removed from the interstate conversation that it "refused to identify ... in any way with the discussion on the substance of the matter or with the draft resolutions arising from it" (A/PV.401, 334). This suggests that some change in circumstances—for example, as measured by mass casualties brought on by local authorities—was not enough to render the status quo so exceptional to warrant clear, unequivocal condemnation.

One can further substantiate this point by considering the United Kingdom's position on Sharpeville. At the General Debate, the United Kingdom acknowledged the occasion as an "annual debate upon the state of the world where we together survey the achievements and the failures of the past twelve months" (A/PV.758, 144). Yet, in 1960, its delegation was not taken aback by the incident. It did not raise Sharpeville—nor the status quo in South Africa more broadly— as a cause for global, multilateral concern (A/PV.877, 223–227). On the contrary, "at every stage of the proceedings in New York, the United Kingdom objective has been to ... prevent action in the Council," as one Indian delegate observed in a telegram to New Delhi (11/60-AFR-I 1960 in Omalley 2020, 216).

Accordingly, the United Kingdom's immediate position at the Security Council was to abstain from a resolution other states brought to the table a month after the incident. That resolution called on South Africa to bring about "racial harmony based on equality to ensure that the present situation does not continue to recur" (S/4300; S/PV.853, 21–23; S/PV.856, 13). At most, the United Kingdom's immediate position on Sharpeville was to express "deep sympathy with all the people of the Union of South Africa in the tragic events which have taken place" (A/PV.853, 21). On the flip side, it was also to recognize the "indisputable right and the duty of any Government to use the forces at its disposal to maintain law and order within its own territory" (A/PV.853, 21). This is to say that the United Kingdom's immediate position was not a clear, explicit stance against apartheid. Sharpeville was thus not an inflection point. It was not a significant empirical conditioning factor in the United Kingdom's move "off the fence"—contrary to the above statement.

This allows for a preliminary, social constructivist interpretation of the above stance against racial discrimination in South Africa. The empirical basis for that interpretation comes from *how* the position articulates a stance against the status quo. The articulation of that stance was influenced by India and other states' efforts at the First Session of the General Assembly and each successive session since then. The first reason is that it echoes a specific set of ideas that those states had long been in favor of. Like the core states, it argues that the status quo in the country was so "unique"—or "grave and momentous," as India's delegation put it in 1946—that it warranted unequivocal condemnation. As those states had done, the position suggests a socially mediated, normative ramification to racial discrimination in South Africa that was so abhorrent that it ought to supersede all other considerations (including procedural considerations on the United Nations competence). This became more apparent when the British delegation emphasized its "repugnance for the theories underlying the practice of racial discrimination in South Africa" (A/SPC/SR.339, 66).

Moreover, like the core states, the position also sees the status quo as so appalling that it warranted unequivocal *interstate* condemnation. It finds that the nature of racial discrimination in South Africa was not a "purely domestic concern" or "by no means a narrow or local," as India put it in 1946. It "concerned all nations of the world," as the Mexican delegation put it that same year (A/C.1&6/SR.1–6, 23). Hence, how the United Kingdom formulated ideas against the status quo suggests that it was moved by the diplomatic pressure that a core coalition of states brought to bear.

A second reason to support this social constructivist interpretation relates to the nature of interstate proceedings from 1960 to 1961. An indication comes from the large membership expansion at the United Nations, as Newell Stultz emphasizes (Stultz 1991, 4–6). From 1960 to 1961, thirteen new member states came from Africa. Furthermore, from 1961 to 1962, all four new member states again came from Africa. Admission of these new member states amounted to a twenty-two percent increase in membership at the United Nations. This expansion of membership matters because those states were seen as ardent about questions of racial discrimination and even more concerning South Africa. Sir Brian Urquhart, then Under-Secretary-General, made a relevant observation:

> The fall of 1960 was a turning point. The balance in the General Assembly was radically changing, reflecting a new and very different world from the polarized East-West state of affairs of the 1940s and 1950s. New interests and new forces were coming into play. Power vacuums were occurring in sensitive areas of the world in the wake of decolonization.
>
> URQUHART 1987, 171

These new states are thus an essential empirical conditioning factor. They added significant momentum to the coalition's diplomatic campaign against apartheid, which exerted its influence with more intensity thanks to their support. This seems apparent in what some delegations—those otherwise on the fence—observed as the "more bitter" tone of interstate proceedings on South Africa (A/SPC/SR.241, 72). More importantly, it also seems apparent in what the United Kingdom made of its position on South Africa before making it public. In 1961, for example, the Foreign Office made the following observation in a confidential telegram to its Permanent Mission in New York:

> Our position, both generally in the United Nations and in relation to the Afro-Asian powers, would be much strengthened if we could vote in favor of the Indian resolution. If we failed to do so, it would be widely resented and misunderstood, particularly in light of the Prime Minister's remarks in the House of Commons (March 22) to the effect that apartheid had become a matter of more than domestic interest in South Africa.
>
> PREM 11/3598, 52

In that telegram, the Foreign Office emphasized the "strong political case for changing our policy regarding the apartheid issue" (PREM 11/3598, 53). There are at least two key points to make in the statement. One is that it evidences a concern for the United Kingdom's position on apartheid vis-à-vis a global, multilateral audience of states. The other point is that it evidences a specific, more newfound concern for that position vis-à-vis an African and Asian interstate audience. The Foreign Office puts the two concerns together to envision an intersubjective sense of wide resentment towards its long-standing position, as well as a subjective sense of rhetorical entrapment given the need to maintain consistency with more recent positions on decolonization set out at the General Assembly in 1959 (A/PV.798, 23). On this last point, the British Mission in New York was more direct, stating in another confidential telegram that the status quo was socially unsustainable: "to continue to abstain would be embarrassing" (PREM 11/3598, 19). This further supports the interpretation that the United Kingdom's eventual position on South Africa was influenced by the more normative aspects of the interstate social environment at the time, which India and other states first brought to bear in 1946.

Further empirical support for this interpretation comes from another confidential telegram written by Alec Douglas-Home, the then Secretary of State for Commonwealth Relations. While on an official visit to Nigeria, the Commonwealth Secretary made the following point to the Prime Minister and Foreign Secretary at the United Nations in support of India's position on racial discrimination in South Africa in April 1961:

> I am sure it would be a mistake to abstain or vote against paragraph 5 of [the] Indian resolution. These resolutions are never wholly satisfactory to everybody and should, I think, be looked at as a whole. The effect of our voting for the first time in favor of a resolution deploring apartheid would be considerably diminished if we started quibbling about the exact wording.
>
> PREM 11/3598, 41

Douglas-Home's observation further supports the idea that the United Kingdom was influenced by the core coalition's diplomatic pressure on South Africa. It suggests that its decision-makers meant to annunciate a stance against racial discrimination in the country based on the significance that other states like Nigeria attached to it. That sense of relevance, the observation suggests, pressured policymakers like Douglas-Home to see the issue in those terms. Those efforts make procedural concerns about competence, wording, and the like relatively unimportant. Hence, the Commonwealth Secretary's main emphasis is on the interstate, social "effect" supporting a position against racial discrimination in South Africa meant to be produced at the United Nations. The Commonwealth Secretary made another, more explicit observation about newly independent states from Africa:

> I spoke yesterday to Abubakar about our future attitude towards apartheid. I said that we would probably be prepared to vote for a suitable resolution condemning South Africa's racial policies provided it did not contain demands for sanctions or other positive measures. He welcomed this and thought there would be great advantage from [the] point of view of our relations with African states if we and they could vote for an agreed resolution drafted on those lines. He added that this would naturally not

repeat not prevent *sic* Nigeria from supporting in addition other resolutions of a stronger kind.

This latter observation refers to the momentum new African states added to the diplomatic campaign against racial discrimination in South Africa. It further substantiates the claim that the United Kingdom moved off the fence, given the position's particular significance to African states. Thus, the Commonwealth Secretary contemplates an intersubjective, "great advantage" vis-à-vis African states as relevant to a stance against racial discrimination in the country.

I consider several secondary sources about the above interpretation of interstate socialization to develop my argument further. The most relevant is Ronald Hyam's and Peter Henshaw's historical account of the United Kingdom's bilateral relationship with South Africa, including attention to the United Nations proceedings (Hyam and Henshaw 2003, 146–167). The two authors make an important point: the United Kingdom's move off the fence in April 1961 was primarily motivated by a need to maintain a sense of "moral leadership" in overseas territories, mainly to ensure that states about to emerge from colonial rule would remain in the Commonwealth (Hyam and Henshaw 2003, 161). That sense of moral leadership "was being so gravely cast into doubt by the British stand on the South African disputes," perhaps even more so given its increased isolation on those issues (Hyam and Henshaw 2003, 161). Hyam and Henshaw write,

> Progress towards independence, instead of being geared to local political development, accelerated under the influence of political changes elsewhere. And with each further grant of independence in Africa or Asia, international pressure on the colonial powers, instead of being eased, intensified as the ranks of the newly independent nations swelled at the UN.
>
> HYAM AND HENSHAW 2003, 161

Hence, Hyam and Henshaw emphasize a concern for moral leadership and suggest an external interstate political context that calls it into question. A concern for moral leadership entails a relational concern for the interstate political context that may or may not recognize it as such. This point supports the above theoretical interpretation that the United Kingdom's position on South Africa was moved by the interstate social environment of the time. Were that not the case, British officials would have been content with their notion of moral leadership and been done with it. However, as the two authors emphasize, that was not the case. The architects of British foreign policy saw that "more harm is being done to our reputation as a Colonial Power by our attitude on these South African items than is being done by any troubles that may occur in the Colonies themselves" (Lloyd 1960 in Hyam and Henshaw 2003, 162).

Hyam and Henshaw also imply a particular concern for some notions of moral leadership vis-à-vis African states because some were former British territories or in the process of becoming independent. Moral leadership on questions of racial discrimination would have been critical to keep those states within the Commonwealth. This lends credence to the previous point on newly independent states adding momentum to the persistent diplomatic campaign on South Africa. A similar perspective comes from Saul Dubow, who suggests that the potential spread of communism throughout Africa was a motive to formulate an eventual position against racial discrimination in South Africa considering Prime Minister Macmillan's 1960 Winds of Change address. "Adoption of a coherent African policy was judged vital in a context where colonial influence was dissipating and where the ensuing power vacuum invited African nationalists to seek the support of communists" (Dubow 2011, 1096). Hence, "Macmillan's disapproval of apartheid had more to do with the difficulties this posed for Britain's position in the rest of Africa, the Central African Federation in particular, than its effects on black South Africans" (Dubow 2011, 1099). To support the claim, Dubow cites the Cabinet Secretary's observation that "it was wise to make our position clear, because of our responsibilities elsewhere in Africa" (PREM 11/3073 in Dubow 2011, 1099). This latter account adds further empirical granularity to the point on moral leadership vis-à-vis African states, suggesting a need to maintain it to avoid the spread of communism throughout the continent.

Nevertheless, one cannot take the point on moral leadership too far and assume that social anxieties concerning African states were decisive enough to move or "lead" the United Kingdom towards its position against South Africa in April 1961. If it were, one would expect it to have backed or "followed" its more extreme position in support of socio-economic and political sanctions that same month. One would thus expect the United Kingdom to have been in some way part of that new interstate campaign, with a new core coalition of states that supported but sought to push the initial campaign in a new direction (e.g. A/SPC/SR.230, 17; A/SPC/SR.239, 59–60; A/SPC/SR.240, 66–67; A/SPC/SR.243, 80–84). However, in 1961 and the immediate years after, the United Kingdom opposed that campaign (e.g. A/SPC/SR.274, 69–70; A/SPC/SR.339, 66–67). The Commonwealth Secretary made that point clear in the above telegram. Moreover, in another confidential 1961 telegram, the Foreign Office made the following observation specific to proceedings at the United Nations:

Three Commonwealth Governments (India, Ceylon, and Malaya) have tabled a moderately worded resolution, while a large number of Africans have tabled one which gets on to such obnoxious proposals as boycotts and the severance of diplomatic relations.

... a failure to support this moderate resolution would be misunderstood both internationally and in Britain. The resolution will be interpreted by world opinion as being no more than a condemnation of apartheid as a policy which is what we should in any case have to say in speaking in the debate. Moreover it seems to us important to give as much encouragement as we can to the moderates and to strengthen our hands in dealing with objectionable resolutions involving proposals for the United Nations action and interference.

PREM 11/3598, 50

This perspective from the Foreign Office further suggests that the United Kingdom was primarily influenced by the "moderate" interstate campaign on South Africa, which dated back to India's and other states' efforts in 1946. In 1961, newly independent states from Africa—all seen as radically opposed to racial discrimination in South Africa—made an influential albeit residual impression on the United Kingdom. These states may have forced the United Kingdom's hand. However, the fact remains that how the United Kingdom formulated ideas against the status quo spoke to India's long-standing position, suggesting that India's efforts were, in the end, most influential. Accordingly, the United Kingdom's position was more consistent with support for the Indian perspective, not the African one.

Further empirical evidence for this interpretation comes from what other state representatives made of India's efforts vis-à-vis the United Kingdom. The most critical observations come from representatives who coordinated with the United Kingdom on issues related to South Africa. Australia, for example, was especially concerned about India's influence on Britain's perspective on South Africa from 1960 to 1961. In a personal letter to his spouse, Dame Pattie, Prime Minister Menzies lamented that "the simple fact is that Harold is much more concerned to be right with Nehru than he is to be right with me" (Menzies 1961 in Martin and Hardy 1993, 428). Menzies also emphasized, "I am really very sick about Harold Macmillan's statements. He will do anything to placate India but thinks nothing of embarrassing me in my own country" (Menzies 1961 in Martin and Hardy 1993, 428). Menzies' Department Secretary evidenced similar discernment:

the truth is that the United Kingdom is defending, somewhat grimly, its standing and authority in the world. For this purpose, which is political rather than economic, it requires a certain amount of keeping in tune with India in particular.

Bunting 1961 in GOLDSWORTHY 2002, 113

These observations again suggest that India's efforts pressured the United Kingdom to adjust its outlook on South Africa in April 1961. As close counterparts, the Australian side would have been well-positioned to see those efforts operate.

3.2   *Australia*

Australia is another example of a state influenced by the core coalition's efforts. Here are some essential facts. Under Prime Minister Robert Menzies (and previously Ben Chifley), Australia did not take a clear, unequivocal stance against racial discrimination in South Africa until April 1961 (e.g. A/PV.315, 532; A/AC.53/SR.32, 171; A/AC.72/SR.36, 182; A/AC.76/SR.44, 211). Like the United Kingdom, the main reason was on procedural grounds: racial discrimination in South Africa was a domestic concern and was, therefore, not other states' business to discuss. That was Australia's position on proceedings at the United Nations, the Commonwealth, and its political context. As Menzies put it, "*apartheid* (or separate development) was a domestic matter and that we in other countries should not interfere" (Menzies 1968, 193). "I felt that, in a multi-racial community, it was a matter for political judgment ... whether development should be based upon the separation of races or their integration" (Menzies 1968, 193). The furthest departure from that position came in 1957 when the Australian delegation at the United Nations reaffirmed a general position against racial discrimination in connection with proceedings in South Africa. As its Permanent Representative put it, "while the Australian delegation had never entered into a discussion of the substance of the item before the Committee, such an attitude did not imply Australia's support for racial discrimination" (A/SPC/SR.15, 67).

In April 1961, however, Australia took an unequivocal and unambiguous stand on the issue. At the committee meetings, its delegation in New York expressed support for India's long-standing position on South Africa "in order to demonstrate its hostility to the policy of *apartheid*" (A/SPC/SR.244, 85). "The Australian delegation ... felt most serious disquiet at South Africa's racial policies and deplored the results of the application of those policies" (A/SPC/SR.241, 72). Moreover, concerning the resolution about the Indian people, the Australian delegation made the broader observation that:

It has become apparent that even abstention is open to the misinterpretation of indifference to the human issues involved. In substance, this issue has affinities with the question of *apartheid* which the General Assembly is also dealing with at the present session. The Australian delegation has already explained its attitude on this point in the First Committee. It does not support or condone the policy of *apartheid*, of which the matter here at stake—the treatment of people of Indian origin—is one aspect. It shares the view that the most hopeful means of a solution to this problem lies in the negotiations which are recommended to the South African Government in the draft resolution before us.

To make this attitude clear, my delegation will vote in favor of this draft resolution.

A/PV.981, 265–266

This sentiment broke with some fifteen-year-old opposition to or abstention on almost identical resolutions. Moreover, for the first time, it also manifests an unmistakable stance on the substantive complaint against racial discrimination in South Africa. As a news piece from *The Guardian* put it, the move was a "volte-face by Mr. Menzies Policy on S. Africa" (*The Guardian* 10.4.1961). "Australia's decision to vote for a United Nations resolution rebuking South Africa for its apartheid policies ... does mean a marked change in Mr. Menzies' attitude" (*The Guardian* 10.4.1961).

The first observation one must make about this "change in attitude" is that it does not represent an inherent, normative "hostility" to racial discrimination as practiced in the Union of South Africa. Empirical evidence for this assertion comes from the absence of such sentiment throughout participation in previous interstate proceedings on the issue from 1946 to 1961 (e.g. A/PV.315, 532; A/AC.53/SR.32, 171; A/AC.72/SR.36, 182). This raises the question of whether the position responded to the March 1960 Sharpeville massacre one year before. There is limited empirical evidence for that interpretation as well. I say limited because from March 1960 to April 1961, the Australian delegation did not emphasize an abhorrence to what happened in Sharpeville. At the Security Council, one month after the incident, the Australian delegation was not among the twenty-nine others to initiate proceedings to condemn what occurred (S/PV.856).

Moreover, at a parliamentary debate in early April 1960, Prime Minister Robert Menzies "refused to condemn apartheid in specific terms, and at a press conference on the 10th of April, he reaffirmed his Government's policy of non-interference in the internal affairs of South Africa" (PREM 11/3112, 11–12). And six months later, in the General Assembly, the Prime Minister did not raise

Sharpeville in the General Debate (A/PV.888, 434–437). Hence, the suggestion is that Sharpeville was not the main reason for Australia's "volte-face" on South Africa. One year later, in April 1961, the Australian delegation observed that "the events which had occurred since 1959 had added urgency to the question being examined before the Committee" (A/SPC/SR.241, 72). Yet that sentiment acknowledges that those events had only "added" significance, not significance enough to sanction a new articulation of position on South Africa.

How Australia expressed a stance against racial discrimination in South Africa allows for a preliminary, social constructivist interpretation. There are two empirical justifications for why. The first empirical justification comes from *how* Australia articulated its position. The reasoning here is similar to what has been covered in the previous subsection on the United Kingdom and does not require further discussion. The main point is that Australia's eventual articulation of position seems influenced by the coalition's efforts because, after years of silence on the substantive question, it echoes a specific set of ideas that those states had long favored.

Furthermore, the position also evidences a response to the trenchant outcry against racial discrimination in the country since "it has become apparent that even abstention is open to misinterpretation of indifference to the human issues involved." Responding to that outcry implies an intersubjective need to "speak out" and reaffirm a stance against the status quo. This suggests that silence on the substantive question became socially unsustainable, taken by other states to represent insouciance (or a "lack of concern in a vital human problem," as India's delegation put it in 1946). A core coalition of states seems to have been influential concerning Australia for reasons like the United Kingdom. It helped inculcate an intersubjective, interstate atmosphere that galvanized otherwise muted normative sentiment against racial discrimination in South Africa.

The second, more direct empirical justification for this theoretical inference comes from what Australian authorities made of the position on South Africa before making it public, particularly before learning about the United Kingdom's move off the fence in April 1961. Australia's views began to change when Arthur Tange (Secretary of External Affairs) received a report from Jim Plim (Permanent Representative to the United Nations in New York). Tange said, "the estimated voting intentions of other countries was a major factor in the final decision" (Tange 1961 in Hearder 2015, 131). "It enabled advice to the Prime Minister that, if a resolution criticizing apartheid was supported by all except Australia, there would be 'serious misunderstanding worldwide about Australia'" (Tange 1961 in Hearder 2015, 131). The Australian Prime Minister Robert Menzies then made that sentiment known in "private and personal" correspondence with Harold Macmillan and Duncan Sandys (the United Kingdom's Secretary of State for Commonwealth Relations). In that correspondence, Robert Menzies set out Australia's reasons to change its stance on the status quo in South Africa. In an April 1961 letter to Macmillan, Menzies made the following point:

> We have been studying to-day the two draft resolutions on Apartheid now before the UN Assembly. I think there will be widespread opposition to the extreme African resolution. However we understand that you may be contemplating only abstaining on the fifth paragraph of the Three Power resolution and thereafter voting in favor. I hope you will not adopt this course. This is substantially the same resolution which you voted against last time (1959) at which time Australia abstained. I want you to realize that if the UK not vote in favor, with New Zealand presumably following suit, it would leave Australia quite isolated. This would render my own position intolerable.
>
> PREM 11/3598, 9

One month later, after adopting a new stance on South Africa, Menzies wrote the following personal letter to Duncan Sandys:

> After considerable reflection, I feel it necessary to put a few matters to you regarding the recent General Assembly of the United Nations, and in particular the three power resolution regarding South Africa. In November, 1959, the United Kingdom voted against this resolution. Australia, rightly or wrongly abstained. This year we were proposing once more to abstain when, without any notice from the United Kingdom and without any United Kingdom consultation with us, our own representative at the United Nations informed us that he had learned that a change of vote by the United Kingdom from opposition to straight out support was being recommended and supported. Having regard to certain events that had happened, this clearly involved me in most grievous difficulties. I at once cabled Mr. Macmillan, but, for all substantial purposes, this proved too late. In the result, we at this end had to make most painful and embarrassing decisions.
>
> Enquires indicated that if we abstained, we would find ourselves alone. There would be serious and world-wide misrepresentations, and Australia would incur a solitary hostility among African and Asian nations. The choice was therefore between my own personal position, which became one of humiliation, and in fact exposed me to considerable ridicule, and

the general repute of my country. Under these circumstances, we decided that, with reservations orally indicated by our representative, we would vote with the United Kingdom.

But I should make it clear that I deeply resent the way in which these circumstances arose. I can see no possible excuse for the failure to consult us, since the United Kingdom government must have known that the question of South African policy would come up, as it had in previous years. I think that you just forgot about us, in a matter in which I had been greatly and unsuccessfully involved in London only a week or two previously.

PREM 11/3598, 8–9

There are numerous essential observations one must draw from Menzies' communications. One is that the United Kingdom was a crucial empirical "conditioning factor" in Australia's eventual stance on South Africa. Menzies felt left behind by Harold Macmillan and, as a result, saw a need for Australia to reevaluate its position on South Africa.

Another critical observation from Menzies' writings is that they also provide evidence of a direct concern for the interstate political context of racial discrimination in South Africa. Given the United Kingdom's new stance, it takes a fresh appraisal of the nature of interstate proceedings on the issue. Given that appraisal, Menzies finds Australia "alone" in that context. As the first passage indicates, Menzies saw the isolation and its subsequent appearance vis-à-vis other African and Asian states as socially unsustainable or "intolerable." This sense of isolation is more apparent in the Prime Minister's writings to his spouse Dame Pattie, in which he intimates that maintaining Australia's long-standing position on South Africa "would give rise to enormous political difficulties and would lend support to the people who are ever ready to say that I have become a "lone wolf" in the Commonwealth" (Menzies 1961 in Martin and Hardy 1993, 428). Note that Menzies' sense of isolation (or being seen as a "lone wolf") was *not* just socially unsustainable or "intolerable" in a relational sense. As the second passage above suggests, it was intolerable to the extent that the substantive issue—namely, racial discrimination in South Africa—was also relevant. Hence, Menzies also expresses a sense of "embarrassment," "humiliation," "ridicule," "hostility" and a challenge to Australia's "general repute" in specific connection with the absence of an affirmative stance against racial discrimination in South Africa. This further sheds light on what motivated Australia's socially mediated, normative sentiment against apartheid. It also supports an interpretation of the interstate social construction of that position.

Annemarie Devereux's *Australia and the Birth of the Bill of Human Rights* is the most relevant secondary account of this interpretation of interstate socialization. The work addresses Australia's stance on South Africa at the United Nations in April 1961. Devereux makes two relevant points. The first point is that Prime Minister Menzies and Garfield Barwick (then Acting Minister of External Affairs) "were reluctant to draw any adverse conclusions about the Sharpeville Massacre" (Devereux 2005, 220). "Both men refused to support a resolution in the House of Representatives condemning South Africa" (Devereux 2005, 220). This supports the assertion that domestic circumstances in South Africa were not enough reason to adopt a position on South Africa. The second relevant point that Devereux makes is that "Australia's decision was taken reluctantly after being taken unawares by the United Kingdom's change of heart" (Devereux 2005, 220). "Faced with the risk of being the only country not to vote for a resolution, and the attendant risk of misrepresentation of Australia's motives, Cabinet authorized Australian delegates to vote in favor of General Assembly action" (Devereux 2005, 221). This latter point supports the interpretation that the United Kingdom's "change of heart" was a significant empirical conditioning factor, leading Australia to reconsider its position on South Africa. Devereux's latter point also allows the interpretation that the interstate political context at the time was a decisive consideration in reviewing that position.

What Devereux's account lacks, however, is the social constructivist assertion that that political context was not "inevitable" in April 1961. On that score, as we have seen, India and other states' efforts had been critical to the "construction" of that context since 1946. These core states were vital to Australia's eventual stance on South Africa. Yet Australia's eventual outlook on South Africa was not just based on a relational need to avoid interstate isolation, as Devereux suggests. It was also based on a socially mediated, normative concern for the issue's content. Robert Menzies, for example, expresses more profound social anxieties of "embarrassment," "humiliation," and "ridicule" about the particular question of racism in South Africa. Menzies' sentiment suggests social concern over Australia's specific stance on racism, not on other issues that Australia was also numerically isolated on at the time. Thus, Australia's change in position took place primarily because of socio-strategic and socially mediated normative concerns for what resounded as "legitimate" at the United Nations.

3.3   *Canada*

Canada is the third and final example of a socialization subject. Consider these facts. From 1946 to 1958, the Canadian delegation did not support India's complaint against South Africa on procedural and factual grounds (e.g. A/C.1&6/SR.1–6, 11–12; A/AC.61/SR.20, 112–113; A/AC.72/SR.35, 177). The closest it went was to reaffirm a general position against racial discrimination throughout those proceedings from 1952 to 1958 (e.g. A/AC.72/SR.35, 177; A/AC.61/SR.20, 112; A/AC.76/SR.47, 231). In 1958, Canada's delegation went further by voting for that year's two resolutions on South Africa (A/RES/1302(XIII); A/RES/1248 (XIII)). The most explicit of those resolutions was (A/RES/1248 (XIII)), which expressed "regret and concern" over the continued policies of apartheid (A/RES/1248 (XIII), 7). Favorable votes on those resolutions were a subtle change in Canada's stance. On one hand, it was consistent with previous positions. The reason is that Canada's delegation saw those resolutions as conciliatory, meaning they did not *per se* outline forthright condemnation of the status quo (DEA/6–1959/2). Moreover, support for the two resolutions was consistent with previous reservations that the "General Assembly should not ignore the provisions protecting States from interference in their internal affairs" (A/SPC/SR.92, 35). On the other hand, however, support for the two resolutions was a break with the past. In contrast with previous years, the Canadian delegation joined the Indian delegation to draft one of the resolutions and at least imply a stance against racial discrimination specific to South Africa.

In April 1961, the Canadian delegation went further. It made the unequivocal and unambiguous point that "Canada felt obliged to protest against the policy of apartheid" (A/SPC/SR.243, 79). Later in November, the delegation went on to insist that:

> The defenders of "apartheid" had spoken of the benefits received by the non-white population in South Africa: low-cost housing, hospital and medical facilities, economic improvements, and educational facilities. Whatever the importance those benefits, however, they did not alter the intrinsic evils of a system which asserted the racial superiority of one group over another within the national community ... the Assembly was faced here with an evil philosophy which could, in the final analysis, be overcome only by moral persuasion.
>
> A/SPC/SR.285, 132

This position was a more explicit turning point in Canada's stance on South Africa at the United Nations. It broke with years of reservation and made known an unmistakable normative position against the status quo.

The first empirical observation about this gradual change in position is that it does not represent an inherent, normative "protest" against racial discrimination in the Union of South Africa. Like the previous two examples, the empirical evidence for this assertion comes from the lack of such sentiment throughout participation in prior proceedings, especially while the policy of apartheid was in force from 1948 onwards (e.g. A/C.1&6/SR.1–6, 11–12; A/ AC.61/SR.20, 112–113; A/AC.72/SR.35, 177). This raises the question of whether the historical circumstances at the time were unique enough to sanction the above change in position. The most apparent change in circumstances was Sharpeville in March 1960. The empirical record indicates that Canada's delegation did not see those events as grounds to change course at the United Nations (DEA/7060–40). Canadian Prime Minister John Diefenbaker was explicit, making the case that "the conclusion of the government is that at this time no beneficial purpose would be served by diplomatic protests or by even more extreme measures to intervene in this tragic situation" (Diefenbaker 1960 in Tennyson 1982, 146). Hence, the empirical record does not suggest that Canada's stance on South Africa was based on a categorical normative abhorrence to apartheid, nor motivated by events in Sharpeville.

This allows for a preliminary, social constructivist interpretation that India and other states' efforts were influential. There are two empirical justifications for this. The first comes from how the Canadian delegation articulated a position on South Africa at the United Nations in April 1961. The reasoning here is similar to the previous two subsections, and so does not require further discussion. The position seems influenced by the Indian coalition's efforts because, after years of reticence on the substantive question, it echoes a specific set of ideas that those states had been agitating for. The second empirical justification comes from how Canadian officials arrived at that position. Empirical evidence for this assertion dates back to 1946 when the Indian delegation first brought its complaint to the United Nations. Substantial empirical evidence does suggest that the core coalition's efforts were gradually influential, particularly in nurturing a sense of contretemps and pressuring the Canadian delegation to change course. In a confidential communication, for example, Lester Pearson (then Undersecretary for External Affairs) emphasized that India's complaint was "an embarrassing one, especially for Commonwealth countries" (Pearson 1946 in Tennyson 1982, 117). Louis St. Laurent (then Prime Minister) made a similar observation:

> Canada's position in regard to the status of East Indians here is not above criticism and we are at present time receiving communications protesting against it. It would be unfortunate, therefore, if we took any initiative which served to concentrate attention on our own position and extend the controversy to include us.
>
> ST. LAURENT 1946 in TENNYSON 1982, 117

In 1952, the empirical record also suggests that Canadian officials felt embarrassed due to India's and other states' resolutions on the "race conflict" question. As Lester Pearson put it (then as Secretary for External Affairs), "the Canadian Delegation might let other delegations know in informal discussions that the inclusion of this item on the final agenda would cause us embarrassment" (Pearson 1952 in PCO 288).

Over the years, Canada's response was "to delay and possibly prevent bitter discussion on the merits of the question" (Pearson 1952 in PCO 288). By the mid to late 1950s, however, Canadian officials saw the sense of "embarrassment" as socially unsustainable and reason to change course accordingly. In 1956, the Department of External Affairs urged a review of Canada's stance on "colonial issues" at the United Nations (Henshaw 1999, 27). They argued that:

> Canada's prestige at the UN and its relations with newly-independent states could only be harmed by the continuation of a reactionary stand on these issues, especially when Canada was placing itself in the company of an increasingly isolated group, most of which were colonial powers.
>
> DEA in HENSHAW 1999, 27–28

In late 1957, the Canadian delegation made a similar observation in a confidential assessment of proceedings:

> At the Twelfth Session there seemed to be renewed interest in these [South African] items probably because of the gradually swelling voice of the African nations ... however, they can be increasingly embarrassing to the European members of the Commonwealth, who will be under constant pressure to take positive steps to induce South Africa to change its ways.
>
> DEA/5475-DW-52-D-40

On proceedings in 1958, when Canada supported a common position on South Africa, Harold B. Robinson (the Special Assistant to the Secretary of State for External Affairs) made a further observation in a policy guidance memorandum approved by then Prime Minister John Diefenbaker:

> International opinion is becoming more outspoken on this question, mainly because South African policies are increasingly antipathetic to current international conditions in which non-white peoples are becoming more important and are demanding recognition of the equality of all races ... Reflecting this changing atmosphere, ten Western nations

(including the United States, New Zealand and Italy as well as Canada) switched their votes from abstention to the affirmative on the apartheid resolution in 1958 and there has been a similar shift on the other two items.

ROBINSON 1960 in DEA/7060–40

These three observations explicate how Canadian officials began to see a reason to change course on South Africa by 1958. Among other things, they suggest some sense of "embarrassment" and demonstrate a manifest concern for how other states—especially states from Africa—saw Canada's position on South Africa. This suggests that social anxieties about how Canada was seen on questions of racial discrimination were a critical empirical conditioning factor in how its officials arrived at the eventual position.

Yet, like with the United Kingdom and Australia, social anxiety concerning new African states alone was *not* decisive enough to move Canada towards an unequivocal and unambiguous national stance on racial discrimination in South Africa. If it were, then one would expect Canada to have been more consistent with its more inordinate position in favor of diplomatic sanctions (e.g. South Africa's expulsion from the United Nations) (A/SPC/SR.86, 7–8; A/SPC/SR.90, 23; A/SPC/SR.91, 29–30; SPC/SR.123, 173–174). New African delegations made such sentiment known throughout proceedings in 1958 and 1959, as well as throughout the General Debate in 1960 (e.g. A/SPC/SR.140, 67–68; A/SPC/SR.146, 94; A/SPC/SR.172, 212–213). Nevertheless, in those years, Canada's delegation still favored a conciliatory approach, namely to "abstain on resolutions directly critical of the Union" and to show "by voting affirmatively on some paragraphs and by our statements in the debate that we in principle disapproved of racial discrimination" (Robinson 1960 in DEA/7060–40). Hence, the influence of newly independent African states was not pivotal in 1958.

This is to say that the core coalition's cumulative efforts were more influential vis-à-vis Canada by 1958. In the first place, those core states were the ones to insist on the annual treatment of the situation in South Africa, creating the focal point around which the interstate response could organize and pressure others to follow suit. In the second place, the empirical record also, in more direct terms, supports the interpretation that India's efforts were influential in exercising a "moderating influence" over the extreme elements of the interstate campaign so that it could in turn appeal to the likes of Canada to join suit. In 1959, Canada's delegation wrote a confidential report that sheds light on how that took place:

With the experience of the thirteenth session in mind, a large group of African-Asian delegations led by India this year introduced a similar resolution in the hope that they would be able to win the support of an equal or greater number of delegations. The Indians and Ceylonese told us (and it may well be true) that the African members of the African-Asian caucus were pressing for a much stronger resolution (and indeed Liberia threatened publicly in committee to introduce a resolution warning the Union of possible expulsion from the UN). However, our informants say the Asians persuaded the Africans that by sticking with the present relatively mild resolution, a sweeping majority vote could be obtained. When it came to be known that Australia and Belgium might switch from a negative vote to an abstention this year, the elated sponsors were anxious not to lose Canada's vote and the Indians went so far as to make formal representations in Ottawa to this effect.

DEA/5475-DW-52-D-40

This latter observation demonstrates the influence that core states like India had on new coalition members and over third states like Canada. It shows that states like India were influential in keeping the focus on a common position against apartheid and providing an avenue through which Canada could support it. Although Canada did not support an identical resolution on South Africa in 1959, against Diefenbaker and the Canadian delegation's express wishes, the empirical point remains that India and other core states' efforts were most influential at the time (Henshaw 1999, 30).

The question remains about how Canada arrived at its forthright national position against apartheid in April 1961. There is some indication that the position had to do with South Africa's withdrawal from the Commonwealth in March 1961. Peter Henshaw, for example, makes the point that John Diefenbaker had been a progressive influence on Canada's apartheid position since he took office in June 1957 (Henshaw 1999, 27–36). With South Africa gone from the Commonwealth, Diefenbaker no longer saw an obstacle to making the Canadian national position unequivocal and unambiguous on apartheid (Peter Henshaw 1999, 35). "This action, taken on 15 March 1961, immediately transformed not only the character of the Commonwealth but also the course of the South African disputes at the UN" (Peter Henshaw 1999, 35). Peter Henshaw's perspective is important to keep in mind. It emphasizes that some Canadian officials, particularly John Diefenbaker, had been uneasy about the status quo for years. It also emphasizes that South Africa's longtime membership within the Commonwealth kept Diefenbaker from elevating those views to the level of Canada's national foreign policy.

I agree, to an extent. On the former point, the empirical record suggests that John Diefenbaker's views against apartheid date back to at least 1952, when he made the point as a member of parliament that "the commonwealth, with five to one of those who are members ... being colored races, should do every-thing possible to assure freedom from discrimination" (Diefenbaker 1952 in Henshaw 1999, 28). As a prime minister, however, the empirical record does not substantiate the interpretation that those personal views were decisive. The reason is that Diefenbaker himself was unwilling to elevate those views to the level of national policy. "On a number of occasions, he intimated that were he not head of government, he would express his own abhorrence of apartheid in stronger terms" (Freeman 1997, 23). Accordingly, under the Diefenbaker government—which assumed office in June 1957—Canada's immediate stance on South Africa did *not* change. This reservation was appar-ent in proceedings at the United Nations in October 1957 (A/SPC/SR.56, 71). It was also apparent elsewhere, such as in September 1957, when Diefenbaker turned down a request by Martin Luther King Jr. and Eleanor Roosevelt to join other world leaders in condemning apartheid (Tennyson 1982, 141). "They were told pointedly that Canada disapproved of racialism everywhere and saw no reason to single out any one country" (Tennyson 1982, 141). This is not to say that Diefenbaker's personal views were insignificant. Diefenbaker's were sig-nificant, but not to the extent that they were a leading influence on Canada's eventual stance on apartheid.

I agree with Henshaw's second point that South Africa's withdrawal from the Commonwealth was critical. However, if that is the case, then one must also emphasize the decisive influence that the core anti-apartheid states—and new states from Africa—in the first place had on the withdrawal and, by exten-sion, Canada's subsequent stance on apartheid at the United Nations. This requires a look at proceedings in connection with the May 1960 and March 1961 Commonwealth conferences, both of which dealt with a custom that states seek majority approval for readmission after a change in the form of govern-ment (Diefanbaker 1989, 220). By 1961, new states from Africa and Asia—all dead set about opposition to apartheid and later South Africa's readmission—became the majority in the Commonwealth (Freeman 1997, 19; Hayes 1980, 472). The main point is that Canada was *not the* most influential in that process, especially given the majority (Freeman 1997, 19–29). The core anti-apartheid states and new states from Africa conjured up the diplomatic atmosphere in which support for—or even perceived equivocation on—South Africa's con-tinued membership became socially unsustainable. As Linda Freeman writes,

In fact, leadership in securing South Africa's withdrawal had been taken not by Diefenbaker, but by the leaders of India, Ghana, Nigeria, and Malaysia (Malaya). In closed sessions, India's Prime Minister Jawaharlal Nehru stood out, leading "with clarity and conviction" [Robinson 1989, 186]. He never wavered in his understanding that South Africa's racial policies were incompatible with a multi-racial Commonwealth, and that this principle was more important than the convention that the domestic policies of Commonwealth members should not be discussed.

FREEMAN 1997, 27

Harold Robinson, who was an advisor to the Prime Minister at the March 1961 meetings observed that:

Although Diefenbaker was the most sympathetic of the white prime ministers to the positions of the non-white, he can hardly be said to have played the leading role in the drama of South Africa's withdrawal from the Commonwealth. The dominant figures were Nehru and Macmillan, the former because he knew his objectives and pursued them with clarity and conviction, the latter because of his chairmanship in a series of exceedingly delicate situations.

ROBINSON 1989, 186

More importantly, a member of South Africa's delegation emphasized that:

The rock upon which South Africa finally came to grief was that same Nehru. We had watched him in conclave with his sister, Mrs. Pandit, then High Commissioner for India in London, and other Afro-Asians, unrelenting and unsmiling, and I for one had the feeling that nothing Verwoerd could propose would meet with their approval.

MEIRING 1973, 165

To be sure, John Diefenbaker's decision to break ranks with Prime Ministers Harold Macmillan, Robert Menzies, and Walter Nash was influential in undermining compromise proposals to altogether avoid even considering the general question of racial discrimination (e.g. Dubow 2017, 299; Freeman 1997, 26; Henshaw 1999, 34). However, Diefenbaker's approach was to "temporize," as Jawaharlal Nehru put it (Menzies 1968, 214). Moreover, as Harold Basil Robinson put it, "nothing had been more consistent in Diefenbaker's approach than his search for a tolerable way of averting South Africa's withdrawal" (Robinson 1989, 187). Hence, India's Prime Minister and other prime ministers from Asia and Africa were most influential in the decision to leave. By extension, these states were most influential in changing Canada's foreign policy on apartheid.

One can retort that the Canadian government—particularly throughout John Diefenbaker's administration—was, in any case, inclined to express an unequivocal and unambiguous stance against apartheid before the March 1961 Conference (CCC 2.3.1961). As early as May 1960, for example, the Prime Minister made that known to South Africa's Prime Minister Eric Louw at the May 1960 Commonwealth Conference. "You can't carry on like this. Your nation's stand will turn the whole continent of Africa, with the exception of the Portuguese colonies and Rhodesia, against you. Your policies are not only wrong but dangerous" (Diefenbaker 1989, 211). I emphasize two points in response. The first point is that the Prime Minister and the Cabinet favored a stance against apartheid only in the context of closed-door proceedings. Hence, days before the March 1961 conference, John Diefenbaker was *not* unequivocal and unambiguous on the position, asserting that "no one would like to sit in judgment on his fellow member" and that "any association that hopes to play an effective role in the world must ... endeavor to bring about cooperation and understanding between races" (Diefenbaker 1961 in Freeman 1997, 25). This suggests that there was still some equivocation in Canada's apartheid position in the lead-up to the March 1961 Commonwealth Conference.

Even if there was no such reservation, substantial evidence suggests that the position was "constructed" by the interstate political context from 1960 to 1961. The empirical justification for this assertion comes from two strands of evidence. The first strand of evidence relates to how Canadian officials—in particular, aids to the Prime Minister—began to advocate for an unequivocal and unambiguous stance against apartheid from 1960 to 1961. The point is that some of those officials urged a change in position based on the views of other state officials from Asia and Africa. Among those former Canadian officials was Robert Bryce, the Secretary to the Cabinet and Clerk of the Privy Council. According to Harold B. Robinson (an aide to the Prime Minister), Bryce took the position that Canada should take a more forthright stand against apartheid, given its implications for the future integrity of the Commonwealth. In April 1960, Bryce suggested to the Prime Minister that "Canada should consider initiating South Africa's withdrawal from the Commonwealth so that its non-white members could hold up their heads" (Robinson 1989, 124). A few months later, Robert Bryce's resolve grew. He met with delegations from India and Ghana, who pointed out that "the presence of South Africa would deter other African and Asian countries from joining the Commonwealth" (Robinson 1989, 178–179). "On the basis of this experience, Bryce remained as convinced as ever

that Canada should take the lead in denying readmission to South Africa"
(Robinson 1989, 179).

Similar perspectives came from the Prime Minister's Cabinet members, emphasizing that "the important thing was to try to keep the colored
nations within the Commonwealth and confident in the Commonwealth"
(CCC 11.4.1960, 3). Given these concerns for the Commonwealth's future, the
Cabinet also urged a strong stance on South Africa on social grounds:

> Although theoretically apartheid and readmission were separate issues,
> in practice they could not be divorced. The apartheid aspect was by
> far more important, and an equivocal position on civil rights would be
> damaging to Canada's international position and to the Prime Minister's
> national position.
>
> CCC 25.2.1961, 3

The same Cabinet Conclusion also made the point that a failure to take this
position "would be damaging to Mr. Diefenbaker and the Conservative party in
Canada because it would seem incompatible with the public position he had
taken for many years on equality of rights" (CCC 25.2.1961, 2). This latter observation also speaks to the Prime Minister's domestic political pressures from
opponents of South Africa. Yet those domestic political pressures also drew
from the interstate political context at the time. The leader of the Liberal Party,
for example, insisted that "the course actually taken set Canada in opposition
to India and damaged Canada's influence in Africa and Asia" (*The Guardian*
6.2.1960).

Hence, the empirical record still indicates that key Canadian officials—
mainly those close to the Prime Minister—were significantly influenced by
African and Asian officials' views on South Africa from 1960 to 1961. The second empirical justification for how Canada's position was "constructed" by
the interstate political context throughout those years relates to the Prime
Minister. The reason is that the Prime Minister justified a position against
apartheid in reference to the interstate political context of the time. In his
memoirs, for example, Diefenbaker recalled the following point made at the
March 1961 Conference:

> On March 13, I told my fellow Prime Ministers there could be no gainsay-
> ing that the long history of close relations between Canada and South
> Africa had recently been clouded by the racial policy of the Union. This
> policy was repugnant to the Canadian people. So long as it was possible
> to regard this as a purely internal affair of South Africa, the Canadian

government had not expressed any serious criticism, but now any racial question was bound to have international repercussions, and the attitude of Commonwealth countries to this question would be closely watched all over the world ... South Africa's racial policies had such far-reaching effect that their impact was international rather than domestic.

DIEFENBAKER 1975, 218–219

Diefenbaker's observation indicates that the intestate political context from 1960 to 1961 was critical to his eventual decision to express an unequivocal and unambiguous stance against apartheid on behalf of Canada. It qualifies a position against the practice, particularly given its normative significance to other states. This again emphasizes the interstate social construction of Canada's position on apartheid, which became unequivocal and unambiguous by April 1961.

4   Part Three

We have just made the case for an interstate socialization process set in motion by a core coalition of states in 1946 and throughout subsequent years. Now, we turn to the third and final step in the research procedure: the cross-check. I weigh inferences from part two against the most prominent theoretical and empirical counterarguments. The theoretical counterarguments come from materialist accounts of international relations, as discussed in Chapter Two. The empirical counterarguments come from the case study's empirical circumstances and the most relevant secondary historical accounts.

Focusing on material side payments can serve as one theoretical counterargument to this chapter. A possible rendition of the account may have to do with a claim that some states—in particular, those states that this section associates as belonging to the core coalition—took it upon themselves to manipulate specific material incentives and disincentives in favor of or against a position on South Africa. Those efforts, according to this theoretical perspective, would then, in turn, shape the eventual constellation of support for the joint position against racial discrimination in South Africa. A potential ring-leader for those efforts was the Soviet Union, which, according to the Canadian delegation, sought to "exploit ... color sensitivity and lingering anti-colonial sentiment in an effort to woo the new nations, particularly in Africa" (Robinson 1960 in DEA/7060–40). One could point to several newly independent African states—particularly from 1960 to 1961—as especially vulnerable to those efforts and brought to support a particular position thanks to some material resource manipulation. To substantiate the point, one could collate the extent of military and economic relations that new states like those had with the Soviet Union before and after independence.

I concede the plausibility of this theoretical interpretation but push back on two key points. The first point is that the third states most vulnerable to the influence of some material resource manipulation were categorical—and seemingly inexorably—opposed to racial discrimination in South Africa for reasons independent of those efforts. One reason is that almost all of those states saw themselves as victims of racial discrimination, not unlike what they saw in South Africa. For reference, the more acrimonious positions taken by Libya, Morocco, Ghana, and Somaliland are among those that substantiate my claim here (A/SPC/SR.92, 33; A/SPC/SR.16, 74; A/SPC/SR.93, 38–39; A/SPC/SR.243, 84). The "experiential commensurability" between what some developing states saw in their national experiences and the ideas in question was profound (Goodman and Jinks 2013, 25). This is apparent in that the positions those states took—upon initial participation in the interstate conversation on apartheid—evidence no hesitation or ambivalence. It also seems apparent in the way those states inveighed against the status quo. As the British delegation observed in 1952,

> Opinions on colonial questions are now so bitter that we fear that the General Assembly, especially the Fourth [Political and Decolonization] Committee, may be tempted to abandon constructive work in favor of deconstructive criticism.
>
> DO35/6964 in O'MALLEY 2020, 212

Some subsequent material resource manipulation would thus not have made a step-change difference. Even if it did, the question would remain as to how more martially capable state subjects—such as Australia, Canada, and the United Kingdom—could have been influenced by those same efforts. Moreover, the question would remain as to why the more materially capable state agents—such as the United States throughout the late 1940s and early 1950s—would not have manipulated material resources to move interstate support towards a position more favorable to NATO allies.

Another relevant materialist counterargument can proceed from the contention that intergovernmental organizations are epiphenomenal, which means that their proceedings reflect some distribution of material power in the interstate system. This point can relate to the previous paragraph and Chapter Two's reference to the English School. In this chapter, this theoretical interpretation would assert that interstate proceedings on South Africa—in particular, from 1946 to 1961—were, in some part, underpinned by the distribution of material threats balanced or balancing against each other at the time. By this account, one would expect to associate some East versus West cleavage with the nature of interstate proceedings and their eventual outcome. There seems to be some traction in this more neorealist theoretical interpretation. For example, one could point to the fact that states in some way aligned with the Soviet Union from the outset took an unequivocal stance against racial discrimination in South Africa. On the other hand, States aligned with the United States were, at the outset, reluctant to do so. One could also point to South Africa's position within an interstate political, economic, and military alliance against the Soviet Union (and the spread of communism, more broadly) as indicative of the epiphenomenal nature of global, multilateral engagement with the issue.

This theoretical interpretation has its merits. It helps understand the initial interstate convergence around support for a position on South Africa. It can also help understand how it was that some self-declared "neutral" states—including Austria—had a lower, subjective "tipping point" on the issue than other states. Nevertheless, this interpretation also falls short in the following two respects. The first respect is that it glosses over the "non-partisan" nature of the core coalition's efforts on the issue from the outset in 1946. As shown in section one, critical to those efforts was a manipulation of an appeal to common notions of "right" and "wrong" that could, in turn, exert diplomatic pressure upon all states. In other words, from the outset, some states—particularly those that would come to form the Non-Aligned Movement in 1961—cast the question of racial discrimination in South Africa as above an east-west divide.

For good measure, those states couched the issue as such to win others over, regardless of the constellation of material threats balanced or balancing against each other at the time. As India's delegation put it in 1946, "there are standards and principles and ideals that transcend ... the exigencies of the kind of power politics that has proved so calamitous in the past" (A/PV.85, 137). This is to say that an emphasis on some material constellation of material capabilities misses out on how the core coalition saw the issue from the outset.

This last point suggests a second critical shortcoming in this latter materialist counterargument: the non-partisan nature of subsequent interstate proceedings. I say non-partisan because the states that took an eventual stand against racial discrimination in South Africa seem to have done so "as if" moved by what it meant for a relationship with a wider interstate community, as the previous section contends. How those states and others expressed support for the cause suggests that certain cross-cutting expectations were critical, seemingly more so than a need to validate a position within a material balance of threats. This seems consistent with the fact that states aligned with the United States supported a common position on South Africa, even though it was a position that states aligned with the Soviet Union had long been associated with. However, if interstate proceedings on the issue were epiphenomenal— reflecting some balance of or balancing in material threats—it is unclear how an almost unanimous interstate consensus would have come about.

The previous points address the most relevant counterarguments to this chapter drawn from international relations theory. One can also level counterarguments based on the unique empirical circumstances and what some historians have said about them. One prominent line of criticism can relate to South Africa's position on apartheid. For example, one can point to its intransigence on the issue as being increasingly "off-color" to states otherwise on the fence. This would frustrate those states' willingness to shield South Africa from global, multilateral censure. It would also make those states more willing to join in that censure. In this chapter, the empirical counterpoint from the last section can be applied to each state subject. Canada and the United Kingdom are the examples where the critique most applies. The reason is that the prime ministers from both countries had both been ticked off at South Africa's intransigence and suggested that they were willing to maintain the status quo had South Africa been willing to make concessions (Diefenbaker 1975, 216; Macmillan 1972, 298). This was especially true at the March 1961 Commonwealth Conference. Harold Macmillan, for example, recalled the following point:

> It was Dr. Verwoerd's attitude and method of arguing his case, as well as the inflexibility of his dogmatic position, which finally turned the balance. Had he made the slightest concession, for instance regarding, the acceptance of diplomatic representatives of African states ... the mood might have easily changed.
>
> MACMILLAN 1972, 298

Prime Minister John Diefenbaker made a similar observation (Diefenbaker 1975, 216).

I agree that South Africa's intransigence was significant to how states arrived at an almost universal interstate consensus on apartheid by April 1961. However, one cannot apportion too much significance to this historical fact. The reason is twofold. First, the empirical record refutes the suggestion that the "slightest concession might have easily changed the mood" of other state representatives. It indicates that India—alongside other African and Asian states—had been unequivocal and unambiguous about its opposition to apartheid and would not, in any case, compromise on the position. Empirical justification for this assertion comes from the South African delegation's views, as shown above, on Canada (Meiring 1973, 165). It also comes from Robert Menzies, who observed that Hendrik Verwoerd *was* willing to accept a conciliatory proposal at the March 1961 Commonwealth Conference.

> The 'kill' appeared to be inevitable. Yet an effort must be made. Accordingly, several of us got together to draft a statement for the communique. The broad idea was that we would set out , in brief terms, the views of those Prime Ministers who were strongly critical and who wanted to go on record against South Africa and her policies; that we would say that these had been conveyed to Dr Verwoerd, that he had said that he would of course give them careful considerations, but that he held out no prospect of agreement. Verwoerd, standing firmly on the ground that this was a domestic matter and should not be dealt with in a communique coming out of the Commonwealth Prime Ministers' Conference, disapproved. We then had a short adjournment, in the course of which Macmillan discussed the matter with Verwoerd. Thirty or forty minutes later Macmillan re-entered the Conference room looking happy, and said to me, in a low voice, "it's all in order. Verwoerd will accept the suggested communique." My pleasure was short-lived. No sooner had Verwoerd said that he would accept the draft, than Nehru was heard to say that he would not; that he was not prepared to temporize; that he would never let the matter rest; that not only at Prime Ministers' meetings but at every opportunity that presented itself, he would wage war on apartheid and the country which practiced it. It was clear to Verwoerd that the day was lost; his application was going to be rejected. So, after the discussion, and with great dignity, he did the only thing he could do; he begged leave to withdraw his application. This, of course, meant that South Africa would cease to be a member of the Commonwealth. The decision was one of expulsion, not in form, of course; but in fact and in substance, it could have no other meaning.
>
> MENZIES 1968, 214

This observation highlights the limits of an empirical emphasis on South Africa's intransigence as a trigger to the United Kingdom's stance against apartheid in April 1961. It suggests that South Africa's position was *not* all that intransigent, according to Harold Macmillan, and that whatever "compromise" communique the former was willing to accept was enough for the latter to maintain the status quo. It, therefore, cannot follow that South Africa's intransigence significantly influenced the United Kingdom's decision to come out against apartheid in April 1961.

In Canada's example, the empirical counterpoint is more persuasive. The empirical record *does* suggest that some key Canadian officials—such as Harold Basil Robinson—saw South Africa's intransigence as one reason to change course. Robinson wrote, "there is no evidence that Canada has influenced South African racial policies in the past or that we are likely to do so in the near future" (Robinson 1960 in DEA/7060–40). One can point to Verwoerd's refusal to make concessions in private consultations with Diefenbaker—that is, in May 1960 and in March 1961—to further support the empirical counterpoint. This would suggest that South Africa's intransigence significantly contributed to Canada's eventual stance against apartheid in April 1961.

Although South Africa's position was influential, it was not decisive for Canada. Successive South African governments were, in any event, not willing to heed or even entertain substantive recommendations from other state counterparts, as proceedings in the General Assembly and Security Council indicate. This was as apparent in 1946 as it was in 1961. At the March 1961 Commonwealth Conference, South Africa was most explicit. "The Prime Minister of South Africa ... deplored the accusations of racial discrimination leveled against South Africa by member countries, which he alleged were themselves guilty of such practices" (Verwoerd 1961 in Hayes 1980, 474). Hence, a suggestion that Canada (or other states) grew impatient—and for that main reason turned on South Africa—rings hollow. South Africa's continued intransigence from 1960 to 1961 may have been "the last straw" for Canada. Nevertheless, the question would remain how South Africa's intransigence throughout those years—in contrast to the years before—became a most relevant consideration to Canadian officials. As the previous section shows, the interstate political context, in the first place, put South Africa on the spot and into a position where it could not make substantive concessions.

Another empirical counterargument to my argument can follow from a focus on the domestic political pressure that government officials from the United Kingdom, Australia, and Canada felt on apartheid. This potential empirical critique speaks to Audie Klotz's analysis of the diffusion of transnational, global norms on racial equality by the mid-1960s (Klotz 1995). According to this potential critique, British, Australian, and Canadian officials would have felt and primarily responded to transnational—and not necessarily international— diplomatic pressure. One could make this critique, especially concerning the Sharpeville massacre and the high-profile public protest that followed. In my view, there is limited empirical evidence for this critique. As this chapter has shown, the historical record suggests that the government officials in question were neither moved by Sharpeville nor the surrounding transnational protest that followed and lent further momentum to domestic political pressure to change course on apartheid. This is to say that British, Australian, and Canadian officials primarily responded to *interstate* social pressure. The primary source work above provides direct evidence for this assertion. An additional piece of evidence comes from a letter written by Prime Minister Harold Macmillan to the Queen, which suggests that domestic political pressure was not a leading concern in the formation of the United Kingdom's stance on South Africa (Macmillan 1960 in Macmillan 1972, 486–487). The Prime Minister wrote the letter a month after Sharpeville on April 3rd, 1960, and referred to a meeting of the Security Council concerning the incident:

> In my absence, although not without frequent communication with me by telegram, my colleagues had to make a decision about the question of the discussion of South African affairs in the Security Council of the United Nations. The dilemma is easy to state, but difficult to escape. If we rest too much upon the legal and constitutional position, we shall certainly please old Commonwealth countries like Australia and of course South Africa itself, but we risk gravely offending the Asian and African members. I was rather alarmed to see Sir James Robertson's report of the feeling in Nigeria ...
>
> I am not anxious about the pressure of public opinion at home, whether in or outside Parliament. We have the strength, I think, to hold to whatever course we think right. I feel my supreme task is to try to street the Commonwealth through this crisis and to avoid anything in the nature of disintegration.
>
> MACMILLAN 1960 in MACMILLAN 1972, 486

The Embargo on Cuba (1991–2016)

> In supporting in 1994 and 1995 the General Assembly resolution of ending the economic, commercial and financial embargo imposed by the United States against Cuba, the Russian Federation was, and continues to be, guided by the firm consensus on the matter among members of the United Nations. Almost the entire world community, with few exceptions, regards the continuing commercial and economic embargo against Cuba as a manifestation of the outdated mentality of confrontation between blocs.
>
> Permanent Mission of the Russian Federation to the United Nations in New York 1995 in A/51/355, 31

∴

0   Chapter Outline

We now turn to another empirical case study: the political, economic, and financial embargo imposed by the United States on Cuba, focusing on interstate opposition to the embargo from 1991 to 2016. The empirical analysis begins in 1991 because that was the year when member states first considered the embargo as an agenda item at the General Assembly. We end in 2016 because that was when the United States changed its stance on the embargo at the United Nations. The chapter avers that a core coalition of states set an interstate socialization process in motion that cumulatively built an unequivocal and unambiguous consensus against the embargo throughout that period. We adhere to the structure in the previous case study chapter.

The introduction provides an empirical background, which acclimates the reader to the empirical context, especially with how Cuba and other core states made the embargo an "issue" for global, multilateral concern at the United Nations. I refer to the collapse of the Soviet Union and the continued application of American sanctions legislation against Cuba. The introductory commentary again alludes to the theoretical argument chapter's analysis of "information politics," requiring that socialization agents specify and categorize an issue.

© NAIF AL-MULLA, 2025 | DOI:10.1163/9789004711938_006

Following the introduction, we then proceed to the chapter's three main parts, each corresponding to the three-step means of analysis in the data and methods chapter. Part One makes the case for a core coalition of states—a support base—against the United States embargo on Cuba. I identify these core states from proceedings on Cuba in 1991, given their stance on the issue in that year and each subsequent year. I also identify these states given their more vocal support for the position throughout those years. Aside from Cuba, the core coalition includes Canada, Brazil, Mexico, Uruguay, and states from the former European Community. The point is to theorize the core states' views opposing the embargo. I closely examine the "rhetorical action" the socializing agents use to pressure others into supporting the cause. As we shall see, agents manipulate common norms to galvanize interstate support against the embargo.

In Part Two, I look at the extent to which the core coalition's diplomatic efforts pressure other states into positions against the embargo over time. I pay close attention to how positions change, particularly to states that were in previous years not in favor of a clear, unequivocal stance on the issue. The Russian Federation, the United States, and several small states are illustrative country cases. I use these states as illustrative country cases for empirical reasons. The first reason is that the Russian Federation, the United States, and the small states in question had been on the fence for years. The second reason is that these illustrative country cases allow access to a wealth of empirical source work.

Close observation of how these positions change suggests evidence for an interstate socialization process set in motion by the core coalition of states. This is to say that the chapter's observable implication comes from meticulous attention to how state representatives expressed changes in national positions on the embargo. The empirical record suggests that interstate social concerns were central to the formulation of these positions. This means that the Russian Federation, the United States, and numerous small states defended positions against the status quo primarily in reference to where other states stood on the issue.

How these state representatives justify a change in position—that is, by suggesting a concern for its interstate social ramifications—makes the difference. I infer that the relevant changes in position comport with a process of collective legitimization, which the core coalition of states set in motion in 1991 and throughout subsequent years. The Russian Federation, the United States, and numerous small states took positions against the embargo primarily in reference to socio-strategic and socially mediated, normative concerns for what resounded as "legitimate." Interstate socialization occurs in the sense that public—but not necessarily private—viewpoints converge around a common, more "legitimate" stance on the issue. Socialization subjects do not necessarily take to heart and change their internal views; at a minimum, they dissociate from what has become a socially unsustainable position.

I again qualify this argument with the assertion that the core coalition's perceived integrity on the embargo made their efforts more influential. Thanks to this perceived integrity, as we shall see, target states were undoubtedly concerned about the political costs of maintaining their long-standing positions on the embargo. Again, this supports the interpretation that socialization efforts are more likely to succeed when proponents are seen as trustworthy—rather than hypocritical—advocates of a cause.

The chapter's observable implication does not come from the fact that "everyone condemned the embargo." What matters is the way in which condemnation of the embargo crystallized into a common position. What also matters are empirical conditioning factors, which are unique to each example and offer further insight into how the respective state subjects arrived at their respective positions. Part Two also corroborates its findings with a collation of secondary source work. This source work helps contemplate the influence that certain empirical conditioning had on the eventual unanimous interstate consensus against the embargo by December 2016. I adduce empirical conditioning factors that are specific to each respective example. For the Russian Federation, the most relevant empirical conditioning factor is the resurgence of Russian nationalism in the mid-1990s. For the United States, the most relevant empirical conditioning factor is Latin American opposition to the embargo and the election of President Barack Obama in 2008. For small states, the most pertinent empirical conditioning factor was the Helms-Burton Law of 1996. To my knowledge, no relevant empirical circumstance was influential across examples.

Part Three cross-checks the chapter's inferences against alternative perspectives. These alternative perspectives come from international relations critiques addressed in Chapter Two. The most relevant point is material resource inducement, which can be a theoretical antagonist to the present social constructivist perspective.

1   Introduction

The United States embargo on Cuba first came onto the United Nations agenda in 1992, at the 47th Session of the General Assembly. The issue did not gain that platform thanks to a unanimous interstate concern for the "extraterritorial" application of American legislation, as may now seem the case from more recent reports of the Secretary-General (e.g. A/RES/73/8; A/RES/72/4; A/RES/71/5). Nor did the embargo become and remain an "issue" worth interstate attention thanks to some universal predilection for "constructive engagement" with Cuba, as may now seem the case from more recent interstate proceedings on the matter (e.g. A/73/PV.30; A/72/PV.38; A/70/PV.40). The issue was, from the outset, disputatious. It became a global, multilateral concern subject due to the specific protest of a handful of member states (A/47/273; A/47/272; A/46/193). In August 1991, the Cuban delegation was the member state to propose that this protest become a subject of discussion at the United Nations the following Session (A/46/L.20; A/46/193; A/46/PV.46, 1–22). Despite explicit, bilateral démarches (or "transparent threats") from the United States Department of State, other states reject the item's inclusion onto the annual agenda. As the State Department put it, support for Cuba's position "threatens your good relationship with the United States" (A/46/PV.46, 3, 16).

The substance of Cuba's initial complaint spoke to a complex, albeit by then a long-standing category of legislation known as the "embargo." The complaint toured some three decades of sanctions policies and provided extensive details to that effect (A/46/193; A/46/193/Add.7). For Cuba, those policies were "the most serious of the diverse forms of aggression that the Government of the United States has been waging against Cuba" (A/47/PV.70, 4–5). By August 1991, the date of the initial complaint, the applicable pieces of legislation were the Trading with the Enemy Act (1917), the Foreign Assistance Act (1962), the Cuban Assets Control Regulations (1963), the Food for Peace Act (1966), and the Jackson-Vanick Amendment to the Trade Act (1974). This body of legislation culminated with the "Toricelli" or Cuban Democracy Act in October 1992, which meant to encourage a "peaceful transition to democracy" in the country (A/47/179, 3). For Cuba, this latter piece of legislation amounted to a "set of new measures geared to[wards] reinforcing the blocade and tightening the siege by which the United States has, for more than three decades, been attempting to strangle Cuba" (A/47/PV.70, 3). It was also further evidence of the embargo's extraterritorial reach, namely that the United States "aimed ... to compel Cuba and other States, as well as companies and individuals outside the territory of the United States, to comply with Washington's political decisions" (A/47/PV.70, 3).

The sense of urgency with which Cuba brought its complaint to the United Nations came from changes to its international relations throughout the early 1990s, particularly those that related to the collapse of the Soviet Union. As the Cuban delegation observed,

For many years Cuba was able to mitigate the consequences of that [embargo] policy through its foreign transactions and the economic and commercial relations that it established with the socialist countries with which it came to conduct 85 percent of its trade.

With the recent break in those relations, Cuba's entire foreign trade is now exposed to the pernicious effects of the blocade policy pursued by the United States, whose Government constantly persecutes each and every one of my country's commercial operations, obstructs Cuba's access to external sources of financing and tries to bloc potential involvement of foreign capital in Cuban development projects.

While this immoral, illegal, and inhuman policy has not been and will never be capable of bending Cuba's will, it is none the less, in the present circumstances, doing severe damage to the economic and social development of the country, to consumption levels and to the general standards of living of the Cuban people.

A/47/PV.70, 16–17

Numerous secondary accounts attest to what the Soviet Union's collapse brought to Cuba. Andrew Zimbalist, for example, documents the decline in trade relations between Cuba and the Soviet Union throughout those years. From 1989 to late 1991, Zimbalist elucidates that Cuban imports from the Soviet Union fell from $5.52 billion to $1.74 billion (Zimbalist 1992, 408). This meant a reduction in Cuba's total import volume by some sixty percent—leading to shortfalls in basic commodities, significant declines in the "productive apparatus in Cuba's economy," and "widespread demoralization" (Zimbalist 1992, 409).

Cuba saw its turn toward the United Nations as an opportunity to organize an international response to the status quo and leverage its social influence on third states. In the Cuban delegation's words,

our intention in proposing this draft resolution is not to put delegations in an uncomfortable position. But—to put in the simplest terms, it is our duty to demand justice for Cuba and for its people and to seek the solidarity necessary to achieve it, and we will carry out that duty in this Assembly and in other international forums.

A/46/PV.46, 16

At the United Nations, the focus of these efforts came from a draft resolution entitled "Necessity of Ending the Economic, Commercial, and Financial Embargo Imposed by the United States of America Against Cuba" (A/47.L.20/Rev.1). As the title suggests, the resolution's point was clear and concise. For some twenty-four consecutive years—from 1992 to 2016—it demanded that the United States embargo end (e.g. A/RES/47/19; A/RES/48/16; A/RES/49/9). It also requested that member states reject the embargo's stringent measures and report annually to the Secretary-General on the resolution's implementation.

2   Part One

2.1   *The Core Coalition*

Building on the introduction's empirical background, we now turn to Part One, where we make the case for a core coalition of states that opposed the United States' embargo on Cuba. Following the first step in the research procedure, we pay close attention to the more vocal members of that coalition and make the case for the strategic manipulation of the norms of liberal internationalism (Hurd 2005; 2008). The main idea is that the interstate coalition manipulated normative rhetoric to win over more support for the cause. Aside from Cuba, the core coalition includes Canada, Brazil, Mexico, Uruguay, and states from the former European Community.

As we have seen, a core coalition of states can manipulate common norms in a global, multilateral context via appeals to some "stamp of political approval or disapproval." This means that the core states attempt to situate an issue within some accepted interstate normative framework such that the two become seen as the same. This is not to push the wholesale development of some new interstate norm but to claim ownership over its space such that the two become seen as the same. The states can tap into and deploy the diplomatic, social pressure that sustains the normative framework at stake. Socialization agents can project a sense of legitimacy into support for a particular cause that appeals to a more palpable perception of legitimacy because it seems to resonate with what states have recognized as such. This projection of legitimacy is critical since other states cannot perceive that legitimacy save through "an assessment of whether the audience acknowledges it" as such (Finnemore 2009, 61–62; Hurd 2008, 31).

The core coalition's efforts speak to this theoretical point in two respects, each relating to a specific international norm. The coalition made two central normative arguments in opposition to the embargo. The first normative point was that the embargo called into question a norm on state sovereignty. The assertion was that sovereign, independent states—namely, those represented at the United Nations—have the right to determine their foreign policy, especially their trade relations with other states (A/47/PV.70; A/47/PV.71). As

Mexico's delegation put it, "a State's decision to establish trading links with another [state] is a full expression of its sovereignty and consequently is not subject to the will of third States" (A/47/PV.70, 29). The issue was, as Tanzania's delegation put it, "about the right of countries, whatever their size, ideological persuasion or level of development, to choose without reference from any quarter, their partners in international economic and commercial relations" (A/47/PV.70, 43). "We don't think one country has the right to tell another who they can trade with," as a French diplomat put it (McGillion 2005, 103 in Morley and Morrison 2005).

According to the core states, the United States embargo was at variance with this norm on free sovereignty because its application had adverse implications for third states or third entities' trade relations with Cuba. The most relevant pieces of legislation were the Cuban Democracy Act of 1992 and, later, the Cuban Liberty and Democratic Solidarity Act of 1996. The 1992 law prohibited any vessel from engaging in trade with the United States if the vessel had entered a port in Cuba during the previous 180 days (A/47/273, 2). The 1996 law included Title III, which allowed lawsuits in American courts against foreign companies that invest in businesses that were once owned by American nationals but seized by the Government of Cuba on or after January 1st, 1959 (U.S. Public Law 104–114, Statute 814–821). For the core coalition, the point is that the embargo was an attempt to "intrude on the sovereignty of third countries and to regulate unilaterally international trade and shipping" (A/47/654). The Canadian delegation emphasized that it amounted to "inappropriate attempts to assert extraterritorial jurisdiction" (A/47/PV.70, 86). Uruguay's delegation drew out the point:

> if every State in exercise of its sovereignty is totally free to decide with which other State it wishes to trade or to cease trading, it is then not possible to accept that a State might seek to extend to other states the effects of its domestic legislation, thus improving *sic* or threatening to impose damages against those third States for trading with the State that was the subject of such domestic legislation.
>
> We are of the view that to apply such a policy is tantamount to seeking to extend the territorial jurisdiction of a State, that it is in effect interference in the internal affairs of other States; and that it runs counter to the principles and norms of international law governing the freedom of trade and navigation.
>
> A/47/PV.70, 87

As the commentary indicates, Cuba, Uruguay, and other core states fashioned the status quo as objectionable, manipulating an international norm on sovereignty, particularly concerning a state's right to determine its own foreign and trade relations. Hence, the embargo was not just objectionable to the core coalition but to "every state in exercise of its sovereignty" given common expectations regarding how it should pursue foreign/trade relations. On this specific point, the Cuban delegation was more explicit in manipulating some "stamp of political approval or disapproval." Its report about the embargo's extraterritorial application emphasized that "no one yet has questioned the accuracy of the information it contains" (A/46/PV.46, 4–5).

This is to say that the anti-embargo coalition attempted to project a sense of legitimacy into a position against the status quo by manipulating its resonance (or "frame") within a norm on state sovereignty and what it entails for international trade/navigation. The coalition also amplified that intersubjective resonance by cuing, prompting other delegations to see an incongruence between the embargo's extraterritorial measures and an interstate free trade/navigation norm. The coalition did this by making that incongruence appear as though it was growing increasingly divergent from the outset, such that the embargo's extraterritorial measures increasingly undermined the given norm. In 1992, Cuba was among the delegations to hammer on the point about the Cuban Democracy Act:

> With regard to Cuba, extraterritoriality is not a recent phenomenon but a characteristic that has been present in the blocade policy since its very beginning and includes the efforts that the Government of the United States has been making for decades to secure the cooperation of other countries with that policy. The difference is that now, by means of a pseudo-legal formula, extraterritoriality is more openly proclaimed and more explicitly extended to those third countries that have links, no matter how legitimate, with Cuba.
>
> A/47/PV.70, 16

Throughout subsequent sessions, the Cuban delegation kept up these efforts with periodic reports on the embargo's effects, including its extraterritorial effects on third states (e.g. A/48/258; A/48/259; A/49/451). One can refute the social construction of this position by suggesting that the embargo was, in its terms, an insult to some international norm on free trade/navigation. One could then point to the embargo's explicit, extraterritorial measures aimed at third-state entities in 1992 (and later in 1996) as evidence (A/47/654).

In my view, there is one critical reason to stick to a social constructivist interpretation: support for certain norms on sovereignty—in particular, as it relates to some right to free trade/navigation—was not equivalent to opposition to the United States embargo on Cuba in 1992. In other words, there was no unanimous interstate consensus on the blocade in 1992, even given those pre-existing norms of sovereignty related to free trade/navigation. The main contention was whether the embargo was an issue "appropriate" for consideration in a global, multilateral context such as the United Nations. As the American delegation put it, "the United States embargo of Cuba is not an appropriate issue for discussion at the United Nations" (A/46/193, Add.7, 1). Japan was among the states to take the same position (e.g. A/47/PV.71, 8; A/48/PV.48, 13; A/49/PV.45, 14). Its delegation emphasized that "this question is very complex, and Japan wonders if the resolution ... properly addresses such complexity. If not, the question will remain unresolved until a better way is found to arrive at an appropriate solution" (A/48/PV.48, 13). This is again to emphasize the social constructivist nature of the core coalition's "rhetorical action." In this instance, the coalition made a consistent effort to manipulate certain norms of international law—in particular, norms of international law on free trade/navigation—in support of a "legitimate" position against the embargo.

The core coalition of states made two central normative points in support of a position against the embargo. The first point was about a norm on sovereignty, particularly as it relates to a state's right to engage in free trade/navigation. The second central normative point is "constructive engagement," meaning dialogue. The assertion was that constructive engagement—rather than "confrontation"—was how the United States ought to work out its differences with the Government of Cuba, including concerning promoting and protecting human rights in the country. In 1992, Brazil was among the delegations to make the assertion:

> The end of the cold war, the disappearance of East-West confrontation, and the strong trend towards democratization, both within and between nations, have opened the way for a changing international situation with renewed prospects for understanding and international cooperation. This international atmosphere has encouraged negotiated solutions of persistent conflicts, as well as the overcoming of historical divergences. The same should apply in the case of Cuba. A renewed dialogue would facilitate change and help resolve pending problems in accordance with international law. In this spirit, Brazil stands ready to cooperate so that

Cuba can more easily overcome its current difficulties in peace, justice, freedom and democracy.

A/47/PV.70, 31–32

A more explicit articulation came from Norway in 1993, which like other European states, was forceful about the position:

Norway to a large extent shares the same objectives the United States is seeking to advance in relation to Cuba ... the Norwegian Government strongly deplores the violations of human rights and the lack of democratic rights that still characterize the situation in Cuba. The experience we have gained in Europe, however, indicates that it would not be appropriate to isolate Cuba. Emphasis should instead be placed on involving Cuba in greater cooperation with a view to bringing about changes in the internal situation that could contribute to respect for human rights and democratic processes.

A48/PV.48, 14

The above two interventions suggest a further normative aspect to the core coalition's diplomatic campaign on the embargo. In this latter instance, the focus drew from an intersubjective sense of how states ought to interact with each other in a real or imagined new "era" of international relations after the Cold War. Steven Holloway and Rodney Tomlinson refer to this as a "spirit of accommodation," which meant a "positive transformation among most states in substituting a policy of cooperation for that of confrontation" (A/46/PV.1, 17; Holloway and Tomlinson 1995, 252). The point is that a core coalition of states made a persistent effort to make others see the embargo as an archaic Cold War issue, belying the normative preference for constructive engagement in the following years.

3   Part Two

We have paid close attention to the core coalition of states that took shape by a shared initial position against the United States embargo on Cuba. I now consider how the coalition's diplomatic efforts influenced other states to assume similar positions, submitting that the Russian Federation, the United States, and a handful of small states were affected by the core coalition's efforts. I qualify this argument with the assertion that the core coalition's perceived integrity on the embargo made their efforts more influential. Thanks to this perceived integrity, the Russian Federation, the United States, and a handful of small states were undoubtedly concerned about the political costs of maintaining foreign policy positions on the embargo. "Our unpopular policy towards Cuba … was an albatross around our necks," Secretary Hilary Clinton observed (Clinton 31.7.2015). "Time after time, meeting after meeting, leaders from Mexico to Uruguay criticized our approach to Cuba, it was a constant drumbeat—a perennial irritant—as we sought greater cooperation with our neighbors," as Ambassador Susan Rice commented (Rice 14.10.16). This supports the interpretation that socialization efforts are more likely to succeed when proponents are seen as trustworthy—rather than hypocritical—advocates of a cause.

3.1   *The Russian Federation*

The Russian Federation is one example of a state influenced by Cuba and other states' cumulative efforts since the 46th Session of the General Assembly in 1991. In terms of context, it is essential to emphasize the following facts. In December 1991, the Soviet Union collapsed, and the new Russian Federation's leadership contemplated a "revolution" in its relations with other states. This change in foreign policy outlook was apparent at the United Nations when President Boris Yeltsin made this observation to the Security Council in January 1992:

> Russia regards the United States and the West not as mere patterns but rather as allies. This a basic prerequisite for, I would say, a revolution in peaceful cooperation between progressive nations …
>
> It is a historic irony that the Russian Federation, a state with centuries-long experience in foreign policy and diplomacy, has only just appeared on the political map of the world. I am confident that the world community will find Russia, as an equal participant in international relations and as a permanent member of the Security Council, a firm and steadfast champion of freedom, democracy and humanism.
>
> S/PV.3046, 48

There are two critical components to this perspective. The first is that Boris Yeltsin saw an improvement in Russia's relationship with the United States (and "West") as central to a "revolution" in international relations. Hence, as Mervyn Bain writes, "in the early to mid-1990s Moscow's foreign policy became much more western looking when compared with the Soviet era" (Bain 2016a, 333). "Boris Yeltsin's government repeated Gorbachev's willingness to embrace new ideas and concepts which … was central to the end of the Cold War" (Bain 2016a, 333).

The second essential component of President Yeltsin's perspective is what it entails for Cuba. The chapter introduction shows that Russia's relationship with Cuba fell apart in the early to mid-1990s. The point here is that this relationship breakdown was inextricable from the new Russian Federation's drive to improve ties with the United States (e.g. Bain 2005, 776–778; 2010, 131; 2016a, 333; 2018, 257). In short, that drive to improve ties "negated close relations with Havana because of the continued strained nature of Cuban-American relations" (Bain 2010, 131). According to another scholar, "to improve political ties, Washington demanded that B.H. Yeltsin cut ties with Cuba. This course of action dominated the 1990s" (Larin 2007 in Bain 2018, 257). Primary source work also substantiates this assertion and dates to at least 1991. Boris Pankin, Soviet diplomat and Foreign Minister from August 28th to November 19th in 1991, explains the perspective in his memoirs:

> our relations with Castro had always had an emotional and romantic content over and above the politics of the situation. In the eyes of the Soviet elite he was a true hero who reminded us of our Soviet traditions of heroism. His appeal was not unlike the appeal of Nelson Mandela in some Western circles: here was a leader fighting for the rights of little people against gigantic forces. All this had to give way to the recognition that we could not longer afford either to sustain him economically, or to exacerbate the American obsession with Cuba. The faithful Fidel had to be sacrificed on the alter of Soviet self-interest.
>
> PANKIN 1996, 116

This "sacrifice" of Cuba was evident in the Russian Federation's support of the United States' initiatives against Cuba at the United Nations, among other things. From 1992 to 1995, for example, the Russian Federation stood four-square behind the United States' resolutions to denounce the human rights situation in Cuba at the Human Rights Commission (Miller 2005, 71). In February 1992, the Russian delegation went as far as to "apologize" for its previous support for Cuba (Miller 2005, 71). Moreover, at the General Assembly, the Russian Federation supported the United States' human rights resolutions against Cuba yearly from 1992 to 1995.

Concerning the embargo, the Russian Federation was silent or abstained on Cuba's resolutions from 1991 to 1994 (e.g. UNYB 1992, 802–803; UNYB 1993, 852–854; UNYB 1994, 1106–1107). At the General Assembly, the Russian delegation supported the United States' position that the "embargo of Cuba is not an appropriate issue for discussion at the United Nations" (A/46/193, Add.7, 1). As Russia's delegation put it in December 1992,

The Russian delegation will abstain in voting on the draft resolution in document A/47/L.20/Rev.1 because we believe that, in order to resolve issues relating to trade and economic relations, it is more appropriate to consider them within the context of bilateral negotiations between States rather than in international forum.

A/47/PV.70, 83

Hence, global, multilateral stricture of the embargo was *not* "appropriate," according to the Russian Federation. For Russia, the issue was primarily a bilateral dispute, as the United States had been emphasizing (e.g. A/47/PV.70, 75–77; A/48/PV.48, 11–12; A/49/PV.45, 11–12). The previous two paragraphs emphasize that a drive to improve ties with the United States significantly influenced Russia's positions on Cuba throughout the 1990s. That influence was not favorable toward Cuba's opposition to the embargo.

A change in position came in October 1994, when the Russian Federation first took a stand against the embargo unequivocally and unambiguously. The empirical evidence comes from correspondence with the United Nations Secretary-General from October 1994 to July 1997. In October 1994, Russia's Permanent Mission to the United Nations in New York made the point that:

In supporting the General Assembly resolution, the Russian Federation based its position on the fact that a consensus on the issue had already emerged in the international community. The Russian Federation, the Latin American countries, the majority of developing countries in Asia and Africa and the Western European States view the embargo as a throw back to the Cold War and an ongoing source of tension between Cuba and the United States.

A/50/401, 25

In 1995, Russia's Permanent Mission made the further point that:

In supporting in 1994 and 1995 the General Assembly resolution of ending the economic, commercial and financial embargo imposed by the United States against Cuba, the Russian Federation was, and continues to be, guided by the firm consensus on the matter among members of the United Nations. Almost the entire world community, with few exceptions, regards the continuing commercial and economic embargo against Cuba as a manifestation of the outdated mentality of confrontation between blocs.

A/51/355, 31

And finally, in July 1997, Russia's delegation again made the same sentiment known:

> In supporting since 1994 the General Assembly resolution on the neces-
> sity of ending the economic, commercial and financial embargo imposed
> by the United States of America against Cuba, the Russian Federation
> takes account of the firm consensus on that matter among members of
> the United Nations.
>
> Almost the entire world community regards the continuing commer-
> cial and economic embargo against Cuba imposed by the United States
> as a manifestation of the outdated mentality of confrontation between
> blocs. Most of the States of the world express their disagreement with the
> attempts by the United States to tighten up the embargo by associating
> the international community with it through the implementation of the
> Cuban Liberty and Democratic Solidarity Act of 12 March 1996. This act is
> rightly described as discriminatory and incompatible with the norms of
> international law and the principles of free trade.
>
> A/52/352, 26

There are several observations one must draw from these communications.
The first relates to what the contacts do not, in their terms, suggest: a sudden
"remembrance" that the Cold War had ended and its implications for international relations with Cuba. The Cold War had been over for almost three years
without the Russian Federation positioning itself with other member states
supporting Cuba's resolutions. This is not to say that some prior sympathy
for engagement with Cuba was irrelevant to the position, particularly in its
post-Cold War context. It was relevant, but not to the extent that it warranted
unequivocal and unambiguous condemnation of the embargo at the United
Nations (e.g. A/50/401, 25–26; A/48/PV.48, A/48/448, 22–23).

This leads to whether there had been some deterioration in the
circumstances—for example, in the embargo's more extensive extraterritorial
application—to encourage the above change in perspective. To my knowledge, there is limited empirical traction in the suggestion given the applicable date of October 1994 (which was two years after the passage of the Cuban
Democracy Act in 1992 and two years before the Cuban Liberty and Democratic
Solidarity Act in 1996). Even if there were, it would pail compared to the Cuban
Democracy Act of 1992, which strengthened an embargo that had been in place
for some three decades. Hence, if the three-decades-old embargo and explicit
measures to enhance it were not enough in the first place, it seems implau-
sible that an incremental increase in sanctions actions could have made the

embargo objectionable *en toto*. As the Cuban delegation put it in 1992, "extra-territoriality is not a recent phenomenon but a characteristic that has been present in the blocade policy since its very beginning" (A/47/PV.70, 16). "The difference is that now, by means of a pseudo-legal formula, extraterritoriality is more openly proclaimed and more explicitly extended to those third countries that have links, no matter how legitimate, with Cuba" (A/47/PV.70, 16).

This allows for a preliminary, social constructivist interpretation of the Russian Federation's move against the embargo in line with a process of collective legitimization. The empirical justification comes from *how* the Russian Federation articulated its position, lending direct empirical support to a theoretical interpretation that the core coalition's efforts on the embargo were influential. I say influential because each communication evidences a manifest concern for an interstate "consensus" on the issue—particularly concerning the previous normative point about "constructive engagement" with Cuba—and stresses its relevance to the Russian Federation's subsequent position. That relevance was decisive, as the commentary indicates. In the first instance, the Russian Federation "based" its position on the positions of other states. In the second instance, it was and continued to have been "guided" by what it saw as a consensus among member states on the embargo. In the third instance, the Russian delegation again emphasized the same point, "taking account" of a "firm consensus" in its formulation of position. The inference is that in each instance, the Russian delegation justifies support for Cuba's resolution, given its significance to the broader "community" of states. Each communication, more specifically, expresses a socio-strategic and socially mediated normative justification to oppose the embargo on "legitimate" grounds. This suggests that the potential political consequences of maintaining the status quo were salient to the Russian Federation. Hence, the empirical record supports the interpretation that the interstate diplomatic context of the time was influential in moving the Russian Federation's stance on the embargo. It also supports the interpretation that the core states were credible and effective, given references to the countries that comprised it: "Latin American countries, the majority of developing countries in Asia and Africa and the Western European countries" (A/50/401, 25).

To be clear, my claim is *not* determinative: that the Russian Federation opposed the embargo *because* of concerns for the interstate social context of the time. At least one other significant empirical conditioning factor one must consider: the rise of Russian nationalism in the mid-1990s. Mervyn Bain makes the point. According to Bain, an "upshot" in Russian nationalism came in December 1995, when Yevgeny Primakov replaced Andrei Kozyrev as foreign minister (Bain 2018, 258). Bain cites several reasons for this rise in Russian nationalism, including discontent with NATO expansion, NATO action in Yugoslavia, and a failure to receive promised aid assistance from the United States (Bain 2010, 135; 2016a, 333; 2016b, 19; 2018, 258). The main point is that the previous foreign minister had been a "strong advocate of the pro-Western foreign policy"; in contrast, the new foreign minister sympathized with Russia's Soviet past and Cuba (Bain 2018, 258). "When coupled with nationalistic tendencies within Russia, the result of this change was Moscow wanting to reassert itself internationally, especially in several areas in which the Kremlin had influence in during the Soviet era" (Bain 2018, 258).

Mervyn Bain further points out that these nationalistic tendencies directly affected Cuba. By improving relations with Cuba, the Russian Federation sought to show the United States that it "once again had global influence" (Bain 2016a, 334). Bain goes on, "it appeared as if the geo-strategic importance of Cuba for the Kremlin was increasing. This is not to suggest it returned to the level of the Cold War, but Moscow did wish to 'tickle the Americans' underbelly' with closer relations with Cuba, achieving this aim" (Bain 2016a, 334; Sosnovsky 1996, 5). Hence, according to Bain, Russian nationalism significantly influenced the Russian Federation's stance on Cuba. Improving relations with Cuba—and, by extension, taking an unequivocal and unambiguous stance against the embargo—would have been a means by which Russia could assert its independence from the United States. Improving relations with Cuba would have also been a means through which the Russian Federation could hedge against American foreign policy positions it saw as objectionable.

In my view, Bain's view makes sense to a certain extent. It points to domestic political circumstances as inspiration for taking a more independent stance on Cuba. The perspective, however, falls short in two key respects. The first respect relates to the time trajectory. If Yevgeny Primakov's becoming foreign minister marked an upshot in Russian nationalism in December 1995 and consequently was a decisive influence on Russia's stance on Cuba, then one would expect the empirical record to indicate as much. On that score, for example, one would expect there to have been a concomitant and contemporaneous recalibration in the Russian Federation's stance on Cuba. The empirical record, however, indicates no such synchronization: the Russian Federation's change in stance on the embargo was in October 1994, over a year *before* Primakov became foreign minister. This was when the Russian Federation still stood in favor of resolutions that the United States underwrote to chastise the situation of human rights in Cuba in 1994 and again in 1995. It is true that Russia's positions on Cuba—namely, on the embargo and human rights—harmonized in 1996 after Primakov became foreign minister. Yet, given the time trajectory, the empirical record cannot suggest that *both* issues were associated with a decisive upsurge in Russian nationalism that peaked in December 1995. Hence, despite an upsurge in Russian nationalism, the empirical record still suggests that it did not decisively influence Russia's eventual stance against the embargo.

The second shortcoming in Bain's perspective pertains to the "smoking gun" touched upon in previous paragraphs. This point does not require further explication, save additional emphasis that the most relevant empirical source work lends explicit support to the interpretation that the interstate social context at the time was the "basis" for the Russian Federation's position in October 1994 (A/50/401, 25). Even by July 1996, an interstate consensus still "guided" the Russian Federation to the position (A/51/355, 31). And by July 1997, "a firm consensus on the issue" was what the Russian Federation "took account of" in the formulation of its position (A/52/352, 26).

3.2 The United States

The previous subsection suggested that the Russian Federation was influenced by the core coalition's efforts to take an unequivocal and unambiguous stance against the United States embargo on Cuba. I now suggest the United States as another example of a state influenced by the core coalition's efforts. The most relevant facts are as follows. Since 1991, the United States' primary justification for the embargo was the lack of democracy and human rights in Cuba. As the American delegation put it in 1992,

> the United States chooses not to trade with Cuba because of our concerns about human rights abuses and the lack of democracy in Cuba. We believe that the future of Cuba should be determined by the Cuban people and not by a regime imposed upon them.
>
> Cubans should be able to enjoy freedom of speech and association and the basic human rights recognized by this institution. Unfortunately, the behavior of the Cuban Government has not become more reasonable with the passage of time. In contrast to the policy of the Cuban government towards its own population, the United States embargo is not designed to hurt the Cuban people.
>
> A/47/PV.70, 73–75

This was the United States' position in 1992 under the Clinton Administration, as well as from 2000 to 2008 under the Bush Administration (e.g. A/56/PV.64, 17–18; A/57/PV.48, 3–4; A/58/PV.54, 5). It was also, for a time, the United States' position under the Obama Administration (e.g. A/64/PV.27, 19; A/65/PV.36, 20; A/66/PV.41, 21–22). As the American delegation emphasized in 2011, "the embargo represents just one aspect of United States policy towards Cuba, whose overarching goal is to encourage a more open environment in Cuba and increased respect for human rights and fundamental freedoms" (A/66/PV.41, 21).

A change in position came some twenty-five years later, in December 2016, when the American delegation abstained from Cuba's resolution and called for an end to the embargo. In clarifying the position, Permanent Representative Samantha Power made the following point:

> For more than 50 years, the United States had a policy aimed at isolating the Government of Cuba. For roughly half of those years, Member States voted overwhelmingly for a General Assembly draft resolution condemning the United States embargo and calling for it to be ended.
>
> The United States has always voted against this draft resolution; today the United States will abstain. Let me explain why.
>
> ... the draft resolution being voted on today is a perfect example of why the United States policy of isolation towards Cuba was not working—or worse, how it was actually undermining the very goals it set out to achieve. Instead of isolating Cuba, our policy has, as President Obama has repeatedly said, isolated the United States, including right here at the United Nations.
>
> Under President Obama we have adopted a new approach: rather than to try to close off Cuba from the rest of the world, we want the world of opportunities and ideas to open its doors to the people of Cuba. After over 50 years of pursuing the path of isolation, we have chosen to take the path of engagement, because, as President Obama said in Havana, we recognize that the future of the island of course lies in the hands of the Cuban people.
>
> A/71/PV.32, 15

Power went on to assert that "the United States and Cuba must continue to find ways to engage, even as our differences persist. Today we will take another small step to be able to do that. May there be many more—including, we hope, finally ending the United States embargo once and for all" (A/71/PV.32, 17). This annunciation of position was significant. It drew cheers from delegations at the General Assembly and broke with some twenty-five years of policy at the United Nations. It was a "big deal," as Erik Voeten put it (Voeten 26.10.2016).

The empirical record directly supports the theoretical interpretation that the core coalition's efforts were decisive in how the United States developed its position. There are two strands of evidence to consider. The first strand of evidence dates to the mid-1990s when the Helms-Burton Law was enacted

1996 under the Clinton Administration. One strand of evidence shows that certain core states had been influential in pressuring successive administrations to oppose specific embargo provisions. A relevant provision included Title III of the Helms-Burton Law (1996), which allowed lawsuits in American courts against foreign companies that invest in businesses that were once owned by American nationals but seized by the Government of Cuba on or after January 1st, 1959 (U.S. Public Law 104–114, Statute 814–821). Another relevant provision is Title IV, which denies entry visas to individuals found to "confiscate" or "traffic" in such property (U.S. Public Law 104–114, Statute 822–824). The point here is that certain core states found the provisions especially objectionable and managed to pressure presidential administrations into waiving them periodically (under the Presidential Suspension of Right of Action). We know those efforts were influential for two reasons.

The first reason is that the core states effectively nurtured anxieties among American officials about how much America's stance on the embargo was socially unsustainable. Dennis Hays, Director of the Office of Cuban Affairs at the State Department, made the following observation about Helms-Burton:

> Oh God, another headache. First it was Iran, now we're going to do more to Cuba and then it's going to be Iraq, and then what about Libya. To these guys it was just one more issue, just one more pariah country and do we really want to piss off the EU over yet another of these matters.
>
> MCGILLION in MORLEY AND MCGILLION 2005, 100–101

Another high-ranking official in the State Department's Office of Cuban Affairs made a similar observation in a confidential interview with Professor Chris McGillion: "whenever senior level officials from the White House, State, or any other agency traveled overseas they were hit with this" (McGillion in Morley and McGillion 2005, 103). The international criticism was "the most undiplomatic language I've ever seen," as another official put it (McGillion in Morley and McGillion 2005, 103). "It was hugely controversial in our relations with the Europeans who were saying 'that sounds like extortion to us'" (McGillion in Morley and McGillion 2005, 103). Stuart Eisenhower, President Clinton's envoy on Cuba, made a similar observation: "it would be hard to overstate to you the level of anger and resentment in Europe and Latin America about this issue based on what they see as the principle of extraterritoriality from their perspective more so than any practical damage to their actual interests" (McGillion in Morley and McGillion 2005, 108).

The diplomatic pressure felt by American officials had observable effects on successive presidential administrations from the mid-1990s onwards. This leads to the second reason to suggest that the core coalition's efforts were influential throughout this period: the Clinton (and later Bush) Administration moved to waive Helms-Burton's Title III given the pressure from core states. Empirical evidence for this assertion has been documented by Chris McGillion, who has conducted original interviews that speak to the matter (McGillion in Morley and McGillion 2005, 97–147). McGillion finds, for example, that an EU threat to bring its complaint against the embargo to the World Trade Organization was influential in the Clinton administration's decision to hold off on Title III. According to McGillion, one State Department official made the following point: "Politically, we couldn't let the EU proceed with the WTO challenge" (McGillion in Morley and McGillion 2005, 108). The official went on, "the WTO was already under fire and being questioned by members of Congress. And our attempt to get others to join the WTO, and our efforts to build the WTO up as a credible organization would have been completely undermined" (McGillion in Morley and McGillion 2005, 108). Another American diplomat made the point that "proceeding further with this matter would pose serious risks [to the WTO, which was still] a very fragile institution" (McGillion in Morley and McGillion 2005, 109). McGillion also refers to John Howard, the U.S. Chamber of Commerce's director of international policy, who questioned why the Clinton Administration was willing to risk "an unnecessary fight at the WTO of our own making, when we have so much else at stake in the global trading system" (McGillion in Morley and McGillion 2005, 123).

In addition, press releases from the U.S. Department of State explicate presidential decisions to waive Title III of the Helms-Burton Law. Some of these press releases also demonstrate that the core states were influential. A 1997 statement by President Bill Clinton is an example:

> Last July, I allowed Title III of the Cuban Liberty and Democratic Solidarity Act (Libertad Act) to come into force but suspended for six months the right it grants to American nationals to bring suit against foreign firms trafficking in confiscated properties in Cuba. I took this step so that we could have time to develop a more common approach with our allies and trading patterns to promote democracy, human rights and fundamental freedoms in Cuba. We and our allies agree on the vital need for a transition to democracy on the island, but differences over how to achieve that aim have often overshadowed the goal itself. That is why I decided to make maximum use of Title III to increase pressure on the Castro regime by working with our allies—not against them—to accelerate change in Cuba.
>
> CLINTON in RANNENBERG 3.1.1997

A July 1999 press release is another example:

> The president allowed Title III into force on August 1, 1996, but suspended
> for six months the provisions that would permit American nationals to
> bring suit against persons trafficking in confiscated properties in Cuba
> claimed by U.S. nationals. He did so in order to work with our friends and
> allies to develop a multilateral approach to advance democracy, human
> rights, and fundamental freedoms in Cuba.
>
> U.S. Department of State 16.7.1999

Although this latter piece of empirical evidence is not direct, it nevertheless
suggests that certain "friends and allies" were central to the decision to modify
aspects of the embargo. More direct evidence for these states' influence on the
decision comes from recently released documents at the Center for Legislative
Archives in Washington, D.C. I found several such documents during my visit
to the Center in the Spring of 2020. The most important document is an email
dated May 28th, 1996. The email is between Senate Committee on Foreign
Relations members and speaks to when the Clinton Administration first opted
to waive specific embargo provisions. On May 29th, 1996, Daniel Fisk wrote
the following about Peter Tarnoff, Under Secretary of State for Political Affairs,
from 1993 to 1997.

> The Administration is expected to announce tomorrow that exclusion
> provision (Title IV) of Helms-Burton has gone into effect.
>   ... Reports have it that senior Canadian and Mexican officials met at
> the White House today on Helms-Burton. I don't know if the meeting
> with them [is] to hear from the Administration or for them to blast the
> US for implementing the law.
>   Marc, rumor has it that tomorrow's State press briefing will concen-
> trate on Helms-Burton implementation.
>   Finally, sources inside State blame Tarnoff for the foot-dragging and
> lack of more forceful enforcement of Helms-Burton. Tarnoff—and oth-
> ers I'm sure—want to do the minimum in order not to offend our "allies"
> (especially the Euro weenies) while pretending, for our sake, that they're
> enforcing the law.
>
> FISK 28.5.1996

This email communication offers further empirical evidence for the theoretical interpretation that certain core states—especially the "Euro weenies"—
were influential in the Clinton Administration's decision to withhold the

application of specific embargo provisions. It presents direct evidence that the Clinton Administration was moved by those efforts and responded accordingly. Mexico's Foreign Ministry emphasized that the Clinton Administration's decision "constitutes an effort to respond to the unanimous opinion of the international community" (Ministry of Foreign Affairs of Mexico in Lippman 4/1/1997).

I extend this same analysis to the George W. Bush Administration's decisions to waive the same embargo provisions based on the Administration's commentary (PBS News 17.7.2001). Empirical evidence for this assertion comes from the Morley and Morrison volume. According to Chris McGillion, European opposition to the embargo was again influential. McGillion cites a State Department European Affairs official who made the following point:

> It's assumed on both sides, or at least on the European side, that the U.S. will continue to renew the Title III waiver ... Now if, for whatever reason, the U.S. was not to renew the waiver again, then of course, the WTO case would come back. But for the moment I don't think anyone in the administration would be advocating that we stop renewing it.
>
> MCGILLION in MORLEY AND MCGILLION 2005, 127

Moreover, McGillion cites an EU official who made a similar point:

> Our assumption is that a regular waiver is part of the understanding. So we're assuming that things are ok and the U.S. is aware that if things, for whatever reason, turn out not to be ok then there's the WTO and other things [that we would do] and that would just sour everything.
>
> MCGILLION in MORLEY AND MCGILLION 2005, 127

This commentary demonstrates that the core states—particularly states from the European Union—were influential in moving the Bush Administration to oppose certain embargo aspects. The officials indicated that the Administration arrived at that stance in response to European interstate opposition.

I have dealt with one strand of empirical evidence suggesting that the core coalition of states had influenced successive administrations to oppose specific embargo provisions. The two relevant provisions were Title III and Title IV. My point was that certain core states found the provisions especially objectionable and managed to pressure presidential administrations into waiving them (under the Presidential Suspension of Right of Action). I made the point that those efforts were influential for two reasons. The first reason was that the core states effectively nurtured anxieties among American officials about how much America's stance on the embargo was socially unsustainable. The second reason is that the Clinton and Bush administrations moved to waive Helms-Burton's Title III, given diplomatic pressure from certain core states.

A discussion remains of how the Obama Administration moved to oppose the embargo at the United Nations by December 2014. Substantial empirical evidence suggests that the core coalition's efforts were influential, given how Obama Administration officials justified the United States' change in position. Consider the following interventions, each of which suggests that the inter-state social context on the issue was a decisive influence on the United States' eventual position. The first intervention comes from a senior official in the Obama Administration:

> There's the annual vote on whether or not the U.S. embargo should be lifted at the United Nations. That took place earlier this year. I believe the vote was something along the lines of 192 to 2. I think we were joined by Palau in that vote. The rest of the world has gone from this set of policies, and I think this will be good for the United States and not just the hemisphere, but in the world and in international fora generally.
> Senior Official, Obama White House 17.12.14

A second critical intervention comes from Roberta Jacobson, Assistant Secretary of State for Western Hemisphere Affairs:

> Our previous approach to relations with Cuba over a half century ... isolated us from our democratic partners in this hemisphere and around the world.
> ... We believe that this policy had become such an irritant in our work with other Latin American countries, with our European allies, that it also enables us to work more effectively with them.
> ... We believe this is going to be an important turning point in countries engagement, especially countries which have a history of working on these issues in the region, which have been afraid to work too closely with us because of not wanting to appear aligned with our previous policy.
> JACOBSEN 15.2.15

A final critical intervention comes from Ben Rhodes, President Obama's Deputy National Security Advisor and lead negotiator on Cuba:

> For more than fifty years, the United States pursued a policy of isolating and pressuring Cuba. While the policy was rooted in the context of the Cold War, our efforts continued long after the rest of the world had changed. Put simply, U.S. Cuba policy wasn't working and was well beyond its expiration date. ... The United States was isolated within our own hemisphere—and in the wider world—which disagreed with our approach.
>
> RHODES 18.2.16

Rhodes made the further point in an interview with the BBC:

> We got an extraordinary amount out of this. First of all, the symbolic anchor of our Cuba policy we cut loose. So our standing in Latin America, our standing in the world improved because of our shift in the Cuba policy.
>
> RHODES 17.12.17

One critical observation must be made about these three interventions: each justifies a position against the embargo by explicitly referencing the interstate social context on the issue. In the first intervention, a senior administration official highlights a roll-call vote at the General Assembly and emphasizes that the "rest of the world has gone on from this set of policies." In the second intervention, Roberta Jacobsen emphasizes that the embargo "isolated us from our democratic partners in this hemisphere and around the world" and that "countries ... have been afraid to work too closely with us because of not wanting to appear aligned with our previous policy." And in the third intervention, Rhodes asserts that "the United States was isolated within our hemisphere—and in the wider world—which disagreed with our approach." This is to say that the empirical record directly supports the interpretation that the interstate political context of the time was a decisive influence on the Obama Administration's position on the embargo. Leading officials saw America's position as socially unsustainable and moved to change course accordingly.

It is important to emphasize that the change in position was not just relational. The Obama Administration also advocates for a socially mediated normative position against the embargo, as the process of collective legitimization set out in this book suggests. President Obama pointed out that "today we are making these changes because it is the right thing to do" (Obama 17.12.14). Some American officials emphasized the novelty of the Obama Administration's "new approach" to Cuba (A/71/PV.32, 15). Yet that approach was not novel at the United Nations. It was to appropriate the same *normative* preference for "constructive engagement" that the core coalition of states had been in favor of since the early 1990s. Samantha Power said, "rather than try to close off Cuba from the rest of the world ... we have chosen to take the path of engagement" (A/71/PV.32, 15). This is to say that the socially mediated, normative content present in the Obama Administration's perspective—that is, its normative preference for constructive engagement with Cuba's Government—suggests that a process of collective legitimization was central to the position. This indicates that the core coalition's efforts were influential to the extent that the issue's substantive content became relevant.

Several secondary accounts would be helpful to consider in this chapter. Professor LeoGrande's "Normalizing US-Cuba Relations: Escaping the Shackles of the Past" is the most relevant. LeoGrande makes two key points concerning the Obama Administration's stance on the Cuba embargo. First, "for years, the diplomatic cost of hostility towards Cuba was relatively low" (LeoGrande 2015, 487). Although the UN General Assembly had voted overwhelmingly against the embargo for each of the past 23 years, most countries were not willing to make bilateral relations with Washington contingent on a change in US-Cuban relations (LeoGrande 2015, 487). The second important point that Leogrande makes is that "the cost of maintaining the status quo went up significantly as US relations with Latin America founded on the shoals of US policy towards Cuba. The depth of Latin America's anger and frustration over the issue became apparent to Washington only during the 2012 Cartagena Summit, a few months before Obama decided to open the secret dialogue with Cuba" (LeoGrande 2015, 488).

I have a twofold response to LeoGrande's perspective corresponding to the two points above. On the first point, I cannot entirely agree with the assertion that the "diplomatic cost of hostility towards Cuba was relatively low" for some twenty-three years and that most countries were unwilling to make bilateral relations with the United States contingent upon the end of the embargo. Certain core states *were* explicit that the blocade—particularly its extraterritorial effects—was objectionable and would stymie bilateral relations if it continued. In 1992, for example, the European Community wrote the following to the Department of State: "The European Community and its Member States consider that the enactment by the US president of this legislation would cause grave damage to bilateral EC/US economic and trade relations" (Delegation of the Commission of European Communities 7.10.1992). Canada, Mexico, and the United Kingdom voiced similar complaints and coupled them with concrete measures to undermine the embargo's application (McGillion 97–147 in Morley and McGillion 2005).

Moreover, as previous paragraphs have shown, we know that those efforts were influential in nurturing a sense of unease among American officials to at least waive some of the embargo's provisions. This applies to both the Clinton and Bush administrations. Hence, LeoGrande's first point about relatively low diplomatic costs to the United States throughout the 1990s and 2000s is misleading.

LeoGrande's other key point is to assign decisive agency to Latin American states following the 2012 Cartagena Summit. For LeoGrande, Latin American states were particularly influential in moving the Obama Administration towards an unequivocal and unambiguous position against the embargo. I agree with LeoGrande's interpretation that Latin American states were effective. For example, empirical evidence for the assertion can come from commentary by Ambassador Susan Rice:

> We sometimes forget, but when Obama took office, the United States standing in Latin America had suffered. Hugo Chavez and anti-American voices were ascendant. And our outdated Cuba policy was a big reason why. Time after time, meeting after meeting, leaders from Mexico to Uruguay criticized our approach to Cuba, it was a constant drumbeat—a perennial irritant—as we sought greater cooperation with our neighbors. Thanks in part to our normalization policy, and an approach to the region based on cooperation and shared values, relationships between the United States and countries in the hemisphere are as good now as they've ever been.
>
> RICE 14.10.16

As Ambassador Rice suggests, social anxieties—especially vis-à-vis Latin American states like Mexico and Uruguay—significantly influenced the United States' stance on Cuba. However, the empirical record does not suggest that these Latin American states' influence on the Obama administration was decisive. My reasoning is twofold.

The first reason is that most Latin American states—including Mexico and Uruguay—had been vehement about their opposition to the embargo from the outset in 1991 and also took explicit measures to counteract the embargo's application (Morley 180–223 in Morris and Morley 2005). For example, Morris Morley writes the following about Mexico:

> The hemispheric clamor against Helms-Burton was even more vociferous and hostile than earlier demonstrations of the CDA [namely, the Cuban Democracy Act]. No government was more scathing of this latest piece

of legislation than Mexico, Washington's partner (together with Canada, another very public critic) in NAFTA. Clinton's decision to sign Helms-Burton outraged the Zedillo government and ended sympathy in Mexico City for America's Cuba policy. In June 1996, the Mexican Congress began drafting "antidote" legislation to protect local companies from the global "reach" of Helms-Burton. At the same time, President Zedillo broached the possibility that Mexico would adopt a law not dissimilar to Canada's, blocking companies from complying with the reporting provisions of Helms-Burton and forbidding them from paying any fines levied by U.S.

MORLEY 200 in MORLEY AND MORRISON 2005

Mexico's staunch opposition to the embargo—which Morley describes as one of "outrage"—remained invariable throughout the Obama Administration's tenure. Hence, if Latin American states were decisive in the United States' eventual stance on the embargo, then it is unclear why they would have been more influential throughout the Obama Administration's tenure rather than in previous administrations. The more significant empirical conditioning factor was the Obama Administration's greater emphasis on restoring America's sense of moral leadership worldwide and, therefore, greater willingness to heed the groundswell of interstate opposition to the embargo. Empirical evidence for this assertion comes from multiple sources, including Secretary Hilary Clinton, who insisted that the Obama Administration "repaired America's tarnished reputation. We shaped old alliances and started new partnerships. We got back to the time-tested values that make our country a beacon of hope and opportunity and freedom for the entire world" (Clinton 31.7.2015).

LeoGrande could retort that Latin American opposition to the embargo grew as more states normalized relations with Cuba, and so was a more significant influence on the United States when the Obama Administration assumed office. With that argument, however, one would still have to contend with the fact that most Latin American states began normalizing relations with Cuba throughout the 1990s, as Morris Morley indicates (Morley 180–234 in Morley and McGillion 2005). Moreover, one would still have to contend with the lack of explicit empirical evidence to suggest that certain Latin American states—those that had recently normalized relations with Cuba—had a decisive influence on the Obama Administration's eventual stance on the Cuba embargo. The empirical record suggests that those states' influence was residual, meaning they added momentum to the mainstay of interstate opposition that had been around since 1991. The evidence for this assertion comes from LeoGrande's work, where he references senior American officials who emphasize the significance of the policy change to Latin America in general and not in particular to Latin American states that had recently normalized relations with Cuba (LeoGrande 2015, 482).

My second reason for disagreeing with LeoGrande's interpretation comes from the empirical source work, some of which became available after LeoGrande's publication in 2015. The point is that much of that source work is explicit in its suggestion that the interstate social context of the time—particularly its global, multilateral reach—was influential in moving the Obama Administration towards its position against the embargo. In other words, the empirical record suggests that concerns for how other states saw the United States in that context were central to how Obama Administration officials arrived at a position against the embargo. The evidentiary basis for the claim comes from the interventions above, each of which apportions prime significance to the United States' standing within that particular social context. An explicit example comes from Josh Earnest, Spokesperson for the Obama White House. In 2014, Earnest made the following point to a news reporter at a press conference:

> But here's the principle, Jon. The sanctions regime that we've had in place against Cuba is unilateral … The rest of the world is actually on the other side of this issue. They criticize our sanctions regime policy against Cuba, and it actually interferes with our ability to bring to bear pressure from the rest of the international community on the Castro regime to better respect human rights in Cuba … And that's why we believe that a strategy—a fundamental strategy change was necessary.
>
> EARNEST 2014

This is not to say that some social concern vis-à-vis Latin American states was insignificant. It is to say that social concerns vis-à-vis Latin American states were just one component of a larger social concern vis-à-vis the "international community" at large.

3.3   *Small States*

We have postulated that the Russian Federation and the United States were subjects of the interstate socialization process that the core coalition of states set in motion in the early 1990s. In both examples, the core coalition of states was influential in moving the Russian Federation and the United States toward an unequivocal and unambiguous position against the Cuba embargo in a manner consistent with a process of collective legitimization. Given particular empirical conditioning factors, the observable implications for the claim were based on how the respective officials expressed positions against the status quo. In both examples, the respective officials were explicit: the interstate social climate of the time was a decisive influence on the eventual positions the two governments took.

We now turn to a third and final empirical example: small states. Wikileaks' 2015 release of confidential diplomatic cables necessitates touching upon small states. The reason is that releasing the documents provides rare insight into diplomacy at the United Nations. However, the nature of the resource is dispersed and does not allow the same depth of analysis that the previous subsections achieve. I accordingly touch upon one small state example and then take a step back to examine research findings more broadly about four other small states. The context for the cables is the United States' petitions (or diplomatic démarches) to other governments, asking that they oppose or abstain on Cuba's embargo resolutions at the United Nations. The cables are between the Department of State, its diplomatic staff abroad, and foreign ministries (particularly international organizations departments). American diplomats abroad meet with foreign ministry officials, deliver diplomatic démarches, and report to the Department of State. The most relevant findings in this research project come from how foreign ministry officials respond to the diplomatic démarches. Consider the following examples from small states.

The Emirates had been among a handful of states in the Middle East that were silent on Cuba's annual complaints against the embargo at the United Nations. This was the case from 1991 to 1998. In its first explication of the vote, the Emirati delegation in New York made the point that:

> The United Arab Emirates emphasizes that all States must enjoy the freedom of trade and navigation in all international sea lanes. Therefore, the United Arab Emirates does not apply any economic, commercial or financial embargo on Cuba and does not allow application of these measures outside the context of international legitimacy.
>
> A/66/114, 95

There are several observations one must draw from this intervention. The first is what it does not suggest: "discovery" of a norm on "freedom of trade and navigation." The embargo had been in place for each of the previous seven years, with a norm on free trade and navigation in question. The United Arab Emirates, however, did not position itself in favor of or against the embargo.

This leads to whether there had been some deterioration in circumstances— for example, in the embargo's more extensive application—to encourage the above change in position. This would be the case had the position change occurred more reflexively in 1992 or 1996. The above statement also suggests that the empirical record does not support that interpretation. Moreover, there is no direct evidence to suggest that either one of those pieces of legislation was an inflection point for the United Arab Emirates. Even if the two pieces of legislation were an inflection point, a focus on them would gravitate towards a "push comes to shove" analysis, whereby some three-decades-old sanctions measures that were in place from the outset were not enough to countenance an unequivocal and unambiguous anti-embargo position. That suggestion is not persuasive: the preponderance of evidence suggests that states that suffered or anticipated suffering from the embargo—such as Canada, states from the European Community, and Latin America—were steadfast about it from the get-go. It therefore seems doubtful that an incremental increase in the embargo's application—for example, via the Helms-Burton Law in 1996— would have made the difference. At most, Helms-Burton may have been influential and qualified as a significant empirical conditioning factor. However, the empirical record cannot suggest it was the basis for how the United Arab Emirates developed its eventual stance against the embargo.

This allows for a preliminary social constructivist interpretation of the above foreign policy change on the embargo. The empirical justification is twofold. The first comes from how the United Arab Emirates articulated its position, which suggests it was moved by the socially mediated, normative aspects of the core coalition's campaign. The reason is that it echoes a specific set of ideas that the anti-embargo coalition had long been in favor of. Like the core states, it finds that a norm on the "freedom of trade and navigation" is relevant to a position against the embargo. The embargo became objectionable, given common expectations on how states should conduct trade relations. Hence, the specific way the United Arab Emirates formulated ideas against the embargo suggests that it was moved by the interstate social influence that a core coalition of states brought to bear.

The more direct empirical justification comes from diplomatic cables in Wikileaks entitled "Démarche Instructions for Cuba Embargo Resolution at the UNGA." The wires include exchanges between American diplomats and Emirati officials at the Ministry of Foreign Affairs, and relate to a request that the United Arab Emirates withhold support for Cuba's complaint at the United Nations:

> Econchief declined reftel démarche to MFA International Affairs Director Yacoub Al-Hosani on October 28, the first day Al-Hosani was available to meet. Econchief highlighted the human rights situation in Cuba and urged the UAE to vote against or abstain on the UNGA resolution.

Al-Hosani asked what the results were on the 2006 resolution. After Econchief explained that the resolution passed by a vote of 183 to 4, Al-Hosani stated that he did not believe the UAE would change its vote ... He added "don't push us" to oppose an overwhelming international consensus, adding it's not logical.

... "He commented: 'people like America, but not your policies'."

ABUDHABI1812_a

This communication highlights the basis of the United Arab Emirates' embargo position. The critical point is that the transmission justifies a stance against the embargo, primarily referencing its interstate social ramifications. The International Affairs Director is explicit: there is "logic" in supporting an anti-embargo position mainly because to do otherwise is to "oppose an overwhelming international consensus." Moreover, Al-Hosani's comments evidence further social concerns: citing what "people like" as further justification to oppose the embargo and not for any other reason (such as the embargo's past or present material effects on trade relations with Cuba). This supports the interpretation that the diplomatic costs of upholding the status quo were credible for the United Arab Emirates. Thanks to the core coalition's efforts, appearing to abstain from or being indifferent to the embargo's consideration became socially unsustainable, decisively influencing how the United Arab Emirates changed course.

The United Arab Emirates is one example of a small state that seems to have based its position on the embargo primarily because of diplomatic pressure. There are several other examples, all of which follow from the State Department's démarche instructions. The following are noteworthy, but for a lack of space will skip ahead to the more direct empirical evidence. Each example includes states that had been silent for years on Cuba's complaint. This cable concerns Jordan:

1(C) Poloff delivered refuel talking points October 30 to Ayman Al-Amiri, Acting Head of the International Organizations Department of the Ministry of Foreign Affairs. Amiri promised to closely review our request to oppose or abstain on the resolution, but admitted that it was "unlikely" that Jordan would break consensus with other Arab states and the European Union on this issue.

03AMMAN7088_a

This cable concerns the Bahamas:

1. (C) Bahamas Prime Minister Hubert Ingraham received reftel démarche from Charge late October 4. PM Ingraham took on-board USG points regarding the UN having great potential for progress if like-minded countries would agree to work together on balanced and reasonable UN resolutions and other initiatives.
2. (C) However, PM Ingraham robustly defended specific Bahamian votes on important resolutions that had differed from USG votes in previous UNGA sessions. Ingraham began by stating that the "U.S. stands alone on the Cuban Embargo."

o8NASSAU709_a

This cable concerns Poland:

1 (C) Pol External Chief delivered refuel demarcate November to Mariusz Lewicki of the MFA UN Department. After consulting widely within the MFA and contacting the Polish Mission in New York, Lewicki responded late in the evening that the GOP had decided the "highest priority was to maintain the common EU position." Poland would therefore ... support the overall Cuba resolution ...

Comment: Poland is attempting to repair relations with EU partners such as Germany and France, while at the same time assuaging concerns in Brussels that the ruling Law and Justice (PiS) party is Euro-skeptical. This is compounded by the perception in Europe since the beginning of OIF that Poland is too much of a U.S. surrogate within the EU ...

o6WARSAW2370_a

This cable concerns Denmark:

Danish MFA Deputy Head of Department for Asia and Latin America (DAS-equivalent) Lars Bredal reaffirmed October 26 Denmark's commitment to a firm EU policy in support of human rights and democracy in Cuba, and indicated that the Danish government welcomes U.S. interest in joint action with the EU (Ref A) ... From Denmark's perspective, Bredal said, the challenge of open U.S.-EU collaboration will be in avoiding the image of the West "ganging up" on Cuba—also in the eyes of other Latin American countries.

COPENHAGEN 000988

And this final cable concerns Romania:

1 (C) Deputy Palcons on 8 November delivered démarche on the Cuba Embargo Resolution (ref a) to MFA Director for UN Affairs Petru Dumitriu and Deputy Director Eugen Mihut …

2 (C) Comment: … Romania even prior to formal EU entry in January 2007 has begun to march in close step with the EU on this matter (and on many other issues), and will want to maintain its bona fides by hewing closely to the EU common position.

   BUCHAREST001706_a

Each of these interventions asserts a stance on the embargo, referencing its wider interstate social implications, meaning how the broader community of states sees the respective positions. The first intervention emphasizes Jordan's refusal to "break ranks with the other Arab states and the European Union." The second intervention emphasizes the Bahama's refusal to withhold opposition to the embargo because the "U.S. stands alone on the Cuba embargo." The third intervention emphasizes Poland's need to oppose the blocade because the "highest priority was to maintain the common EU position," and avoid the "avoid the perception in Europe … that Poland is too much of a U.S. surrogate within the EU." The fourth intervention emphasizes similar social anxieties, emphasizing the significance of "avoiding the image of the West 'ganging up' on Cuba—also in the eyes of other Latin American countries." And the final intervention again highlights social concerns, indicating Romania's need to "march in close step with the EU." In each example, the respective state actors justify a position on the embargo primarily given concerns for its interstate social ramifications and not for any other main reason. Hence, the communications demonstrate a manifest concern for how other states—especially member states from the European Union—see their position, suggesting that social concerns were a decisive influence on the respective state subjects.

4   Part Three

Moving forward, we now arrive at the third and final step in the research procedure: the cross-check, which weighs inferences from the previous section against the most prominent theoretical and empirical counterarguments. The theoretical counterarguments come from materialist accounts of international relations, as discussed in the argument chapter. The empirical counterarguments come from the case study's empirical circumstances and the most relevant secondary historical accounts.

A theoretical focus on material side payments serves as one theoretical counterargument. A possible rendition may have to do with a claim that some states—particularly those we associate as belonging to a core coalition—took it upon themselves to manipulate specific material incentives and disincentives in favor of or against a position on the embargo. According to this theoretical perspective, those efforts would shape the eventual constellation of support for a common position against the blockade. A potential ringleader for those efforts is Cuba, which, according to Morley, sought to expand its trade relations with other countries following the collapse of the Soviet Union. Numerous states would have been susceptible to those efforts, especially in Latin America. Morley emphasizes that "in 1990, Cuba conducted only 5 percent of its total trade with the region; by 1994, the figure increased sevenfold to 35 percent" (Morley 199 in Morley and Morrison 2005). An example is Argentina, which struck a future investment accord with Cuba, enabling it to remove some $1.25 billion in debt (Morley 198 in Morley and Morrison 2005). The implication is that a deal of this magnitude would have made Argentina more sympathetic towards a position against the embargo than otherwise.

I concede the plausibility of this theoretical interpretation and allow the possibility that numerous states had their material reasons to oppose the embargo. Nevertheless, I push back on two key points. First, even if Cuba were successful in some form of resource manipulation, it would pale compared to what the United States could achieve. The reason is axiomatic: the United States' material capabilities far outweighed that of Cuba's. Moreover, we know that successive American administrations *did* manipulate those resources to ensure that other states did not oppose its position on Cuba. An explicit example comes from Chile:

> When Chile announced the exchange of ambassadors with Cuba in April 1995, Washington combined expressions of "disappointment" with the threat of economic sanctions. One State Department official warned that it "won't make things easier" for Chile's application to join the North American Free Trade Agreement (NAFTA).
>
> MORLEY 191 in MORLEY AND MORRISON 2005

Thus, if some material resource manipulation significantly influenced how states positioned themselves on Cuba, we would expect states to have been more sympathetic to the United States' stance throughout the 1990s and 2000s and not Cuba's.

Another materialist critique can relate to the neorealist assertion about the "epiphenomenal" nature of international organizations, as set out in Chapter

Two. The critique would emphasize that the eventual constellation of opposition against the embargo reflected some material balance of threats balanced or balancing against each other. The most relevant rendition of the critique would proceed along the lines of the uni-polar, anti-American analysis set out in Chapter One (e.g. Bailey, Strezhnev, and Voeten 2017; Potrafke 2009; Voeten 2004). There is some traction in this potential critique in that opposition to the embargo was almost exclusively, by definition, an anti-American position.

The problem with that perspective, however, is twofold. The first respect is that it glosses over the "non-partisan" nature of the anti-embargo coalition's efforts since 1991. As shown in section one, central to those efforts was a manipulation of *common* notions of "right" and "wrong" that could exert diplomatic pressure upon all states. In other words, a coalition of states from the outset cast consideration of the embargo as above an anti-American cleavage. Moreover, those states couched the issue as such to win others over, regardless of the constellation of material threats balanced or balancing against each other at the time. This is to say that an emphasis on some constellation of material capabilities overlooks how the core states saw the issue from the outset.

The second limitation of the neorealist critique pertains to how the relevant state subjects formulated a position against the embargo. The reason is that states that took an eventual stand against the blockade seem to have done so "as if" moved by what it meant for a relationship with the wider interstate community, as the previous section argues. The empirical record suggests that the primary concerns were social; the applicable state subjects took stands against the embargo in explicit reference to its significance to the broader community of states. When pressed to justify his views, for example, Vietnamese diplomats' central defense on Cuba was that "the GVN position is consistent with the majority of countries that support the Cuba embargo resolution" (06HANOI2833_a). One can make a similar point based on interventions from the previous section. This is to say that this chapter's "smoking gun" evidence lends direct empirical support to the theoretical argument that this book advances.

Another potential materialist critique of this chapter can come from an emphasis on "sanction's fatigue" (Haas 1998). This critique may run along the following lines. Maintaining sanctions policies against Cuba was expensive in material terms and perhaps increasingly so as their effects remained elusive. In this case study, the basis to oppose the embargo would be material and not social. I concede that sanctions are expensive and that there was an evident material incentive not to support the United States sanctions policies against Cuba. I also recognize the possibility that there would have been more material inducement to oppose sanctions policies against Cuba as its economy recovered following the Soviet Union's collapse.

In defense of the empirical argument, consider these two points. First, the nature of the relevant changes in position cannot be accounted for without the anti-embargo coalition's efforts (Hurd 2005, 521). How certain states opposed the embargo suggests that the coalition's efforts were influential. As Hurd would suggest, the coalition gave the other states the "tools" to fight an essential aspect of American foreign policy. As Hurd would also suggest, some states might still have opposed the embargo, but at a more significant cost to their relationship with the United States. Hence, the coalition gave rise to an inter-subjective "safe space" within which third states could oppose the embargo without appearing to confront the United States.

One could extend the sanctions fatigue argument to the Obama Administration's decision to oppose the embargo. Yet, there are also limitations to this potential critique. The reason is threefold. First, the Obama Administration's decision to oppose the embargo was not conditioned on the embargo's demise. Embargo legislation has remained in place until today. Second, given that lifting the embargo was never an immanent possibility, it is doubtful that material interests significantly influenced the Obama Administration's decision. Professor William LeoGrande makes a similar point, emphasizing that the "Cuban market was small and poor ... once US agricultural interest won an exception to the embargo in 2000, allowing them to sell food to Cuba, business pressure for a policy change receded" (LeoGrande 2015, 487). The third reason comes from what the "smoking gun" evidence demonstrates, lending direct support to the present social constructivist assertion that material interests were not a decisive influence on the respective state positions.

A historical critique may relate to President Trump's election and subsequent change in stance on the embargo following the Obama Administration's departure from office. The Trump Administration reportedly undertook over 200 initiatives to tighten the embargo (Marsh 3.3.2021). At the United Nations, the American delegation once again opposed the annual embargo resolutions (A/72/PV.38; A/73/PV.30; A/74/PV.28). This reverts to long-standing policy on the embargo would seem to refute the suggestion that the core coalition's diplomatic pressure was influential. My response to this potential critique refers to the limitations of my theoretical argument in the theoretical argument chapter. Recall that my theoretical argument hinges on how much a state subject attaches significance to its stature on a particular issue. I referenced Giovanni Mantilla to support the point that certain states may care more (or less) about the "consequences of public embarrassment to their self-image, status, and reputation" (Mantilla 2020b, 177). The former states are more "socially vulnerable" because they wish to be seen as having "'good' standing as members of the 'international community', 'particularly among social competition'" (Mantilla 2020b, 177).

On the other hand, the latter states are less socially vulnerable, so diplomatic pressure cannot affect these states. This includes states that maintain a certain position despite the prevailing negative interstate social repercussions. A state that does not care about that diplomatic pressure—in particular, as it relates to maintaining an intersubjective sense of legitimacy on the issue—will not, for that reason, come around. More importantly, if a state commonly adopts a "renegade attitude" against international norms—for example, by boasting about its status as an outcast on the issue—it is unlikely to be moved by diplomatic pressure (Mantilla 2018, 331).

This theoretical caveat is relevant to the United States' position on the embargo under President Trump for two reasons. The first reason is that we have strong reason to believe that American officials during the Trump Administration—like officials under previous administrations—still felt the weight of diplomatic pressure to oppose the embargo. As evidence, I suggest communication between several senators and President Trump. The communication is dated October 31, 2017, and was authored by Patrick Leahy, Chris van Hollen, Sherrod Brown, Elizabeth Warren, Jeff Merkley, Amy Klobuchar, Jack Reed, Edward Markey, Al Franken and Sheldon Whitehouse. The senators made the following observation before the General Assembly voted on the embargo in the fall of 2017:

> Next month, the UN General Assembly will vote on a resolution calling for an end to the United States embargo against Cuba for the 26th time. As you know, last year the United States abstained from voting on the resolution for the first time, as it has become abundantly clear that our effort to isolate Cuba has instead isolated us from the international community and particularly from allies and partners in this hemisphere. We recognize that because the embargo is still U.S. law, the Administration is unlikely to support the resolution. However, as one of the only two nations that did not vote in favor of the resolution, we urge you to direct our UN Ambassador to again abstain in order to prevent further isolation of the United States.
>
> Our failed embargo against Cuba has been repeatedly and publicly condemned by the international community as ineffective and harmful

to the people of Cuba. The longer we maintain this outdated Cold War policy the more our international regional credibility suffers.

... One vote on a UN resolution cannot replace the legislation required to end the embargo. Only Congress can repeal this outdated policy. It does, however, signal to the international community that the United States remains open to dialogue and further negotiation with Cuba.

U.S. Senate 31.10.2017

The senators point to the United States' diplomatic isolation on the embargo and the damage to America's intersubjective sense of credibility worldwide. As the senators importantly emphasize, these interstate social ramifications warranted renewed opposition to the embargo.

My second reason is that abundant empirical source work suggests that the Trump Administration adopted a "renegade attitude" towards the international community on the embargo despite the diplomatic pressure on the issue. As we have seen, this attitude sharply contrasts with the Obama Administration's, which attached the utmost significance to maintaining an intersubjective sense of legitimacy to the embargo. Consider the following observations by Ambassador Nikki Haley, the Trump Administration's Permanent Representative to the United Nations in New York. One such observation comes from remarks to the General Assembly in November 2017.

One year ago, the United States abstained in the voting on resolution 71/5, under this item. The reason given was that the continuation of the embargo was not isolating Cuba but was, in fact, isolating the United States. It is true that we had been left nearly alone in opposition to this annual resolution. No doubt there will be some here who do not understand how we can take such opposite positions, separated by just 12 months. They will wonder how we could passively accept this resolution last year and energetically oppose it this year. To those who are confused as to where the United States stands, let me be clear. As is their right under our Constitution, the American people have spoken. They have chosen a new President, and he has chosen a new Ambassador to the United Nations. As long as the Cuban people continue to be deprived of their human rights and fundamental freedoms and as long as the proceeds from trade with Cuba go to prop up the dictatorial regime responsible for denying those rights, the United States does not fear isolation in this Hall or anywhere else. Our principles are not up for a vote. They are enshrined in our Constitution. They also happen to be enshrined in the

Charter of the United Nations. As long as we are Members of the United Nations, we will stand for respect for human rights and fundamental freedoms that the Member States in this body have pledged to protect, even if we have to stand alone.

A/72/PV.38, 92

Another observation comes from remarks at the following Session in November 2018.

Last year, we were joined by just one nation in voting against resolution 72/4, and that is fine; we were in very good company. We have no problem with standing alone on behalf of the things that we believe in and will proudly do so again today if necessary. But the most regrettable fact of this draft resolution each year is not that the United States may not stand alone in opposing it, but that the draft resolution is a waste of everyone's time. It is one more time that countries feel they can poke the United States in the eye. But they are not hurting the United States when they do this; they are literally hurting the Cuban people by telling the regime that their treatment of their people is acceptable.

To the people of Cuba, I once again say that the United States will continue to stand with them, regardless of what others do. We will stand with them until the day comes that we can stand together as free peoples in our shared neighbourhood.

A/73/PV.30, 8–9

And finally, Haley expressed the following observation in an op-ed in the *New York Times*:

The unfortunate thing is not that the United States was left, once again, standing virtually alone on behalf of human dignity at the United Nations. To the contrary. We are proud to buck the mob when it comes to the principles we believe in.

HALEY 3.11.18

Each one of these observations, in contrast to the Obama Administration, demonstrates a sense of pride in being seen as an outcast on the annual embargo resolutions at the General Assembly. The first intervention acknowledges a sense of being "alone" but nevertheless emphasizes a commitment to principles that the United States supports "even if we have to stand alone."

The second intervention is more explicit, emphasizing that "we have no problem with standing alone on behalf of the things that we believe in and will proudly do so again." And the third intervention is even more explicit, insisting that "we are proud to buck the mob when it comes to the principles we believe in."

CHAPTER 5

The Ban on Nuclear Weapons (1946–1961)

For some time much emphasis had been placed upon the existence of a moral opinion among the smaller nations that could
be brought to bear, and thus restrain the main protagonists in the
struggle between the Communists and the free world. Many who
were aware of the difficulties inherent in the conduct of bilateral
negotiations on the disarmament issue hoped that nations not
immediately aligned side or the other might prove helpful ... Yet
when the Soviet Union suddenly resumed tests on an extensive
scale, and action with threats of 100-megaton bombs, the reactions
of the neutral or non-aligned countries at Belgrade and again, to
some extent, at the General Assembly of the United Nations were
so mild as to be wholly inconsequential. As a result, their position as
"guardians" of the world's conscience was greatly weakened.

MCCLOY 1962, 343–344

∴

0   **Chapter Outline**

In contrast to the previous two case studies, we now move on to examine an
issue area where the "dog does not bark." My adaptation of the term refers
to the coverage of an issue where interstate socialization does not occur: an
almost unanimous, unequivocal, and unambiguous interstate consensus does
not eventuate. The point of presenting an inconclusive case study speaks to my
research design. The idea is to sharpen my general argument for the conditions
under which socialization will and will not occur. Recall my proposition that an
agent's perceived integrity on an issue can make socialization efforts more (or
less) influential. Specifically, socialization efforts are more likely to fail when
proponents lack that integrity—and are therefore seen to be hypocritical—
because the target states do not see a political drawback to maintaining the
status quo. By integrity, I meant a social constructivist (and not a rationalist)
version of "reputation," which refers to the extent to which a socialization subject regards a socialization agent as a trustworthy advocate of a cause. I stressed

© NAIF AL-MULLA, 2025 | DOI:10.1163/9789004711938_007

that my use of the concept is intersubjective. It asks to what degree a potential socialization subject views a socialization agent as meaning what they say—namely, "talking the talk" *and* "walking the walk"—on the specific issue.

The chapter tests this theoretical proposition concerning nuclear weapons proceedings at the General Assembly. Studying the issue can be complex, encompassing some seventy-five years of intensive discussion from 1946 to the present. For simplicity, I focus on one clear and concise issue: the moral right to use or threaten to use nuclear weapons in war. In response to James Mahoney and Gary Goertz's commentary on the possibility principle, I also pay particular attention to the same period as my first case study—from 1946 to 1961. As we have seen, that principle asks for nonpositive case studies that resemble positive cases to "control for background features and thereby achieve greater leverage for causal analysis" (Mahoney and Goertz 2004, 655). I thus examine the same period to replicate the conditions under which socialization took place in my first study and control for a host of historical factors that can affect the success of that socialization. In the two case studies, the most prominent of these historical factors is decolonization, which led to a substantial increase in membership at the United Nations in 1960 and 1961. These new member states—from Africa and Southern Asia—lent further support to the core coalition's diplomatic efforts on apartheid, as well as on the nuclear weapons ban. Controlling for decolonization thus controls for the added potential social effects—such as those that can follow from an increased sense of isolation—that a core coalition's numerical expansion can have on an interstate audience. I also allude to the same agents and subjects of socialization as case illustrations as much as the source work allows. This allows me to control for a host of actor properties, such as those relating to regime characteristics at a particular period.

Nonpositive case studies are most valuable when they address empirical contexts where the outcome of interest has a "real possibility of occurring—not just those where the outcome has a nonzero probability" (Mahoney and Goertz 2004, 654). I accordingly also examine the time from 1946 to 1961 to ensure that interstate socialization on the issue had a "real possibility of occurring," as per my first case study. Some may question whether a state's possession of nuclear weapons would have altogether abnegated support for the ban. Here, I emphasize that the two are *not* necessarily incompatible. A state can possess the means to engage in specific modes of warfare but believe that doing so runs counter to select common norms.

This chapter follows the structure of the previous case study chapters with an introduction and three parts. The introduction has two components, the first of which provides an empirical background for the case study. This acclimates the reader to the empirical context, especially with how certain core states—particularly India and the Soviet Union (as well as states associated with the Eastern Bloc)—made the nuclear weapons ban an issue for global, multilateral concern at the United Nations. My prefatory commentary again alludes to the theoretical argument chapter's analysis of information politics, requiring that socialization agents specify and categorize an issue (Rosert 2019). The second component considers the literature on nuclear weapons from the social constructivist research tradition in international relations. The most relevant work comes from Professor Nina Tannenwald, who zeroes in on the role of a "taboo" on the use of nuclear weapons (Tannenwald 1999; 2005; 2007; 2018a; 2018b). By taboo, Tannenwald means a "normative inhibition against the first use of nuclear weapons" (Tannenwald 2018a, 89). In response to Tannenwald's work, I emphasize the limits in that taboo, drawn from my empirical focus on the United Nations. I suggest that there has long been some general aversion to nuclear weapons at the interstate level. More importantly, I also emphasize that this general aversion to nuclear weapons has not been synonymous with a diminution in the belief in the moral right to use (or threaten to use) nuclear weapons in self-defense. Put differently, a unanimous interstate consensus against the right to use nuclear weapons does *not* exist. Interstate socialization has accordingly not occurred on this issue.

Part One makes the case for a core coalition of states' diplomatic efforts as advocates of an unequivocal and unambiguous stance against the right to use (or threaten to use) nuclear weapons in war. The chapter identifies the coalition from proceedings on nuclear weapons at the United Nations, which date back to 1946. The leading proponents of the position were the Soviet Union (as well as states associated with the Eastern Bloc) and states that later formed the Non-Aligned Movement. India and the latter were among the coalition's most vocal proponents. Part One suggests the existence of a core coalition that took shape by a shared, initial stance against the moral right to use (or threaten to use) nuclear weapons in war. Like the previous two case studies, the main task is to theorize those views by scrutinizing "rhetorical action": the discursive practices that the potential socialization state agents use to influence other states. As we shall see, these agents manipulate common norms to pressure an audience to support a cause.

Part Two considers how the core coalition's diplomatic efforts on the nuclear weapons ban were unsuccessful. My point relates to the Soviet Union and India's sense of integrity on nuclear weapons as advocates of the ban. I submit that these states' perceived integrity was in significant doubt and consequently undermined the extent to which their efforts could have influenced other states' positions. This is to say that the campaign to ban the bomb failed because those leading it lacked integrity in the eyes of target states—that is, NATO member states—thanks to their own nuclear arsenal or potential to develop one. My general conclusion is that socialization efforts fail when proponents are seen to be hypocritical. Empirical evidence for this argument comes from observations made by American, British, and Canadian officials about the Soviet Union and India as advocates of the ban. I use these three states as illustrative country cases for empirical reasons. The first reason is that Canada, the United Kingdom, and the United States had long opposed the ban in contrast to the Soviet Union, states associated with the Eastern Bloc, and states that later formed the Non-Aligned Movement. The second reason is that these three country cases allow access to insightful empirical source work, as we shall see.

Part Three moves on toward the third and final step in this book's research procedure: the cross-check, weighing points from the previous section against the most prominent theoretical and empirical counterarguments. The theoretical counterarguments come from materialist accounts of international relations. The main materialist counterargument to the chapter would proceed from the assertion that intergovernmental organizations are "epiphenomenal," meaning that their proceedings reflect some constellation of material power in the interstate system. This theoretical interpretation would assert that interstate proceedings on nuclear weapons—particularly from 1946 to 1961—reflect the East-West Cold War cleavage of the time. Hence, interstate proceedings on the issue were not amenable to a divergence from that cleavage as long as the states in question saw themselves as aligned with one side or another. The point is that the national defense imperatives would define positions on nuclear weapons. A potential socialization agent's perceived integrity on nuclear weapons would therefore have little or no influence on other states' positions. I make two points in response to this potential critique. The first point is that the Cold War's end has not been associated with an arresting change in positions on the issue, particularly by states that have not opposed the right to use (or threaten to use) nuclear weapons from the outset. The second point is that the critique overlooks the social anxieties that potential socialization subjects expressed upon evaluating the issue at the United Nations.

1   Introduction

The question of nuclear weapons first came before the General Assembly at its First Session, when member states unanimously voted to create the Atomic Energy Commission in 1945. Among the Commission's aims was to make "specific proposals" on disarmament efforts, including nuclear disarmament efforts (A/RES/1(I), 9). Yet the Commission did not set out to outlaw the use or threat of use of nuclear weapons. In 1946, the Soviet Union was the member state to first raise and advocate for that proposition in a communication entitled "Draft international convention to prohibit the production and employment of weapons based on the use of atomic energy for the purpose of mass destruction" (AEC/7). The draft convention referred to the status quo in undesirable terms: the "great scientific discoveries in the sphere of atomic energy carry with them a great danger, first of all, for peaceful towns and the civilian population in the event of these discoveries being used in the form of atomic weapons for the purpose of mass destruction" (AEC/7, 1). The document also sorted the issue into a broader category of problems posed by other weapons that had been banned because of their especially destructive nature. "International agreements have already prohibited the use in warfare of asphyxiating, poisonous and other similar gases, as well as all similar liquids, substances, and processes, and likewise bacteriological means" (AEC/7, 1). At the time, however, the Soviet Union's efforts were a minority viewpoint. In 1948, for example, the Soviet draft resolution to ban nuclear weapons was rejected by the General Assembly, with forty member states against the proposition (A/PV.157, 468–469; UNODA 1970, 22).

The Atomic Energy Commission was eventually dissolved and replaced by the Disarmament Commission in 1952, which envisioned a "system of guaranteed disarmament [where] there must be progressive disclosure and verification continuingly of all armed forces ... and all armaments including atomic" (A/RES/502(VI), 2). The creation of this commission was more controversial, with eighteen out of sixty member states not supporting the resolution to establish it (A/PV.358). One reason for the controversy, as the Soviet Union put it, was that the "resolution contains nothing that could give any kind of ground for regarding it as an attempt to prohibit atomic weapons" (A/PV.358, 300). The Soviet delegation went on,

> You will see how cunningly all this is worded, so cunningly that it may be searched completely in vain for any actual prohibition of atomic weapons, for the simple reason that there is no question here of any real prohibition ... Its purpose is the legalization of further uncontrolled production of atomic weapons and the use of atomic bombs for the mass destruction of people.
>
> If the delegations headed by the United States which sponsored this resolution indeed wished to prohibit atomic weapons ... why can they

not say so clearly and definitely in their resolution, as is proposed in the amendment of the USSR delegation.

A/PV.358, 300

For reference, the United States' position had been to withhold support for a ban on nuclear weapons until the establishment of an effective international control regime (e.g. A/PV.358, 309–311; A/PV.17, 260–263; UNODA 1970, 12–13).

At the Fifteenth Session of the General Assembly (1959–1960), the Soviet Union and other member states again pushed for acceptance of a draft resolution that would condemn the use of nuclear weapons in November 1960 (UNYB 1960, 24; A/C.1/L.254). Vote on the draft resolution was held off until the following Sixteenth Session in 1961 when new non-aligned member states added further political support to the cause (A/4942/Add.3, 4–5). Secretary-General U Thant saw these new, non-aligned member states as exercising a "moderating and catalytic influence" (Thant 1962 in Cordier and Harrelson 2010, 206). The resolution was entitled "Declaration on the prohibition of the use of nuclear and thermonuclear weapons" (A/RES/1653(XVI), 4). A journalist from *The Guardian* referred to the motion as the "ban the bomb" declaration (Pick 10.11.1961). Among its key propositions was the by-then familiar assertion that the "use of nuclear and thermonuclear weapons is contrary to the spirit, letter, and aims of the United Nations and, as such, a direct violation of the Charter of the United Nations" (A/RES/1653(XVI), 5). Another key proposition was a request that the Secretary-General "consult the Governments of Member States to ascertain their views on the possibility of convening a special conference for signing a convention on the prohibition of the use of nuclear and thermo-nuclear weapons for war purposes" (A/RES/1653(XVI), 5). These two provisions and others were again controversial. Fifty-five delegations voted in favor of the resolution, while fifty-six delegations either abstained or outright opposed it (A/PV.1063, 808). The United States, for example, did not mince words about its opposition to the declaration. The American Permanent Representative, among other things, emphasized that it was "suicidal" for states to give a blanket pledge not to use (or threaten to use) nuclear weapons (*The New York Times* 11.11.1961).

The controversial "ban the bomb" declaration was an inflection point in the diplomatic campaign against nuclear weapons at the General Assembly. Since then, the resolution has been a reference for similar efforts at the United Nations. These efforts include the Sixteenth Session in December 1962, when the same coalition of states reaffirmed the content of the ban on the bomb declaration and again pushed for the convening of a conference where member states would commit to prohibit the use of nuclear and thermonuclear weapons (e.g. A/5174; A/5174/Add.1; Add.2). In that session, the issue was again controversial (A/RES/1801(XVII); A/PV.1192). It was again controversial in the following Seventeenth Session in 1963 (A/RES/1909(XVIII); A/PV.1265), as well as in the Twenty-first Session in 1966 (A/RES/2164(XXI); A/PV.1484). The focus on the moral right to use (or threaten to use) nuclear weapons in war returned in 1978 during the Thirty-third Session, with a resolution entitled "Non-use of nuclear weapons and prevention of nuclear war" (A/RES/37/71B; A/33/PV.84). In substance, the resolution was not new. It was a more concise formulation of the 1961 resolution. One hundred and three member states supported the resolution, while forty-nine did not. The resolution remained controversial throughout ten more subsequent sessions (e.g. A/RES/34/83G; A/RES/35/152D; A/RES/36/92I).

In 1982, another reaffirmation of the 1961 ban on the bomb declaration came from another resolution entitled "Convention on the Prohibition of the Use of Nuclear Weapons" (A/RES/37/100C; A/37/PV.101). This resolution has been considered for some thirty-five subsequent sessions at the General Assembly (e.g. A/RES/38/73G; A/RES/39/63H; A/RES/40/15F). A corollary to these diplomatic efforts was a request for (and subsequent follow-up on) a legal opinion from the International Court of Justice in 1994 (A/RES/49/75K; A/49/PV.90; A/49/699). Seventy-eight member states supported the initiative, while one hundred and seven did not (including forty-three that directly opposed the request) (A/49/PV.90). The diplomatic campaign against nuclear weapons at the United Nations has culminated in partial support for the 2017 Treaty on the Prohibition of Nuclear Weapons (A/CONF.229/2017/8; A/RES/72/57). Some seventy out of one hundred and ninety-three member states did not vote in favor of the motion (A/72/PV.62). Forty delegations even boycotted the subsequent proceedings on the Treaty (Aljazeera 27.3.20).

It should now be apparent to the reader that diplomatic efforts to "ban the bomb" have been controversial at the General Assembly. Against this empirical backdrop, the next paragraphs discuss social constructivist literature on nuclear weapons. The most relevant reference is Professor Nina Tannenwald, who emphasizes the role of a taboo in the non-use of nuclear weapons since 1945 (Tannenwald 1999; 2005; 2007; 2018a; 2018b). By taboo, Tannenwald means a "normative inhibition against the first use of nuclear weapons" (Tannenwald 2018a, 89). The taboo "stems from a powerful sense of revulsion associated with such destructive weapons" (Tannenwald 2018a, 890). The main argument is that this normative prohibition on nuclear weapons has "developed in the global system, which, although not yet a fully robust norm, has stigmatized nuclear weapons as unacceptable weapons of mass destruction" (Tannenwald 1999, 433). Tannenwald writes,

> The normative branding of nuclear weapons as "unacceptable" and "inhumane" weapons is strong today, and has been actively reinforced in recent years by the campaign at the UN that has sought to highlight the devastating humanitarian consequences of any use of nuclear weapons.
>
> TANNENWALD 2018a, 92

Without this sense of normative stigma, nuclear weapons might have been used more often since 1945 (Tannenwald 1999; 2005; 2007; 2018). Tannenwald makes this argument concerning the United States' experience with nuclear weapons and further references other international relations studies to support the argument (Tannenwald 2018a, 90). Nevertheless, Tannenwald qualifies the taboo by emphasizing its controversial nature: the "delegitimization of nuclear weapons has always been incomplete" (Tannenwald 2018a, 93). "Although widespread support for the further stigmatization of nuclear weapons—as the achievement of the nuclear ban treaty in July 2017 shows—the general opprobrium is far from universal" (Tannenwald 2018a, 93).

I make two points that underscore the taboo's limitation in response to Nina Tannenwald. The first point is that there has long been some general moral revulsion associated with nuclear weapons at the interstate level. Empirical evidence for this assertion dates to at least 1946, with proceedings on the Atomic Energy Commission (A/PV.17; A/12). Those proceedings—as well as those throughout subsequent years—demonstrate unanimous interstate agreement on nuclear weapons belonging to a most destructive class of weapons that should be eliminated from national arsenals (e.g. A/PV.17; A/PV.101; A/PV.155). For this reason, member states empowered the Commission to make proposals for the "elimination from national armaments of atomic weapons and of all other major weapons adaptable to mass destruction" (A/RES/1(I), 9). Thus, the destructive nature of nuclear weaponry—and its especially harmful humanitarian effects—has not been in dispute. In other words, there has not been a time when member states saw nuclear weapons as "just another weapon." Even the United States, the world's most known nuclear power at the time, was not an active proponent of nuclear weapons use. In 1946, its delegation drew attention to the "problems presented by the discovery of atomic energy and the other forces capable of use for mass destruction" (A/12, 4). The American delegation also called for "measures which would permit and promote the use of these forces for peaceful and humanitarian purposes under security conditions which will protect the world against their use for destructive purposes" (A/12, 4).

This section's second point in response to Nina Tannenwald's perspective is to emphasize that a longstanding revulsion associated with nuclear weapons has *not* diminished the belief in a moral right to use (or threaten to use) nuclear weapons in self-defense. This is to say that a belief in a moral right to use nuclear weapons—that is, despite their especially destructive potential in war—has been the position of many states for some seventy-five years. Empirical evidence for this assertion comes from proceedings on the controversial resolutions referenced above. More recently, France, the United Kingdom, and the United States made the following observation about the Treaty on the Prohibition of Nuclear Weapons in 2017:

> France, the United Kingdom, and the United States have not taken part in the negotiation of the treaty on the prohibition of nuclear weapons. We do not intend to sign, ratify, or ever become party to it. Therefore, there will be no change in the legal obligations on our countries with respect to nuclear weapons ...
>
> This initiative clearly disregards the realities of the international security environment. Accession to the ban treaty is incompatible with the policy of nuclear deterrence, which has been essential to keeping the peace in Europe and North Asia for over 70 years. A purported ban on nuclear weapons that does not address the security concerns that continue to make nuclear deterrence necessary cannot result in the elimination of a single nuclear weapon and will not enhance any country's security, nor international peace and security.
>
> US Mission to the United Nations New York

The 2017 Treaty was historic because an unprecedented number of member states expressed support for a ban on nuclear weapons. Yet the statement—like others—demonstrates the limits of that support, which has never applied to more than two-thirds of the membership of the United Nations. Moreover, the continued public nature of the sentiment also undermines the suggestion that nuclear weapons have been stigmatized as "unacceptable weapons of mass destruction." This is to say that the issue remains controversial in a global, multilateral context. An interstate consensus against a moral right to use nuclear weapons does *not* exist. Hence, interstate socialization has not occurred in relation to this issue area.

2   Part One

I now suggest the existence of a core coalition of states as proponents of a ban on the right to use (or threaten to use) nuclear weapons in war. I pay close

attention to the more outspoken states in that coalition as potential socialization agents. In 1946, the most vocal proponents of the position were the Soviet
Union (and states associated with the Eastern Bloc) and states that later formed
the Non-Aligned Movement in 1961. These latter core states include India. The
ban's detractors, to be clear, were NATO member states such as Canada, the
United Kingdom, and the United States. This section theorizes the views
the core states express supporting the ban on nuclear weapons. The chapter
does this by closely examining the norms that the core states manipulate to
influence the target states' views on the issue.

As set out in the theoretical argument chapter, one specific way that a core
coalition of states can achieve this is via collective legitimization, via an appeal
to some "stamp of political approval or disapproval" concerning a particular
situation. This means that the core states attempt to "frame" an issue within
some already accepted *interstate* normative framework, such that the two
become seen as the same. The coalition's efforts in the present case study can
speak to this theoretical point. Since the First Session of the General Assembly
in 1946, some states have agitated for an unequivocal and unambiguous normative stance against the right to use nuclear weapons in war. The assertion
was that the use of nuclear weapons in war entails excessive human suffering.
The scale of that human suffering is so abhorrent (or "inappropriate") that it
negates the membership's highest aspiration: to "save succeeding generations
from the scourge of war," as the Charter's first sentence outlines. This precludes
a state's right to use (or threaten to use) nuclear weapons in war. In 1946, the
Soviet Union was the leading proponent of this position. Its Minister of Foreign
Affairs, Vyacheslav Molotov, made the point to the General Assembly:

> It is common knowledge that the atomic bomb was used against such
> towns as Nagasaki and Hiroshima. The populations of these Japanese
> towns experienced the cruel effect of the atomic bomb. But the atomic
> bomb has not yet been used anywhere for action against troops. And this
> is not fortuitous. If, however, there are plans to use atomic bombs against
> the civilian population of towns and, moreover, to use them on a large
> scale, as certain newspapers babble, one should not foster any illusions
> with regard to the international effect which would result from the carry-
> ing out of atrocious plans of this kind. Justified indignation would sweep
> over honest people in all countries, and the sanguine hopes regarding
> the decisive importance of the atomic bomb in a future war may lead
> to political consequences which will mean the greatest disillusionment,
> above all for the authors of these plans.

... After the first World War, already, the nations agreed to prohibit
the use for military purposes of poisonous gases, bacteriological preparations, and other inhuman means of war. It is all the more necessary
to prohibit the use for military purposes of atomic bombs as well as
any other means for the mass extermination of people, which in this
case means the wholesale destruction of the inhabitants of towns and
civilians in general, since a merciless blow will fall mainly on children,
women, sick persons and old men.

    A/PV.46, 842–843

In 1946, the Soviet Union's delegation coupled this sentiment with a proposal
to create a draft convention banning the use (or threat of use) of nuclear weapons in war. This is an excerpt from the preambular paragraphs:

Fully realizing that the great scientific discoveries in the sphere of atomic
energy carry with them a great danger, first of all, for peaceful towns and
the civilian population in the event of these discoveries being used in the
form of atomic weapons for the purpose of mass destruction.

    Recognizing the great significance of the fact that international agree-
ments have already prohibited the use in war of asphyxiating, poisonous and other similar gases, as well as all similar liquids, substances and
processes, and likewise bacteriological means, rightly condemned by the
public opinion of the civilized world, and considering that the international prohibition of the use of atomic weapons for the mass destruction
of human beings corresponds in still greater measure to the aspirations
and the conscience of the peoples of the whole world.

    AEC/7, 1

These two interventions encapsulate the crux of the interstate campaign
against the right to use nuclear weapons in war. Similar sentiment has been
advanced by states that later formed the Non-Aligned Movement. The most
outspoken sentiment came from consideration of the "ban the bomb" resolution in 1961 (e.g. A/4680; A/4942/Add.3; A/PV.1063), as well as communications
to the Secretary-General in response to it (A/5174; A/5174). India was among the
more outspoken proponents, emphasizing that it has "always been, and continue to be, totally opposed to the use of nuclear and thermo-nuclear weapons" (A/5174, 22). "The total prohibition of such use is essential to the welfare
and, indeed, the survival of humanity" (A/5174, 22).

    As the interventions suggest, a core coalition of states pushed for a norma-
tive stance against nuclear weapons. The core states did this by framing the

issue within a common notion of appropriateness drawn from abhorrence to excessive human suffering in war, as had most recently been seen in World War Two. The right to use nuclear weapons was not just objectionable to the core states; it was objectionable given common humanitarian concerns about how states ought to conduct war. Hence, the interventions above are explicit in an appeal to common notions of appropriateness to support the cause. They point to interstate agreements on "inhuman means of war," nuclear weapons use as producing "indignation ... [among] honest people in all countries," and nuclear weapons non-use as corresponding to the "aspirations and the conscience of the peoples of the whole world." This is to say that a core coalition of states attempted to project a sense of legitimacy into a position against nuclear weapons by manipulating the position's resonance within a more widespread abhorrence to inordinate human suffering in war.

A coalition of states also amplified that intersubjective resonance by "cuing," prompting other delegations to see the dissonance between the right to use nuclear weapons and humanitarian concerns. Some states have done this by calling for studies that investigate the humanitarian (and later environmental) effects of nuclear weapons (e.g. A/C.1/L.260/REV.1; A/RES/33/91/D; A/RES/43/75N). At the General Assembly, the first initiative for a study into the humanitarian aspects came from the Soviet Union and states associated with the Eastern Bloc (e.g. A/C.1/SR.1119; A/C.1/SR.1120; A/C.1/SR.1134). In November 1960, Poland's delegation was the one to make the request with a draft resolution entitled "Universal dissemination of information on the consequences of nuclear war" (A/C.1/L.260/REV.1). The resolution called for a "team of consultants specialized in the theory and practice of physics, chemistry, medicine and technical sciences" (A/4680, 10). The team's task was to "prepare a report on the consequences of the use of nuclear weapons, particularly concerning human life and health and the material and cultural heritage of mankind" (A/4680, 10). It then fell upon delegations to "widely distribute the report ... and to disseminate it by all possible means" (A/4680, 10). This is to say that "cuing" was also an aspect of the core coalition's efforts to cast doubt on a moral right to use nuclear weapons. Other states have been behind similar initiatives in subsequent years (e.g. A/RES/31/70; A/RES/33/91/D; A/RES/43/75N).

3   Part Two

We have so far emphasized that a unanimous, interstate consensus against a right to use nuclear weapons does *not* exist. We can now contemplate how the core coalition's efforts on nuclear weapons were unsuccessful. I suggest that certain theoretical conditioning factors were not prevalent nor influential to interstate socialization. The applicable theoretical conditioning factor relates to the Soviet Union and the non-aligned states' perceived integrity on nuclear weapons as advocates of the ban. These states' integrity was in significant doubt and consequently undermined the extent to which their efforts could have influenced other states' views. The campaign to ban the bomb failed because those leading it lacked integrity in the eyes of target states—namely, NATO member states—thanks to their own nuclear arsenal or potential to develop one. The general conclusion is that socialization efforts fail when proponents are seen to be hypocritical by the relevant audience. Empirical evidence for my argument comes from observations made by Canadian, British, and American officials about the Soviet Union, India, and non-aligned states as advocates of the ban. I use these three states as illustrative country cases for empirical reasons. The first reason is that Canada, the United Kingdom, and the United States had opposed the ban in contrast to the Soviet Union, states associated with the Eastern Bloc, and states that later formed the Non-Aligned Movement. The second reason is that these three country cases allow access to insightful empirical source work, as we shall see.

As for the Soviet Union, the empirical record suggests that its integrity as an advocate for a ban on nuclear weapons was in significant doubt, undermining the extent to which its diplomatic efforts could have been influential. As we shall see, the impression was that the Soviet Union's views on nuclear weapons were insincere, especially given its continued nuclear weapons development and testing. Empirical evidence for this interpretation comes from the United States, the United Kingdom, and Canada. These three states were among those that did not support the ban since the General Assembly's First Session in 1946 and throughout subsequent sessions. They shared a moral aversion to the use (or threat of use) of nuclear weapons in war but would not support the ban. The idea was that international control measures were more appropriate and should precede commitments to a prohibition (e.g. A/PV.17; A/PV.358; A/PV.1063).

Empirical source work from the United States includes commentary by its delegation to the United Nations in New York and officials from the Department of State and Department of Defense. The commentary addresses the Soviet Union's perceived integrity on nuclear weapons. The following interventions are noteworthy. In January 1961, Secretary of Defense Thomas Gates made the following observation before the House of Representatives. The observation concerns Nikita Khrushchev's diplomatic efforts on disarmament, including his "general and complete disarmament" proposition to the General Assembly on September 18th, 1959 (A/PV.99, 31–38). According to foreign officials, one of Khrushchev's main ideas was that "nuclear weapons would continue to be produced until Western powers agreed to a ban" (Burns 1972, 39). In response, Secretary Thomas Gates offered the following reflection:

> I do not think people are going to take very seriously the idea that the Russians are going to throw away all their arms and have a foreign policy based on no military strength. We are not taking it very seriously in the Department of Defense ... In the disarmament proposal be made to the United Nations it was pretty blanket elimination of every bit of military power. I think this is only a tactic and that the long-range objective remains unchanged.
>
> GATES 1961 in BURNS 1972

Another relevant observation comes from American Ambassador Arthur Dean, a diplomat in the American delegation to the United Nations in New York. The observation relates to the Soviet Union's support for the "ban the bomb" declaration at the General Assembly in 1961:

> Of at least incidental interest to this Assembly might be the fact that the Soviet Union has carried out not some thirty nuclear tests in the current series, starting on 1 September, but instead has carried out approximately fifty—I repeat, fifty—nuclear tests in its recent series in the months of September, October and November. No one of course, except the Soviet Union, because of its secret society, knows precisely how many nuclear tests it has carried out, or in precisely what environments.
>
> A/PV.1063, 799

Ambassador Dean also commented that:

> I say this carefully because the Soviet Union, as it has indicated in this Assembly, has not the slightest intention of paying any attention to this draft resolution, despite the enthusiastic support which the Soviet Union gave to it in the Committee. How do I know this? We know it from the Soviet representative's own statements in the Committee that the Soviets openly intend to use nuclear weapons at the sole discretion of the Soviet Union, if that country considers the use necessary. The delegation of the United States and other delegations quoted Mr. Khrushchev's statement to this effect. So there can be no doubt of the Soviet intentions in this matter. So, just as in the case of the uninspected, uncontrolled moratorium resolutions on the subject of nuclear testing, the Soviet Union votes

for this draft resolution with every intention of violating it, if for its sole purposes it suits it to do so.

A/PV.1063, 798

Ambassador Dean further emphasized that the Soviet Union "will continue to rattle its rockets and to threaten other countries with thermonuclear destruction" (Brewer 25.11.1961). The United States Permanent Representative Adlai Stevenson offered a similar sentiment, emphasizing that "we have seen the double-dealing of the Soviet Union in respect to nuclear testing, and now the detonation of an enormous *sic* with the consequence—the dire consequences for the human race" (Wagganer 13.11.1961).

Source work from Canada and the United Kingdom suggests further support for this interpretation and reaffirms the Soviet Union's perceived lack of integrity on the issue more generally. A 1961 observation by J.B. Godber—a member of the United Kingdom's delegation to the United Nations—serves as an example:

> The arguments which have been advanced by Soviet representatives in the First Committee seeking to justify their vote in favour of such vague declarations as that envisaged in the draft resolution before us are specious. The point quite clearly made by Mr. Khrushchev himself ... [was] that the Soviet Union would use nuclear weapons in self defense if it found itself at a disadvantage in any war, including what is usually called a conventional war. I find it impossible to understand how any representative of Mr. Khrushchev or his Government can then justify casting a vote in favor of a draft resolution which says among other things that "... any State using nuclear and thermonuclear weapons is to be considered to violate the Charter of the United Nations ..." This must surely be taken as a declaration by the Soviet Government of their readiness to violate the Charter. It can mean nothing else.
>
> ... I cannot call other than hypocrisy actions which are, in fact, hypocritical in this way. We are told that the Soviet Union is supporting this draft resolution, in light of these remarks of Mr. Khrushchev, then I cannot see any other explanation for that action.
>
> A/PV.1063, 803

Other relevant observations come from Canadian officials. In 1961, Canada's Secretary of State for External Affairs wrote the following in a confidential memo to its Permanent Representative in New York. The memo also addresses the Soviet Union's efforts on nuclear weapons at the United Nations:

Since the end of the 15th Session, Soviet policy on questions of disarmament and nuclear tests has reflected an uncompromising position which it will be important for the Western Powers to attack effectively at the forthcoming session. The latest Soviet move in unilaterally abandoning their commitment to abstain from nuclear tests makes forceful Western action even more imperative. Moreover, in view of the degree of international tension engendered by the Berlin crisis—which may well increase during the period of the General Assembly—it will be important for the Western allies to be as united as circumstances will permit in their approach to problems of this kind, where the Soviet Union is not on firm ground and is likely to try to discredit the Western position by "unmasking" an alleged unwillingness to get on with disarmament and by seeking to "uncover" points of difference within the Western side.

GREEN 1961 in DEA/50189-C-40

Lieutenant General E.L.M. Burns, leader of Canada's delegation on all disarmament proceedings between 1960 and 1968, evidences another relevant observation about the Soviet Union's international standing on nuclear weapons:

What comes through very clearly, in the annual debates in the United Nations General Assembly and in the innumerable conferences and demonstrations held throughout the world is the nations which don't possess nuclear weapons want the nuclear powers to abolish them ... From the beginning of these negotiations, in 1946, the Soviet Union, by its continuous advocacy of the prohibition of all use of nuclear weapons, and their total abolition, has presented itself in a favorable light to the non-possessing nations, especially in the Third World. The United States, in contrast, has often been made to look as if its policy was really "love the Bomb." But the Soviet Union's continued build-up of its nuclear armory has somewhat eroded, as of recent years, the noble image that its "Ban the Bomb" propaganda may have created.

BURNS 1972, 8

These latter observations suggest further empirical support for the assertion that the Soviet Union's integrity on nuclear weapons was in significant doubt and consequently undermined the extent to which its diplomatic efforts could have been influential. The United Kingdom's representative emphasizes the Soviet Union's "hypocrisy" as a reason to cast doubt on the integrity of its efforts in support of the ban. Canadian officials make a similar observation. The Soviet Union is "not on firm ground" on nuclear weapons, as Canada's Secretary of

State for External Affairs put it. Moreover, the Soviet Union's "noble image" as an advocate of the ban had increasingly "eroded," as Canada's chief advisor on disarmament put it. This suggests that the Soviet Union's stature on nuclear weapons was indeed in significant doubt and undercut its diplomatic efforts in support of the ban.

So far, we have treated empirical evidence for the Soviet Union, a more proactive member of the coalition of states that stood against the right to use nuclear weapons in war. Other more proactive coalition members included states that made up the Non-Aligned Movement in 1961. Like the Soviet Union, the empirical record suggests that these states' integrity on nuclear weapons had fallen into disrepute. This lack of integrity also undermined the extent to which its diplomatic efforts on nuclear weapons could have been influential. The most relevant empirical evidence for this assertion comes from diplomatic sources, particularly the United States and Canada. Useful source work from the United States includes observations made by John J. McCloy, President John F. Kennedy's Advisor on Disarmament. McCloy's observations address states from the Non-Aligned Movement's standing on nuclear weapons. This observation addresses non-aligned states' perceived integrity on nuclear weapons:

> For some time much had been placed upon the existence of a moral opinion among smaller nations that could be brought to bear, and thus the main protagonists in the struggle between the Communists and the free world. Many who were aware of the difficulties inherent in the conduct of bilateral negotiations on the disarmament issue hoped that nations not immediately aligned side or the other might prove helpful. All through 1960 and 1961 movements were developing in many parts of the world against any resumption of nuclear or thermonuclear testing, and some of them were couched in rather high moral tones. These were mainly directed against the United States. It appeared one reason for this was to counteract the mounting criticism within the United States against continuing a self-imposed, unpoliced moratorium on testing. Yet when the Soviet Union suddenly resumed tests on an extensive scale, and action with threats of 100-megaton bombs, the reactions of the neutral or non-aligned countries at Belgrade and again, to some extent, at the General Assembly of the United were so mild as to be wholly inconsequential. As a result, their position as "guardians" of the world's conscience was greatly weakened.
>
> The tendency of these nations seems to have been to moderate their criticism against those whom they fear and to direct their main blasts against those whom they do not fear; or at best to seek to equate

differences in action between the powers rather than to judge them. This, too, has substantially compromised the force of neutral and non-aligned opinion as a helpful factor in the solution of the disarmament problem. The Goa incident did not help. A leading neutral's cynical attitude with respect to the use of force, and the tacit acceptance of the dangerous doctrine of good wars and bad wars, put still more in doubt whether a strong moral opinion in fact exists among the neutrals and whether even where it does exist it counts for very much. It may have been a delusion from the beginning to suppose that the newer independent nations would, in a pinch, act otherwise than in what seemed to them, however shortsightedly, their own self-interest. At any rate, some rather elaborate pretensions were shattered and what had been a hope for helpful objectivity has been weakened.

MCCLOY 1962, 343

John McCloy also makes another relevant observation about the non-aligned states' integrity as advocates for the ban on nuclear weapons. This observation relates to the non-aligned states' competence on the issue:

A word may be in order as to the role of other countries, whether they participate in these negotiations or express their views from the outside. Unfortunately, very few of them have done or are prepared to do the work which is involved in making a real contribution to the subject. Very few have even one man, much less an adequate staff, whose whole time and preoccupation are applied to the problem. Such a highly technical and frequently abstruse subject demands knowledge, thought and considerable research. Those who sit on the sidelines and merely chant "general and complete disarmament" without putting their minds to mastering the difficulties of the problem neither make much of a contribution nor are they apt to influence those whose efforts are more serious.

It would be a real mistake for these nations to assume that their only role is to press others to take action or merely to line up with one side or the other. In addition to doing the independent homework needed for making a real contribution, they can in several cases, by their own concrete example, indicate the affirmative steps which they believe the international community must take. Such action would be much more persuasive than an exhortation to others to take risks they are not prepared to take themselves. The situation of Pakistan and India is only one of many cases which come to mind. The full disarmament process will take a long time to complete.

MCCLOY 1962, 358–359

Other American officials add credence to John McCloy's assessment. Ambassador Arthur Dean, for example, made two relevant observations that corroborate McCloy's account. The first observation concerns India and other non-aligned states' integrity as advocates of "general and complete" disarmament:

> there are those who have impatiently advocated speed in dismantling the defenses of the West and have brushed aside efforts to ensure specificity in the agreements as unnecessary and even deliberately provocative. It should be noted that these states often do not advocate equal speed in their own disarmament or in solving their own regional disputes. Nor do many of them refrain from asking for U.S. military aid or economic aid for projects which release their own funds for armaments. These remarks are not made to be querulous or critical but merely to point out that the intimate connection between national security and disarmament clicks into focus easily enough when it is one's own problems that are involved, as in the case of India's and Pakistan's concern with Kashmir.
>
> DEAN 1966, 66–67

Dean makes another especially relevant observation, which relates to India and other non-aligned states' response to the Soviet Union's nuclear weapons testing.

> This is not to say that we relied on a misty, vague "world opinion" to deter the would-be violator. We realized well enough that the nation which will be curbed by world opinion is usually the one that least needs curbing. Furthermore, we had before us the example of the conference of the nonaligned at Belgrade in September 1961, the members of which had protested only very mildly when the Soviet Union broke the voluntary moratorium on testing that had been in effect for almost three years, and also the example of the session of the UN General assembly that year where India, a self-proclaimed "nonaligned" state, led the fight against any censure of the Soviet Union.
>
> DEAN 1966, 82–83

Arthur Dean makes the same point again to emphasize India's hypocritical stance on nuclear weapons:

Khrushchev had declared on earlier occasions that the first country to break a moratorium on nuclear weapons testing would take upon itself an enormous moral and political responsibility and expose itself in the eyes of all nations. Now, in 1961, the Soviet government would resume nuclear weapons testing. The text of the statement and the rapidity with which the tests followed revealed that the talks had been deliberately misused as a screen for rest preparations—a situation which we had begun to suspect early in the spring of 1961. We persevered in our efforts in spite of this action; on September 3, 1961, President Kennedy and Prime Minister Macmillan joined in calling upon the Soviet Union to cease further atmospheric testing, to accept a treaty barring such tests without any international controls, and to return to the discussion table to work out a comprehensive treaty. On September 9, 1961, Premier Khrushchev categorically refused. Our ears were assailed that fall with the reverberations of continued Soviet testing, which the UN General Assembly only "noted with regret," as Krishna Menon of India did his best to prevent any criticism of the Soviet Union's flagrant violation of the moratorium.

DEAN 1966, 89–90

The above source suggests that the non-aligned states' sense of integrity on nuclear weapons was doubtful, undermining the potential influence their diplomatic efforts could have as advocates of the ban. Further empirical support comes from Professor George Perkovich's work on India, a putative leader of the Non-Aligned Movement. Perkovich's findings are apposite in two respects. The first respect is that India's stance on nuclear weapons was seen as duplicitous. As Perkovich writes,

Indian legend and commentary generally deny that the quest for nuclear power was ambiguous from the beginning. Typically it is said that Nehru intended for India to use nuclear technology and know-how exclusively for peaceful purposes ...

Perhaps Nehru's image as a world leader of singular moral stature, the heir to Mahatma Gandhi, would have been tarnished if he were shown to have embraced the military usefulness of nuclear power. Thus, according to conventional wisdom, it was Bhabha, the brilliant and ambitious physicist, not Nehru, who gave the dual military and civilian purpose to the Indian nuclear program ...

Closer scrutiny, however, reveals that Nehru also accepted, albeit reticently and ambivalently, the potential military deterrent and international power embodied in the nuclear weapons capability.

PERKOVICH 1999, 13–14

George Perkovich references a 1946 speech by Prime Minister Jawaharlal Nehru to support the argument:

> As long as the world is constituted as it is, every country will have to devise and use the latest scientific devices for its protection. I have no doubt India will develop her scientific researches and I hope Indian scientists will use the atomic force for constructive purposes. But if India is threatened she will inevitably try to defend herself by all means at her disposal.
>
> NEHRU 1946 in PERKOVICH 1999, 14

Perkovich also references a 1948 speech:

> if we are to remain abreast in the world as a nation which keeps ahead of things, we must develop this atomic energy quite apart from war—indeed I think we must develop it for the purpose of using it for peaceful purposes. It is in that hope that we should develop this. Of course, if we are compelled as a nation to use it for other purposes, possibly no pious sentiments of us will stop the nation from using it that way.
>
> NEHRU 1948 in PERKOVICH 1999, 20

The second relevant point that Perkovich makes is that foreign officials—including from the United States—were aware of India's contradictory stance on nuclear weapons. Perkovich provides numerous sources as empirical evidence. The following two examples seem most important. The first involves an exchange with Gerard Smith, the State Department's atomic energy advisor:

> The physicist Isador Rabi, serving as chairman of the U.S. Atomic Energy Commission's General Advisory Committee, conveyed concerns about India's intentions to the State Department's atomic energy adviser, Gerard Smith, in a 1955 discussion: "Rabi said that we must get these controls [safeguards] working before our reactors are constructed abroad. He believed that even a country like India, when it had some plutonium production, would go into the weapons business."
>
> PERKOVIC 1999, 31

A second example involves a conversation between the Chairman of the Indian Atomic Energy Commission (Dr. Homi Bhabha), Prime Minister Jawaharlal Nehru, and the senior army member of the Military Liaison Committee to the Atomic Energy Committee (General Kenneth D. Nichols) (Perkovich 1999, 36).

The exchange took place in 1960 in India. It concerns a meeting to discuss plans for building India's first nuclear power reactor. For that meeting, Dr. Bhabha asked General Nichols to elucidate in the "advantages of opening competition to the U.S. suppliers." General Nichols then recalls that Prime Minister Nehru turned to Dr. Bhabha to ask,

> "Can you develop an atomic bomb?" Bhabha assured him that he could and in reply to Nehru's next question about time, he intimated that he would need about a year to do it. I was really astounded to be hearing these questions from the one I thought to be one of the world's most peace-loving leaders. He then asked me if I agreed with Bhabha, and I replied that I knew of no reason why Bhabha could not do it. He had men who were as qualified or more qualified than our young scientists were fifteen years earlier. He concluded by saying to Bhabha, "well, don't do it until I tell you to."
>
> PERKOVICH 1999, 36

These two exchanges provide further empirical evidence of India's contradictory stance on nuclear weapons. The point is that India's leadership was actually *not* categorical about its opposition to nuclear weapons. Foreign officials were aware of the ambiguity and saw India as a potential nuclear weapons state. India's efforts to ban the bomb were thus seen to be hypocritical, as John McCloy's commentary suggests. This manifest sense of hypocrisy rendered the core coalition's diplomatic pressure ineffectual. The campaign's target interstate audience—that is, NATO member states—accordingly did not perceive a significant political downside to maintaining positions against the nuclear weapons ban.

George Perkovich's commentary on India's dual stance on nuclear weapons resonates with other historians. Bharat Karnad, for example, lends further empirical support to the assertion that Indian officials had entertained the idea of developing nuclear weapons—that is, in conversation with other governmental officials—since the 1950s at the United Nations (Karnad 2008; 2018). Karnad writes,

> Western policy-makers and strategic community alike have portrayed the resumption of testing by India and its decision to come out of the closet as a nuclear-weapon state in 1998 as both unexpected and unsettling and contrary to expectations and the Indian government's pronouncements, and as a result, India was dubbed a "nuclear pariah." The surprise is that there was this kind of reaction at all considering that Indian

representatives had since the 1950s consistently iterated in nonprolifera-
tion and disarmament forums that India would acquire nuclear weapons
if the nuclear-weapon states did not disarm fully ... Nehru's confidante
and the country's Defense Minister, V. K. Krishna Menon, spearheaded
the campaign in international circles. In a speech, for example, before
the UN General Assembly in October 1954, he laid down disarmament
markers. Other than declaring that measures such as the 1954 Partial
Test Ban Treaty were not a substitute for disarmament, Krishna Menon
asked for "general and complete" disarmament, with the elimination of
nuclear weapons to be realized in lockstep with conventional military
drawdowns on the basis of "equitable reduction" in terms of "quantums
and qualities." This was to ensure that a world freed of nuclear weapons
was not made safe for conventional war, and did not advantage states
with superior conventional military might. As an interim measure, he
demanded that an agreement on the nonuse of nuclear weapons—the
first faint intimation of India's subscribing to the No First Use principle as a nuclear weapon power—be speedily facilitated along with an
"armaments truce." He also specifically warned that if these disarmament
goals were not met, India could and would acquire nuclear weapons at
one-tenth the cost, given the labor and other comparative advantages it
enjoyed. India could not have been clearer about what it intended to do.

KARNAD 2008, 60

Karnad's analysis goes further than Perkovich's in that it highlights that Indian
officials went as far as to openly annunciate an openness to develop its own
nuclear weapons, specifically in conversation with other diplomats at the
United Nations in New York. This came at a time when Indian officials also
advocated for a blanket ban on nuclear weapons. Hence, India's stance on
nuclear weapons, as John McCloy and Arthur Dean suggest, did not inspire
confidence; it smacked of hypocrisy and in turn, cast significant doubt on its
integrity as an advocate of the ban.

There is also strong reason to believe that India—as well as other non-
aligned states—was not seen as a whole-hearted proponent of the ban on
nuclear weapons, especially in comparison to other issues before the United
Nations throughout the early 1960s. In my first case study chapter, I emphasized that these years saw a large membership expansion at the United Nations.
From 1960 to 1962, eighteen new member states were admitted, seventeen
from Africa. Admission of these new member states amounted to a twenty-two
percent increase in membership at the United Nations. Recall that this membership expansion mattered because those states were especially passionate

about questions of racial discrimination and added substantial momentum to the diplomatic campaign against apartheid. My point now is that these non-aligned states were seen to be hypocritical, as well as less committed to the cause of a nuclear weapons ban in 1961. Sir Brian Urquhart, then Under-Secretary-General, made the following observation:

> A constituency was emerging which had little direct interest in European affairs, disarmament or in the East-West relationship. It was a radical, angry constituency, in which newly acquired independence had only served to accentuate the feeling of vital time and opportunities lost through colonial status. It was a constituency which strongly resented the established, profitably industrialized, dominant Old World.
>
> URQUHART 1987, 171

Urquhart's observation suggests that non-aligned states were less committed to the ban on nuclear weapons than other issues at the time. This perceived lack of commitment to the cause compared to other causes would have furthermore reduced the political downside for target states to oppose the ban.

4   Part Three

I now turn towards the third and final step in my research procedure: the cross-check. I weigh points from the previous section against the most prominent theoretical and empirical counterarguments. The theoretical counterarguments draw from materialist accounts of international relations, as discussed in Chapter Two. The main materialist counterargument to this chapter would proceed from the assertion that intergovernmental organizations are "epiphenomenal," meaning that their proceedings reflect some constellation of material power in the interstate system. This chapter's theoretical interpretation would assert that interstate proceedings on nuclear weapons—particularly from 1946 to 1961—reflect the East-West Cold War cleavage of the time. Hence, interstate proceedings on the issue were not amenable to a divergence from that cleavage as long as the states in question saw themselves as aligned with one side or another. Empirical evidence for this potential critique can come from the history of voting patterns on the issue, which to an extent, demonstrate an interstate cleavage along East-West lines. Empirical evidence for the critique can also be drawn from the nuclear defense policies that certain states have espoused, especially states associated with NATO and the Warsaw Pact. The point is that the national defense imperatives of the time would, by and

large, define state positions on nuclear weapons. Therefore, a potential socialization agent's integrity on nuclear weapons would have little or no influence
on other states' positions.

There are at least two limitations to this critique. The most apparent is that
the Cold War's end has *not* been associated with a pointed change in positions
on the issue, particularly by states that have not supported the ban on nuclear
weapons from the start. Those views remained unchanged, as the chapter's
introduction has shown. Hence, one would expect a more incontrovertible
change in views if the Cold War was a more decisive influence in the formation of positions on nuclear weapons. The second main limitation of the above
critique is that it overlooks the social anxieties that potential socialization subjects expressed upon evaluating the issue at the General Assembly. The potential socialization subjects were manifestly concerned about the interstate social
ramifications of their stance on nuclear weapons and saw a need to adjust,
although not change, the position given the core coalition's diplomatic efforts.
This is also to say that the potential socialization subjects saw the core coalition as an audience whose general approval they sought (Petrova 14.10.21, 3).
Harold Macmillan demonstrates the point in his memoirs (Macmillan 1972).
Macmillan recalls a communication that relates to Nikita Khrushchev's efforts
at the Fourteenth Session of the General Assembly in September 1959:

> Mr. K has made a speech about disarmament in the U.N. "Scrap the lot" is
> his policy. The passages about "control" are vague. But as a "propaganda"
> effort it seems pretty good. We must, however, follow it up (along the lines
> of the Foreign Secretary on Thursday at U.N.) and not seem to oppose K.
> but rather to pin him down to concrete plans.
>
> MACMILLAN 1959 in MACMILLAN 1972, 90

Although Macmillan goes on to call Khrushchev's intervention a "great propaganda performance" and a "Russian trap," he still emphasizes that "it sets us
quite a problem. We must not be cynical about it, but we must not be naïve"
(Macmillan 1959 in Macmillan 1972, 91). The point is that mere rhetoric at the
United Nations would not pose "quite a problem" to other delegations at the
highest level of government were the social ramifications *not* a central concern. On the contrary, one would expect more unambiguous opposition to the
diplomatic campaign on nuclear weapons, including in relation to efforts on
the ban.

Further empirical support for this point exists in governmental records from
the United States and Canada. Examples of American sources include a formerly confidential document written by Harlan Cleveland, Assistant Secretary

of State for International Organization Affairs. The document is entitled "U.S. Strategy in the 16th General Assembly" and notes a confidential conversation between President John F. Kennedy, Assistant Secretary Harlan Cleveland, Ambassador Adlai Stevenson, and Arthur Schlesinger Jr. (Special Assistant to President Kennedy). The notes record the following exchange in August 1961:

> Ambassador Stevenson thinks it is very important for the United States to be for disarmament in a very positive way. We must take the initiative on this and put the Soviets on the defensive.
>   Mr. Schlesinger and Mr. Cleveland argued these two points of view are readily reconcilable: an attractive vision of Utopia must be featured, but it must not be confused with practical next steps or be regarded as related in some way to next year's Defense budget.
> CLEVELAND 5.8.1961

Cleveland's commentary is pertinent in demonstrating a concerted attempt to navigate the interstate social ramifications of the United States' stance on nuclear weapons. Ambassador Stevenson emphasizes the importance for the United States to be "for disarmament in a very positive way" and for the Soviet Union to be put "on the defensive." Similarly, Schlesinger emphasizes the importance of the United States' association with "an attractive vision of utopia." This is to say that Stevenson and Schlesinger's emphasis on projecting a "positive" (or even "utopian") perception of the United States on nuclear weapons is social in nature. Considering how to maintain such an image would not be necessary were it not to appeal to the wider global, multilateral audience at the United Nations. On the contrary, one would expect a more forthright defense of nuclear weapons regardless of how "positive" or "negative" it made the United States appear on the issue.

I suggest two more American sources to demonstrate the point further. The first is a formerly confidential national intelligence estimate report—"Attitudes of Key World Powers on Disarmament Issues"—which supports the interpretation that American officials were concerned about the interstate social ramifications of their stance on disarmament issues, including nuclear disarmament issues. The report was published on April 6th, 1961, and was prepared by the Central Intelligence Agency and the intelligence organizations from the State Department, the armed forces, the Joint Staff, the Atomic Energy Commission, and the National Security Agency. The report's assessment states,

It is clear that the Soviet leaders see, in agitation of the disarmament issue, a prime opportunity to further their political purposes in the non-Communist world. What is not so clear is the extent to which they may actually desire to conclude agreements on disarmament ...

... the Soviets have a most lively sense of the political uses of talking about disarmament. Realizing that the intricacies of the subject are little understood, they have hit upon their proposal for general and complete disarmament as a way to capture the universal yearning for peace and, at the same time, to label the West as "against" disarmament. It is not a proposal which they expect to make good on, but it is a highly potent instrument of political warfare.

NIE 4-2-61, 35–37

The second source is an observation from Ambassador Arthur Dean, who had served at the United Nations in New York.

We suggested to Washington that the United States put forward a proposal for general and complete disarmament. Though hardly a practical proposition for negotiating under existing conditions, it would vein our own deep interest in ending the arms race and in reducing tensions. It would also cut down the propaganda returns which the Soviet Union was at the time reaping from its declared position as an advocate of general and complete disarmament, while we appeared in the role of a reluctant suitor or captious quibbler in favor only of "arms control" or "arms reduction" or "limitation."

DEAN 1966, 24–25

Note that the first document acknowledges the potential social influence that the Soviet Union's diplomatic efforts could have, suggesting that its diplomacy could have been a "highly potent instrument of political warfare." The second document makes a comparable assessment, evidencing an explicit concern for how the United States "appeared" thanks to Soviet diplomacy. Hence, the core coalition's efforts, although unsuccessful, nevertheless heaped diplomatic pressure on the likes of American officials. As the observations above suggest, that pressure gave rise to manifest social concerns that American officials at least felt a need to navigate. This interpretation is consistent with the American delegation's general approach to the Sixteenth Session of the General Assembly (1961–1962), which was in essence, social:

On September 19, 1961, nearly every major issue of American foreign policy will be before the Sixteenth General Assembly of the United Nations.

This would be largely true even if we did not want it that way. It is all the more true because we have deliberately decided, on some very important matters, that the United Nations must be the central forum in which to pursue our objectives.

... The United Nations is the only loom on which the western world and the Southern Hemisphere can "weave the fabric of common interests" so wide and so strong that it can some day contain—and then suffocate—the East-West struggle.

CLEVELAND, SISCO AND WILSON 22.7.1961

The previous paragraphs treated primary source work from American and British officials relating to nuclear weapons proceedings at the General Assembly in 1961. The point has been that this section's critique overlooks the manifest social concerns that potential socialization subjects expressed upon evaluating the issue. A more detailed primary account comes from a Canadian source: Harold Basil Robinson, an aide to Canada's Prime Minister John Diefenbaker. Robinson's account specifically relates to diplomatic efforts on nuclear weapons at the General Assembly in 1961. Robinson references the following Canadian officials: Howard Green (Secretary of State for External Affairs), General E.L.M. Burns (advisor and lead disarmament negotiator), and Douglas Harkness (Minister of National Defense).

Despite reminders from the president and the impatience of the defense authorities in both countries, no progress was made on nuclear policy in the late months of 1961. A partial reason for this lay in the agenda of the UN General Assembly, where a series of resolutions aiming to end nuclear testing, prohibit the use or spread of nuclear weapons, and advance the prospects for disarmament required decisions with clear implications for Canada's defense policy ... For the most part, it fell to the minister of external affairs to decide how Canada would vote, and since Green was personally so devoted to the cause of peace through disarmament, it was to be expected that under his guidance the Canadian delegation would be instrumental in or associated with "peaceful" initiatives. The minister took full advantage of this state of affairs.

Apart from being frustrating for Harkness and the Department of National Defense, the situation was also uncomfortable for the prime

minister. It was Green's normal practice to seek Diefenbaker's approval
for votes on tactical moves which had policy implications. Occasionally
the two did not connect. Once, for example, there was a contretemps
over a resolution urging a complete prohibition of the use of nuclear
weapons. The resolution had been put forward by a group of non-nuclear
countries and it was clearly at cross purposes with NATO defense policy,
which depended on its effectiveness on the US nuclear deterrent. The
obvious choice from the defense point of view would have been to cast
a vote against it. But Green, strongly pressed by the government's disarmament adviser, General E.L.M. Burns, instructed the Canadian delegation to abstain in the vote, a middle course that placed Canada in the
company of a group of political moderates but fell short of unswerving
solidarity with the prevailing NATO line.

... On 23 November, before the final vote, I noted: P.M. called at 5:30
p.m. and I gave him the latest items including the current dilemma over
whether we should change our vote in the General Assembly on resolutions dealing with the use and spread of nuclear weapons ... P.M. is obvi-
ously doubtful of the wisdom of voting in a way which throws doubt on
our solidarity with NATO defense policy. The minister of national defense
is not drawn into this and I think the P.M. hopes the U.N. votes can be left
in a special compartment and not treated as creating an inherent contradiction in our foreign and defense policies. At the time that note was
written I was not aware of what, if anything, the Prime Minister would do.
I presume (but cannot be certain) that he persuaded Green to alter the
Canadian position because, when the final vote was taken, General Burns
was obliged to explain the change in Canada's vote from an abstention to
a vote against the resolution. It was a tactical defeat for Green which did
not go unreported in the Canadian press.

ROBINSON 1989, 232–234

Harold Robinson's account is apt to provide insight into how Canadian officials
arrived at a position on the nuclear weapons ban at the General Assembly. As
Robinsons's commentary indicates, formulating a stance against the ban was
not an "obvious" accord with defense policies vis-à-vis NATO. On the contrary,
the issue was "frustrating," "uncomfortable" and posed a "dilemma." Among the
reasons for this, Robinson suggests, is because "it was to be expected ... that
the Canadian delegation would be instrumental in or associated with 'peaceful
initiatives'." The implication is that opposition to the ban was at variance with

these expectations. Accordingly, the Prime Minister goes as far as to entertain a contradiction in Canada's foreign and defense policies, suggesting that the issue "be left in a special compartment." This is to say that the *social* ramifications of opposing the ban were a manifest concern for Canadian officials. The empirical record would evidence more unambiguous opposition to the ban were this not true.

Conclusion

This book advanced a novel social constructivist theory on interstate socialization. It drew upon diplomatic history at the United Nations—and especially the General Assembly—as the locus for that socialization in a global, multilateral context. The research question concerned how states can initiate a socialization process that synergistically builds a consensus on an issue over time. By consensus, I meant an overwhelming public—and not necessarily private—extent of agreement among states on an issue.

My argument was that a core coalition of states can create a spotlight of diplomatic pressure that draws into focus an issue. That diplomatic pressure sets in motion a process of collective legitimization, which assumes a life of its own and creates common expectations that make support for a particular position legitimate. Over time, these expectations can incline other states—in particular, those opposing or otherwise "on the fence"—towards joining in on a common position, leading to a convergence in expectations concerning the issue. An interstate socialization process accretes in the sense that public—but not necessarily private—viewpoints converge around a common, more "legitimate" (or "socially sustainable") stance on a particular issue. The outcome reflects a social compromise in which socialization subjects dissociate from the "illegitimate" or (socially unsustainable) position. I qualify this argument with the assertion that an agent's perceived integrity on an issue can make socialization efforts more (or less) influential. Socialization efforts are more likely to fail when proponents lack that integrity—and are therefore seen as hypocritical—because the target states do not see a political downside to maintaining the status quo.

As we have seen, states can act in coalition with each other to mobilize diplomatic action on issues in international relations. A general conclusion from my case studies is that coalitions of states can initiate global, multilateral socialization processes in a manner that is independent of the constellation of material power relations at a given point in history. Coalitions among materially weaker states can pressure third states—including materially stronger third states—into acceptance of certain positions that they would otherwise disagree with. Hence, numerically superior coalitions, often among states from the developing world, have the potential to act as protagonists in global, multilateral diplomacy. My conclusion does *not* entail that the "power of ideas" prevails in these diplomatic contexts. I will return to this point in the following subsection. The critical implication is that diplomatic pressure can mediate the influence of norms on an interstate audience; fortunately, or unfortunately,

© NAIF AL-MULLA, 2025 | DOI:10.1163/9789004711938_008

it can operate in favor of certain norms (and issue areas) at the expense of others. Another important implication is that the architects of socialization processes tend to include the more illiberal and non-democratic states in international relations. These are states—identifiable, for example, from Freedom House's annual "Freedom in the World" report—that may not strike scholars as the most authentic believers in the norms of liberal internationalism. This supports Ian Hurd's assertion that the most authentic believers in norms have relatively less freedom of action in international relations (Hurd 2008, 166).

1   Lessons Learned

I take away several lessons from my research experience. One lesson relates to the availability of primary source work, which limits the extent to which we can conduct studies on states as subjects of interstate socialization. In short, regime type matters. More liberal and democratic regime types—including Australia, Canada, the United Kingdom, and the United States—are more amenable to this line of research than other regime types. A basic definition of a liberal and democratic regime is a "political system marked not only by free and fair elections, but also by the rule of law, a separation of powers, and the protection of basic liberties of speech, assembly, religion, and property" (Zakaria 1997, 22). In my research experience, these regimes tend to disclose confidential source work after specified periods. The same is not true of less liberal and democratic regimes. One potential reason for this difference may relate to divergent norms on public accountability: liberal and democratic regimes are often more accountable to their public and, therefore, may see greater value in allowing public insight into their diplomatic activities at some point in time. The practical research implication is that most of the world's states often cannot serve as subjects for the analysis of interstate socialization in a global, multilateral context. Giovanni Mantilla makes a similar point for reference (Mantilla 2020b, 178). This is a challenge that future interstate socialization studies must contend with.

I see two potential ways to navigate this empirical research challenge. One is to maintain an empirical focus on the more liberal, democratic states as subjects of socialization—especially in more distant historical contexts such as those in chapters six and eight. There is still much ground to cover at the United Nations, as the primary source work available is voluminous. We will return to this point. Another way to navigate is to rely on the personal accounts of former diplomats from less liberal and democratic regimes. Personal memories and interviews can be helpful in this respect, provided that researchers have adequate foreign linguistic resources. Evaluating source work of this nature requires caution, given the political background of officials from more autocratic regimes. A paramount concern is self-censorship; divulging otherwise private information can entail significant personal risk to the official and researchers, especially if the information is collected within the applicable national context. I advise obtaining sought-after information from former officials who have relocated to more liberal, democratic countries. Another way to navigate the research challenge is by paying fastidious attention to diplomatic leaks, such as those made by Wikileaks. These leaks can be insightful, as seen in Part Two. Identifying subjects in as much detail as possible can lend credibility to the information. I am not saying—to be precise—that the more liberal, democratic regimes are always transparent and, therefore, more apposite to studies on interstate socialization. There are specific more recent issues in international relations where transparency is absent and poses comparable challenges to research.

Another lesson learned from my research is that "truth"—for example, as established by more independent fact-finding or investigative bodies at the United Nations—alone seems a relatively inconsequential influence on how states formulate changes in positions in a global, multilateral context. Consider the empirical evidence in the case study chapters, closely documenting how the applicable state changed positions on the issues. As we have seen, references to independent facts are limited despite extensive factual studies being presented to the respective interstate audiences. In brief, facts seem to matter only in as much as the interstate audience wants them to matter. Accordingly, further studies on interstate socialization should focus on *social* facts, meaning facts that exist by interstate agreement only because state representatives believe them to exist (Searle 1995, 1).

More importantly, further socialization studies should also focus on what state representatives make of those social facts. Paying less attention to extensive factual reports—and more attention to what states make of the facts—can save international relations scholars valuable time and energy. A related point is that norms are a relatively inconsequential influence on how states formulate position changes on the issues. As we have seen, state representatives often associate normative concerns with these foreign policy changes. Yet as we have also seen, claiming these normative concerns as justification for foreign policy changes can alone seem rich given that they are *not* timely—addressing issues that are at the time familiar, longstanding, and based on empirical circumstances that have not undergone significant changes. Hence, the diplomatic context of the time mediates the significance (or insignificance) that a norm can have for a particular issue. As we have seen, diplomatic pressure—which operates via collective legitimization—is a critical avenue by which norms gain international currency.

Another important lesson from my interstate socialization studies is that tracing state positions on an issue can involve a cacophony of source work. One cannot count on an international organization's delineation of agenda items alone to curate the issue's consideration over time since the issue may come up in more than one organizational context. An example is the annual General Debate at the United Nations, where delegations often touch upon issues they later raised in the more substantive intergovernmental committees at the General Assembly. Scholars who conduct studies on interstate socialization—particularly in an institutional context—need to be aware of this. The depth and breadth of primary source work may be more considerable than initially thought. I suggest considering source work referenced in the Index to Proceedings of the General Assembly, which contains a subject and delegation speeches index. This resource helps pinpoint where delegations discuss issues across organizational contexts. Another valuable primary resource is the United Nations Yearbook.

2   Further Theoretical Questions

My theoretical argument has emphasized how a core coalition of states can mobilize diplomatic pressure to support a cause, which can set in motion a composite socialization process. I qualified my argument with theoretical limitations, theoretical conditioning factors, and empirical scope conditions. I also suggested that an agent's perceived integrity on an issue can make socialization efforts more (or less) influential.

I suggest that further research consider additional theoretical conditioning factors relevant to studies on socialization in a global, multilateral context. My suggestions are twofold. First, further research could benefit from a closer look at the composition of interstate coalitions and consider how it influences the extent to which a coalition can bring diplomatic pressure to bear on third states. Based on my two positive case studies, my hunch is that socialization is more likely the more representative the core coalition is of what Ian Hurd calls the "'mainstream' international opinion" (Hurd 2005, 512; Hurd 2008, 153). One way to conceptualize representativeness is geographically. I propose that the more geographically representative a core coalition of states—for example, as measured by membership in regional intergovernmental organizations—the more it can generate interstate diplomatic pressure with universal reach. By contrast, interstate coalitions that consist *only* of states from a more antagonistic geopolitical bloc-like formation would seem less capable of extending diplomatic pressure to third states. Empirical examples of these latter coalitions may include the Eastern Bloc or the Western Bloc. A more recent example may consist of member states from ALBA, the Bolivarian Alliance for the Peoples of our America. For reference, Nicole Deitelhoff and Linda Wallbott make a similar point concerning negotiations that led to the establishment of the International Criminal Court:

> The coordinated strategies of the coalition, especially in the regional forums, diminished the role of traditional lines of confrontation within the negotiations. In multilateral settings, negotiations are often characterized by an almost rigid confrontation and mistrust between different groupings such as the Western group, the non-aligned movement or the Arab group. Usually, in such settings outcomes reflect the lowest common denominator. In the Rome process, however, regional allegiances played a negligible role owing to the emergence of the LM coalition as a coalition of small and middle states from all regions, thus cutting across traditional cleavages.
>
> DEITELHOFF AND WALLBOTT 2012, 354–355

More recently, Giovanni Mantilla has made a similar point in an interview with the *Cambridge Journal of Political Affairs*.

> you have to look at what happened in the room to understand the multilateralism's social dynamics beyond Great Power leadership or heavy-handedness. There are for instance social categories of states that are recognized at different points of time as being "undesirable" to vote with. Thinking about the 1970s, there were a few clear "pariah" states then— Israel, South Africa, and Portugal. There were states that were allied with these "pariah" countries that disagreed with these negative notions, but which still recognized their social validity at the international level. I suppose that is simply trying to understand social positioning in the context of negotiations; to understand how, in terms of social groupings and positioning, where are the markers of legitimacy and illegitimacy. But there is no formula for it; you just sort have to triangulate in different ways.
>
> MANTILLA 13.4.2021

Some may take the proposition here to suggest that a more successful core coalition must represent a "median" preference among states, which is another way to view the point (Thompson 2006; 2015). Professor Aaron Rapport suggested this to me in August 2018 at Cambridge (14.8.2018). Given its association with rationalist perspectives on international relations, I hesitate to embrace the term.

Robert Keohane implies two other ways to conceptualize a coalition's representativeness (Keohane 1966). One way is to consider how often a state has voted alongside the majority at the General Assembly. States that have in the past taken positions more in line with the majority may appear more representative of "mainstream" international opinion (Keohane 1966, 14). These states' positions can signal to third states where mainstream opinion stands and will continue to stand on the issues. Hence, the presence of these states in a diplomatic coalition would seem to help generate social pressure with universal reach. Keohane also suggests that the absence of a colonizing history is another way to conceptualize an interstate coalition's representativeness. This characteristic can facilitate an appearance of representativeness in that it can mark a sense of solidarity with a more widespread historical experience among states. In other words, Keohane suggests that a core coalition that consists of almost exclusively present or former colonizing powers would seem more likely to appear as representative of some conspiratorial project than of mainstream public opinion. Some may retort that there are numerous interstate experiences—that it, other than a colonizing history—that are more representative than others and so may also enter the present conversation. I agree. Yet what matters most is what counts as representative in an intersubjective, interstate context. Fortunately, or unfortunately, the absence of colonial history at particular times seems to be among the foremost factors at the United Nations. As Keohane suggests, states without such a colonial history can appear as *not* having an "ax to grind" and, therefore, would seem more capable of having others defer to them on some issues (Keohane 1966, 35).

The previous theoretical proposition relates to socialization agents. Further research should also contemplate the characteristics of potential socialization subjects and the extent to which they make them more (or less) prone to succumb to diplomatic pressure. I suggest two theoretical characteristics that serve as further conditioning factors in socialization processes. One relates to a state subject's administrative capacities, precisely its "dearth of the requisite scientific, technical, bureaucratic, and financial wherewithal" (Chayes and Chayes 1993, 193–195). My suggestion is that the more capacity limitations a state has, the less able and, by extension, willing it is to consider the purview of common issues at length. These states, therefore, seem more amenable to diplomatic pressure on specific issues, particularly on issues that they see as lacking immediate application to their own national contexts. My commentary on small states in the second empirical case study supports this. A potential way to identify certain capacity limitations would be to consider the composition of a state's permanent mission to the United Nations. Another way would be to consider how much a national delegation participates in proceedings from session to session. On this latter point, one could look to the Index of Proceedings—notably the Member State Speech Index—to collate how often certain states make interventions across the gamut of issues.

3   Further Empirical Research

My research is most interested in how diplomatic activism can set in motion a socialization process that cumulatively builds an interstate consensus on an issue over time. That consensus is political in the first instance; it can but does not necessarily have to culminate with the promulgation of an international legal instrument. My theoretical focus on consensus thus allows for capacious empirical latitude in selecting case studies, especially at the United Nations. I am confident that my argument can be applied to more such issue areas and that the Appendix's scope conditions are met.

My preliminary suggestion is to explore further "decolonization" politics at the United Nations. By decolonization politics, I mean coverage of issue areas where materially weaker, developing world states act as rigorous (and often bellicose) advocates of a cause, as we have seen. I suggest further coverage of this diplomatic context because it coincides with the substantial growth in membership at the United Nations—most notably since the late 1950s—and the formation of majoritarian interstate coalitions on specific issues. These numeric increases can accentuate diplomatic pressure and enhance socialization prospects. This empirical focus will help advance the latest research on interstate socialization. Giovanni Mantilla, for example, has recently suggested a similar empirical focus (Mantilla 2018; 2019; 2020a; 2020b). Specifically, Mantilla attends to the "'golden era' of international law-making—i.e. the immediate postwar decades, 1950–1980—which often featured fierce and effective Third World participation and opposition vis-à-vis the leading Great Powers amid Cold War tensions" (Mantilla 2020a, 11). Similarly, Margarita Petrova comments that "decolonization changed the dynamics of international politics by ushering in a new significant audience, something that may help understand why international agreement starts growing from the 1960s" (Petrova 14.10.2021, 3).

At the General Assembly, further interstate socialization studies may include proceedings that relate to South Africa like the question of Southwest Africa (Namibia), assistance to or solidarity with the anti-apartheid movement in South Africa, and support for international sanctions against the apartheid government. One can break down the "universe" of other potential case studies according to thematic issue areas. I suggest four substantive categories: self-determination, disarmament, human rights, and general norms of interstate relations. Socialization studies on self-determination may include Southern Rhodesia, territories formerly under foreign administration, and select issues in the annual agenda item "Question of Palestine." Studies on disarmament may include various nuclear disarmament questions such as bans on nuclear weapons in certain geographical regions (such as in Latin America), declarations of nuclear-free zones (such as in the Indian Ocean), nuclear non-proliferation globally and in certain regions (such as the Middle East), and the comprehensive ban on nuclear weapons testing. Other disarmament issue areas may include the placement of arms in outer space, chemical, and biological weapons, and the development of new weapons of mass destruction. Studies on human rights may include proceedings that call into question the relationship between human rights and disarmament, globalization, and "unilateral coercive measures." And finally, socialization studies on general norms of interstate relations may include the declarations on the "Definition of Aggression," and "Friendly Relations and Cooperation among States in accordance with the Charter of the United Nations."

We have seen that the General Assembly can serve as a focal point for interstate socialization in a global, multilateral context. I am also confident that the book's theoretical argument can extend to diplomatic focal points outside the United Nations, provided that my scope conditions are met. My argument requires that a core coalition of states engage in rhetorical action—manipulating the common norms of a particular interstate community—as part of a persistent diplomatic campaign to gain an audience's acceptance of a cause. Attention to proceedings of less universal intergovernmental organizations may prove theoretically helpful. A potential use, for example, would be to shed further light on a coalition's composition and focus on how its participants coalesce around support for a cause in a more regional context. One could then further delve into how this support can percolate to diplomacy in a global, multilateral context and become a focal point for socialization.

Future research could also address the prospects for socialization at the Security Council. This book has done much work on the matter and has a basis to hypothesize for future research. Refer to the manuscript's case study scope conditions: universal participation of states, decision-making by majority vote, and publicity. Recall that these conditions act as enablers and sharpeners of socialization. How much or little the conditions are met can affect the prospects for socialization. Yet, socialization prospects are not necessarily lower in less universal procedural settings like the Security Council. If the proceedings take place against a political backdrop where an inescapable majoritarian coalition otherwise exists on an issue, the prospects of socialization can remain higher. Security Council proceedings that address issues considered in the General Assembly can serve as a case and point. Many such issue areas would make for rewarding case studies, and I encourage them.

Data and Methods

> Basic to the interpretative or hermeneutical understanding of sci-
> ence is that the very human action which counts as significant in the
> social world, cannot be apprehended without interpretation, that
> is, without understanding the meaning that is given to it (Weber,
> 1988 [1922]) ... In other words, meaning is not limited to the actor
> itself, but must comprise the significance given to it by other actors,
> and also observers (Sparti, 1992: 102–103). Meaning is not something
> idiosyncratic to be studied through empathy.
>
> GUZZINI 2000, 160–161

∵

0   Outline

This Appendix allows the reader more insight into the steps of my novel
research process in successive order. I address an empirical puzzle derived
from Chapter One. My point was that the literature suggests a thematic focus
on interstate bloc politics at the General Assembly. I then present a broad
overview of diplomacy at the General Assembly—consistent with a social
constructivist research orientation—emphasizing interstate social consensus.
I suggest that there has been a general increase in the number of resolutions
states have agreed upon over time. There has also been a general rise in the
proportion of resolutions unanimously agreed upon. Hence, interstate consensus has become an increasingly prominent feature of diplomacy at the General
Assembly and should receive more scholarly attention.

I then outline the scope conditions for my empirical case studies. These
scope conditions suggest empirical issue areas embodied in resolutions where
my theoretical argument applies. The scope conditions require a survey of
resolutions presenting a clear and concise issue with a recurring character. In
addition, I also suggest institutional scope conditions drawn from Giovanni
Mantilla's analysis on forum isolation (Mantilla 2018). The requirements are
the universal participation of states (featuring a one-state-one-vote rule),
decision-making by majority vote (or consensus procedures in the shadow of

© NAIF AL-MULLA, 2025 | DOI:10.1163/9789004711938_009

majority vote), and publicity (Mantilla 2018, 329). Based on these scope conditions, I suggest three empirical case studies: racial discrimination in the Union of South Africa (1946–1961), the United States embargo on Cuba (1991–2016), and the ban on nuclear weapons (1946–1961). I also consider the critical question of selection bias, drawn from scholars who point out the limits of selecting on the dependent variable (e.g. Achen and Snidal 1989; Geddes 1990; King, Keohane, and Verba 1994). I contend with this literature and point out the variance in my research design, which includes attention to a "nonpositive" case study in my third empirical chapter on the diplomatic campaign to ban nuclear weapons.

Next, I outline the three-step research procedure for my empirical case study chapters. In general, the process is to zero in on the diplomatic agitation that a core coalition of states undertakes to support a cause, consider the extent to which this activity influences a target interstate audience, and then consider empirical and/or theoretical counterarguments to my claims.

I finally present my primary sources and consider their limitations. The main limitation relates to how one can infer genuine intentions from foreign policy statements in a global, multilateral context.

1   What's the Puzzle?

Puzzles in international relations are "pieces of information, the belief that pieces fit together into a meaningful picture but the inability to fit the pieces together initially" (Zinnes 1980, 316). This book speaks to a puzzle. To see how, recall my commentary from Chapter One. The chapter suggested a thematic focus on interstate bloc politics at the General Assembly. My suggestion was that the research focus has been incomplete. It tends to focus on potential conflicts of interest among states. However, it pays less attention to how states can find common causes on the issues, despite the position one may associate them with within a bloc or bloc-like formation. The main research focus thus overlooks the extent to which socialization can take place among states overall and follow from diplomatic pressure that transcends the political or otherwise bloc formations that may exist at the time. This is to say that the primary research focus does not give rise to an expectation that such socialization can prevail and shape how states relate to common issues. This shortcoming seems most outstanding, where the common ground appears to expand among states on specific topics. Conflicts of interest—such as those defined by political or otherwise allegiance formations—may prove inherent to that consensus. Nevertheless, the focus on those cleavages overlooks the extent to which exogenous social effects can operate and exert overall pressure upon the states in question.

My second point concerning the puzzle relates to my prior discussion of side payments (or "gift exchanges") at the United Nations. To recap, these accounts deal with certain states using material resources to exact support for or at least acquiescence to specific positions. Yet the agents of such activity can nevertheless see interstate support take shape against their positions, despite, at times, explicit material threats made against target states that are, to some extent, dependent on specific economic and/or military relationships with the agents in question. Hence, more widespread positions can take shape and move against what we would expect if the usual suspects were to employ the side payments successfully. This, in turn, suggests that using side payments has either minimal effect on these positions or that the unusual suspects have been using them to their advantage. The latter point entails that the materially less capable states—rather than materially more capable states—are the ones that manage to leverage material resources toward outcomes in their favor. That perspective is not compelling and does not dovetail with what one would expect from the material capabilities-based focus in the literature on side payments in global, multilateral diplomacy at the United Nations.

2   Diplomacy at the UNGA

According to the Charter, the General Assembly is the "chief deliberative, policymaking, and representative organ" of the United Nations. Central to the history of diplomacy at the Assembly has been the development and, perhaps at times, even solidification of bloc politics among states, as the empirical literature review chapter has shown. Yet also central to diplomacy in this context has been a parallel, overall expansion of the extent of consensus its member states reach over time. This becomes apparent upon taking a step back from the ocean of quantitative information available on bloc politics to examine the big picture, which indicates a general broadening of common ground among states over time. I use summary statistics to provide a general overview of diplomacy at the General Assembly.

Refer to Table 1, Figure 1, and Figure 2. The number of resolutions states have agreed upon has increased since the First Session (1946–1947). This is apparent given that the median number of resolutions adopted exceeds that of each of the first thirty-two sessions and that the highest three-quarters of resolutions passed per session have come after the Fifteenth Session (1960–1961) with just one exception. It also seems apparent given that the lowest quarter of resolutions passed per session occurred before the 22nd Session (1967–1968). Most of the resolutions passed per session in the General Assembly have come towards the latter end of its history, further confirmed by the positive slope of the trend line and leftward skew presented in Figure 1.

The frequency of interstate agreements has generally been increasing since the General Assembly was established. A look at the proportion of resolutions per session that met unanimous interstate approval suggests that the extent of that agreement has also expanded. As we can see, the slope for this figure (Figure 2) is also positive, and the upper quartile proportion of unanimous resolutions passed per session falls within the last twenty-eight years. Hence, the General Assembly has, for better or worse, become the scene of increasing interstate transactions over the years. Therefore, some extent of interstate agreement seems to have become a more prominent diplomacy feature in that context.

This takeaway requires emphasis and should not be taken for granted—perhaps, as some might suggest, as an accumulation of sunk costs over the years that has amounted to a natural growth in work activity (e.g. Keohane 1984, 100–103; Stinchcombe 1968, 119–129; Koremenos, Lipson and Snidal 2003, 315–332). There are no material, coercive measures imposed on states to converge on the United Nations year after year to participate in its proceedings and with increasing frequency. Nor are there manifest, materially coercive circumstances that cannot but lead states to weigh in on and eventually express support for resolutions session after session. Where these suggestions lead—that is, towards disengagement from the United Nations, towards decreasing or perhaps even a general erosion of agreement among states over time—are not hypothetical conjectures, as the 19th Session (1964–1965) demonstrates. That session culminated in a halt to the General Assembly's work, dragging states through what the then Secretary-General U Thant described as a "dark valley of discord and enmity" (Thant in Cordier 2010, 5). Some scholars then went as far as to question whether the year would "go down in history as the beginning of gradual atrophy or debilitation" of the United Nations (Nathanson 1965, 623). The crisis suggests that the general increase in the frequency and extent of the agreement reached among states over time has not been an inevitable, steady progression (or digression) down a path-dependent route without a break in sight.

Path dependence may have been relevant by helping ensure a pattern of continued engagement given the alternative costs of establishing a new, more effective general assembly. A path-dependency critique offers insight into why states may continue engaging other state counterparts yearly for some seven decades. Yet the question remains about how that activity results in a general conclusion of more (and not less or a roughly equal number of) agreements throughout this same period. The specific nature of interstate engagement—namely, its positive, rather than neutral or negative direction—problematizes the critique as alone incomplete, as a significant strand of sociological literature on formal institutions suggests (e.g. Barnett and Finnemore 1999; Finnemore 1996; Meyer and Rowan 1977; McNamara 2002; Parsons 1960; Suchman 1995). In this literature, one finds traction in perspective on how certain common expectations can sustain interstate engagement and push it in the direction my theoretical commentary suggests. One finds, for example, accounts that make the case that "legitimacy leads to persistence because audiences are most likely to supply resources to organizations that appear desirable, proper, or appropriate" (Suchman 1995, 574).

A further challenge to the path-dependence critique is the strong, positive relationship between the number of resolutions agreed upon per session and the expansion in membership at the United Nations. The increase in membership has been strongly associated with the increase in resolutions agreed upon per session at the General Assembly. Note the Pearson's correlation coefficient in Figure 1. A possible implication is that newly independent states have broadened the gambit of issues at the forum and contributed to the conclusion of more resolutions among its members. It is not apparent that a relationship of this nature comports with a path-dependent logic, as new member states would not have been "bound" by concerns for sunk costs incurred throughout previous sessions of the General Assembly. Hence, a path-dependent logic does not seem most applicable to newly independent member states, mainly their reasons for bringing new priorities to the platform.

3   Scope Conditions and Case Study Selection

This book considers specific resolutions as case studies, each of which falls within the below scope conditions. These conditions make qualitative requirements for the project and suggest the kind of issue areas that the book can address. The first condition is that we must examine issues with a consistent recurring character, especially as embodied in the resolutions above. This condition addresses an empirical limitation: issues that do not come up for consideration repeatedly lack periodic updates on state positions that some resolutions provide. These recurring issues or resolutions need not necessarily extend across a specified tract of time. Nor do they need to encompass subject areas that come up for consideration verbatim under the same resolution title or even as points of discussion inside the United Nations context. This condition only ensures a constant record of states' positions on the same issues over time. The criteria, therefore, addresses a theoretical assumption: periodic evidence of state positions on similar, if not identical, issues is essential to weigh a perspective on interstate socialization.

The second scope condition is that a clear and concise issue must be apparent within the applicable resolutions. This condition addresses the need to evaluate a theoretical perspective on interstate socialization, which also requires attention to how state positions converge (or fail to converge) on an issue over time. Hence, the requirement is that there is indeed an issue area that serves as a constant focal point for interstate consideration, helping concentrate on and perhaps even accentuate the surrounding interaction. This, in turn, allows insight into what effect this state-to-state interaction has on the subsequent positions states take on the particular issue. It also, to some extent, controls for alterations in a focal point of discussion that may or may not enter the conversation among states. However, this second condition does not dismiss the importance of the precise wording of a resolution that states may or may not respond to. It instead helps ensure that the language central to the resolution does not undergo significant changes such that its substantive point assumes a new direction. This allows peripheral variance in language to factor into (or fail to factor into) the conversation, though not to the extent that it changes the focal point of proceedings. Therefore, the second scope condition relates to a resolution's specific focus, providing that it must address a consistent point throughout its consideration with some underlying consistency.

Giovanni Mantilla suggests a further relevant set of institutional scope conditions in his analysis of forum isolation (Mantilla 2018, 329). The conditions are the universal participation of states (featuring a one-state-one-vote rule), decision-making by majority vote (or consensus procedures in the shadow of majority vote), and publicity. Nicole Deitelhoff and Linda Walbott suggest empirical support for Mantilla's first two conditions (Deitelhoff and Wallbott 2012, 363). "Small states coalitions' ability to impact on negotiation outcomes will increase in negotiations operating with majority decision rules (and decrease in those that rely on consensus or unanimity)" (Deitelhoff and Wallbott 2012, 364). Mantilla goes on to suggest that these institutional conditions "work both as enablers and 'sharpeners' of diplomatic pressure when a contingent phenomenon occurs: the formation of majority (or supermajority) coalitions during negotiations" (Mantilla 2018, 329). I agree. These institutional conditions are relevant to my empirical case studies. The formation of a majority coalition can be but is not necessarily applicable to my current empirical focus on the General Assembly, where member states can adopt resolutions without the support of an absolute numerical majority in principle. The reason is that the procedural requirement for a resolution to pass—and therefore come up for consideration again—is two-thirds of member states only "present and voting" (Rule 83, Rules of Procedure). Present and voting refer to member states that cast an affirmative or negative vote, not those that abstain or are absent from voting (Rule 86, Rules of Procedure). Thus, abstaining or absent member states can outnumber those present and voting.

Considering the above scope conditions, we can now contemplate the book's selection of empirical case studies. The "universe" of resolutions to base these studies is capacious, with some twenty thousand to date at the General Assembly alone. My suggestion is to select these series of resolutions: (i) racial discrimination in the Union of South Africa from 1946 to 1961, (ii) the United States embargo on Cuba from 1991 to 2016, and (iii) the ban on nuclear weapons from 1946 to 1961. My research interest in the former two cases is how a core coalition of states can build an interstate consensus on the issues over time. This is to say that my focus is on how the process unfolds in those two positive cases of interstate socialization. For reference, my focus on process resonates with other social science works (e.g. Elster 2007, 35–42; Hedström and Swedberg 1998, 7–11; Merton 1968, 39–45). The first two case studies address "positive" examples of interstate socialization, while the latter covers a "nonpositive" or inconclusive example.

I select these three issue areas as case studies for methodological and theoretical reasons. My methodological reason is that the three cases meet the scope conditions above. My theoretical reason is that the two positive studies present relatively "hard" cases for social constructivists but should have been relatively "easy" cases for empirical or theoretical approaches that emphasize material power (Petrova 2016, 391; 2019, 617–618). As we have seen, the former two positive studies relate to interstate socialization that proceeds against the wishes of the more materially capable states or states closely aligned with them. In the first case study, a core coalition of states helped build an almost unanimous consensus against apartheid from 1946 to 1961. This consensus took shape despite staunch opposition from many of the more materially capable states at the time, including each of the world's former colonial powers. Similarly, in the second case study, a core coalition of states helped build an almost unanimous consensus against the Cuba embargo from 1991 to 2016. This consensus also took shape despite staunch opposition from the United States, which included explicit material threats toward third states to refrain from supporting a common position against the embargo. Thus, both positive case studies showcase the limits of a materialist focus on diplomacy at the United Nations.

For now, the selection of the first two case studies begs the question of selection bias since interstate support increases for the respective issues over time. Numerous scholars comment on the limits of "selecting on the dependent variable" in social science research (e.g. Achen and Snidal 1989; Geddes 1990; Lieberson 1991; King, Keohane and Verba 1994). A standard caution is the lack of variation in outcomes allowed in such studies. This lack of variation prevents researchers from understanding the independent effects of the suggested causal variables on the outcome of interest. Researchers can only generalize valid inferences from case studies selected by some rule or criteria not correlated with the outcome (Geddes 1990, 135). I acknowledge this critical body of scholarship, but nonetheless, I see promise in proceeding with the work set out for the following reasons.

First, other social science scholars acknowledge the value of selecting on the dependent variable as a valid research practice (e.g. Dion 1998; Collier 1995; Collier and Mahoney 1996; Garfinkel 1981; Most and Starr 1982; Rogowski 1995; Seawright and Gerring 2008). David Collier and James Mahoney, for example, contend that:

> No-variance designs play an invaluable role in generating new information and discovering novel explanations, which in terms of a larger research cycle provides indispensable data for broader comparative studies and new hypotheses for them to evaluate.
>
> COLLIER AND MAHONEY 1996, 73–74

I am particularly interested in Collier and Mahoney's reference to Alan Garfinkel's concept of "contrast space," which advocates some examination of nonpositive cases to create a frame of comparison and gain more analytic leverage within the particular research design (Collier and Mahoney 1996, 67–69; 74; Garfinkel 1981). I incorporate the concept into my research design in my third case study chapter on nuclear weapons. Studying this latter inconclusive case study also responds to Jeffrey Checkel's call to examine empirical circumstances where the "dog does not bark" (Checkel 1998, 339). I want to gain more insight into the conditions under which socialization will and will not occur by weighing in on the extent to which certain independent theoretical factors are influential. Chapter Two refers to these independent theoretical factors as "conditioning factors." The term comes from Professor Nathalie Tocci (Tocci 2008a; 2008b).

Yet, studying an empirical context where the "dog does not bark" requires caution. A secondary investigation of this kind runs the risk of examining a theoretically inconsequential case where the outcome of concern is both not present and applies to a lesser proportion of cases. This can raise an unavoidable question about the relevance of the examination, as the project would spend time and energy on the circumstances of a case that somehow rendered the outcome impossible (Clarke 2002; Mahoney and Goertz 2004). A way to navigate this potential challenge is to adhere to James Mahoney and Gary Goertz's "possibility principle," which suggests that studies on nonpositive cases examine contexts where the outcome of interest has a "real possibility of occurring—not just those where the outcome has a nonzero probability" (Mahoney and Goertz 2004, 654). It follows that "nonpositive" case studies are most valuable when they resemble positive cases to "control for background features and thereby achieve greater leverage for causal analysis" (Mahoney and Goertz 2004, 655).

Thus, my third nonpositive case study on the nuclear weapons ban replicates—to the extent it is possible—the conditions under which socialization took place in the first positive case study on apartheid. I allude to the same agents and subjects of socialization as case illustrations as much as the source work allows. This enables me to control for various actor properties, such as regime characteristics at a particular period. I also examine the same period—from 1946 to 1961—in both my positive and nonpositive case studies to control for a host of historical factors that can affect the success of socialization. In the two case studies, the most prominent of these historical factors is decolonization, which led to a substantial increase in membership at the United Nations in 1960 and 1961.

Notably, almost all these new member states—hailing from Africa and Southern Asia—supported the core coalition's diplomatic efforts on the respective issues. Controlling for decolonization thus controls for the added potential social effects—such as those that can follow from an increased sense of isolation—that a core coalition's numerical expansion can have on an interstate audience. I also examine the time from 1946 to 1961 to ensure that interstate socialization on the issue had a "real possibility of occurring," as per my first case study. Some may question whether a state's possession of nuclear weapons would have abnegated support for the ban. Here, I emphasize that the two are *not* necessarily incompatible. A state can possess the means to engage in specific modes of warfare but hold that doing so runs counter to select common expectations.

One may question my choice of the Cuba embargo from 1991 to 2016 for my second positive case study chapter. Margarita Petrova, for example, suggests that selecting all three cases from the same period could control for "world time" and help draw into focus theoretical factors relevant to socialization dynamics (Finnemore and Sikkink 1998, 909; Petrova 4.10.2021, 4). I make two points in response. First, I refer to numerous country case illustrations within my positive case studies. This allows me to test theory across distinct empirical country examples while ensuring sufficient historical consistency. My second point is that a positive case study on an alternative empirical context provides that my theory tests are not just contingent upon a particular historical context and thus have greater external validity.

4   Means of Analysis

I require an interpretive approach to understand how diplomatic pressure can operate. This primarily draws me to exchanges between diplomats, which, for the most part, have been recorded in the written documentation that I outline below. I pay close attention to "what actors say, in what contexts, and to what audiences," as Krebs and Jackson call for (Krebs and Jackson 2007, 36). Analyzing these exchanges requires the use of discourse analysis: a means of research most concerned with the interpretation of "social reality," examining empirical evidence against the "horizon" of inter-subjective meaning (e.g. Bos and Tarnai 1999; Elo and Keingas 2008; Holsti 1968; Hsieh and Shannon 2005; Krippendorf 2004; Neuendorf 2016; Weber 1990.). Although serving various research purposes, this approach shares a theme in its attention to the inference of social phenomena from the text. As Klaus Krippendorf writes,

> A text means something to someone, it is produced by someone to have meanings for someone else, and these meanings therefore must not be ignored and must not violate why the text exists in the first place. Text—the reading of text, the use of text within a social context, and the analysis of text—serves as a convenient metaphor in content analysis.
>
> KRIPPENDORF 2004, 19

Analytic deconstruction or "unpacking" of written documentation to the point where one gets a sense of what inspired its creation is central to content analysis and the line of work set out in this work. Each piece of the text addresses a particular audience in a specific context at a certain time. As Darren Weinberg suggests, such text is not a "thing that exists independently of the occasions of its use but as an element of social life" (Weinberg 23.1.2018, 2). It is a social practice in action; the conversation it expresses consists of "practices that systematically form the objects of which they speak" (Foucault 1972, 49). This is to say, to paraphrase Jennifer Milliken, that things do not mean but rather people construct the meaning of things in conversation (Milliken 1999, 229). The catalog of possible meaning becomes more constrained to the social context. Meaning is accordingly not, as Stefano Guzzini argues, "limited to the actor itself, but must compromise the significance given to it by other actors, and also observers" (Guzzini 2000, 161). Although the actors in question need not see meaning the same way, there nevertheless seems to be some essential acceptance as to what it entails for the conversation to exist in the first place.

This book conducts discourse analysis via a novel three-step procedure in each case study chapter. My entry point for the research is a "belief" of how a particular process has come about and how it comports with some meaningful picture (Zinnes 1980, 312). That belief is the subject of my investigation and, as the reader knows, suggests a role for a coalition of states in exerting diplomatic pressure on other states to forge acceptance of a common viewpoint on an issue. From this entry point, the first step in the empirical investigation has two parts. The first part of step one relates to making the case for a core coalition of states supporting a particular issue. In connection with the United Nations, such a coalition can take shape upon the issue's initial consideration. This can be apparent in that it comes up for review in connection with a resolution with an explicit reference to certain member state cosponsors. It can also be evident that certain states, alongside others, act as "spokespersons" for the cause (for example, by being especially vocal about a particular position). However, this does not necessarily imply that these spokespersons—thanks to the support of their member state counterparts—enjoy some acceptance of their moral leadership on the issue. As the previous chapter suggests, socialization agents can take on the role *ipso facto*, owing to the relative silence of others who support the given position.

My point in this latter paragraph is *not* that the composition of a core coalition needs to remain constant. The composition of a coalition can change, especially given the many newer actors that have become independent states throughout the latter half of the twentieth century. This is apparent in the membership count at the United Nations, which grew almost four-fold from fifty-five in 1946 to one hundred and ninety-three in the present. There are numerous examples where one could make the case for a particular core coalition's existence and its composition change along these lines. The case study related to the Union of South Africa is an example. What matters most is how a change in a coalition's composition can affect its campaign in support of a cause, particularly as it relates to its momentum and/or the extent to which it marks the start of a new interstate campaign with an alternative direction. Whatever the case, one can draw insight from a careful focus on the specific issue some states create and have others evaluate over the years.

The second part of step one in the research procedure is to make sense of the positions for which the spokespersons campaign. This involves applying my discussion on content analysis to the primary source work under examination to identify core positions advanced by the support base. There can be some degree of variation across miscellaneous positions. Nevertheless, that these states converge on support for the same general position suggests that there are certain baseline elements in common. Accordingly, I zero in on how states express these positions. The task is to encapsulate normative rhetoric that the coalition manipulates to support a cause. This task is analytic rather than descriptive; the coalition of states will not themselves theorize their views, complete with reference to the literature. That is for me to infer by applying the above discussion on content analysis to the primary source work available. Note that the analysis does not require that the coalition pushes for positions based on the facts. Their activity can very well amount to humbuggery: a "performance of delusion," "theater of absurd," "shameful lies," "parade of hypocrisy," propaganda salvos, and so on (e.g. Haley 3.11.18; Hehir and Neuer 25.1.18; Green 2017; Netanyahu 2017; Udayakumar 2017).

Step two in the investigation procedure looks to zero in on the effects of the core coalition's diplomatic activity on other states. This second step looks at states that have either opposed or have been otherwise "on the fence" on the issue in question. It attaches primary importance to how these states express newfound positions in ways they have not done before. However, these positions may or may not be associated with changes in a particular voting option. What matters is *how* these more recent state positions get expressed and to what extent they seem to develop in response to other state positions already established on the issue. This emphasis on "how" states express themselves— including about changes in state position—is similar to Ian Hurd's focus on Libya's strategic activity's effects on other states meant to uphold a Security Council sanctions regime (Hurd 2002; 2005; 2008). For Hurd, and similarly for my empirical investigation, observing how states express changes in position suggests empirical evidence of these social effects.

Similarly, Ronald Krebs and Patrick Jackson contend that "we cannot observe directly what people think, but we can observe what they say and how they respond to claims and counter-claims" (Krebs and Jackson 2007, 42). Hence, how states express changes in position is the observable implication for my theoretical argument. What counts most are changes in position that echo and thereby respond to the interstate conversation that prevails. This step in the research procedure also considers corroborating detailed primary and secondary source work supporting my theoretical interpretations.

The final step in my research procedure is to cross-check inferences against the broader historical context and especially consider counterarguments from alternative theoretical perspectives on international relations. This step is, in part, a response to calls for process tracing methods to "consider a wide range of alternatives despite the effort it entails" (Bennet and Checkel 2010, 21). More importantly, it is also a response to those scholars who emphasize that social science cannot "see" in minute detail social action as it happens, even in connection with some phenomena that seem more analogous to that of a "chain of events" or "domino effect" (Bennet and Checkel 2012, 12; Bennet 2010, 2; Mahoney 2012, 587). This latter point suggests that alternative takes on the phenomenon of interest can appear at every witch-way and that the most this investigation can do is remain open to potential counterarguments, grapple with them (or, as some argue, "soak and poke" about their implications), and put together the most compelling case for what has happened (Bennet and Checkel 2012, 22). Therefore, this final step addresses skepticism that seems to mostly occur to the reader, considering how certain circumstances—including "exogenous shocks"—intervene and render the analysis more (or less) compelling. I anticipate this skepticism from specific perspectives in international relations theory (like those covered in Chapter Two), studies on the practice of the United Nations (in particular, the General Assembly and Security Council), work on the historical context of the case study in question, and conversations with faculty members at Cambridge: including Jason Sharman, Ayse Zarakol and Aaron Rapport.

5   Primary Sources

Most of my source work is available online via the United Nations Bibliographic Information System (UNBISNET), Official Document System (UNODS), Audiovisual Library, Digital Library, Yearbook, Webcast, and Meetings Coverage and Press Releases. The lion's share of source work comes from resolutions, reports, statements, "explanations of the vote" (before and after the vote), rights of reply, verbatim records, notes verbales, press briefs, and interview transcripts related to the specific issue. Moreover, the previous section's emphasis on state actors permits the research investigation to cast its empirical "net" beyond the United Nations archival system to include news outlets, governmental sources (online and otherwise), historical archives, and my own written and oral exchanges with the applicable representatives if necessary. This allows an interstate conversation to extend beyond the United Nations, including articulations in foreign policy positions from as broad a slate of state actors as possible. On this latter point, state actors' increasing use of specific online platforms in recent years helps. Twitter is a good example. Online platforms like these provide further opportunities to engage in the kind of interstate conversation analysis that my project addresses.

It is worth considering the potential limitations of my primary sources. Numerous scholars have cautioned against examining national statements made by states, especially in connection with diplomacy in a global, multilateral context. The criticism seems to run along the lines of a view that "talk is cheap" and so cannot serve as a reliable way to consider what states mean or mean to communicate. Concerning the United Nations, critiques on garrulous proceedings seem to come mainly from scholars concerned with the international legal status of states' pronouncements in the form of resolutions. Arangio-Ruiz suggests that member states tend to ingratiate themselves with the wider interstate audience, trying to "get away from every session with as good an image as possible" (Arangio-Ruiz 1972, 457–459). "Potential or natural opponents are often reluctant to face the risk of besmirching their image by opposing a proposal openly or casting a negative vote" (Arangio-Ruiz 1972, 457–459). Stephen Schwebe similarly comments that delegations often express support for "much of which they actually disagree"; they do so "because it is politically unpopular to do otherwise" (Schwebel 1979, 301–302). And Michael Byers emphasizes member states "saying things which are different from what they do" (Byers 1999, 40–43, 135–136). These scholars, alongside others with more generic views on the subject, suggest a challenge in looking at public statements to consider what states (or social actors more broadly) "really think" on the given issue.

Yet this challenge is "serious, but not unsurmountable" for at least the following two reasons (Elster 2015, 48). First, the criticism highlights rather than detracts from my central concern: the social construction of interstate relations. Unlike the above scholarship—which seems held back by concerns for evidence of general practice accepted as law—my research investigation takes head-on intersubjective notions of "image," "popularity," and "hypocrisy" in international relations. We remain in business if delegations tend to pontificate and make much of how they are "seen" by other state counterparts. I am interested in where intersubjective concerns like these can come from and how to expect them to shape states' ideas on the issues.

That some states prevaricate or misrepresent their positions out of concern for besmirching their image, losing popularity, and coming across as hypocritical seems to be affected by the time's interstate social context. The insincere use or misuse of language in the presentation of governmental positions makes my investigation all the more interesting. It suggests that mere conversation can pressure states to accept positions they otherwise would not. Ian Hurd makes a similar point (Hurd 1999, 381, 392; Hurd 2008, 164; Hurd 2015, 54). More recently, Giovanni Mantilla suggests that hypocrisy can act as a "productive engine" of socialization (Mantilla 2020b, 177). The attractive theoretical proposition is that governmental positions do not develop exclusively within some national context but are, in some part, constituted (or "constructed") by the broader interstate social context. I accordingly see the challenge as a further invitation to international relations research analysis, including wherever a need to "read between the lines" appears.

This leads to a second point on the available primary source work. There are several ways to grapple with what national statements mean and do not mean. Even so, there is no definitive, formulaic solution to the concern that talk is cheap. The best way to address the matter is to examine the source work as judiciously as possible and by a straightforward step-by-step procedure for others to scrutinize. Therefore, I emphasize explicating the due diligence in my research procedure. One way to do this is by examining what states say in the conversation's context and considering how it is consistent with prior positions or positions taken in other contexts. If, for example, a state expresses a position as a matter of principle, one should expect to find prior consistency in that position on the issue or set of issues under consideration. If that is not the case, and the position taken in principle seems to have come about more suddenly, then it can very well seem that something is up. The position that the state expresses—if, among other things, an echo of that same principle—can then seem in some part a response to some interstate social circumstances rather than its wholesale expression of the position. Whatever the case, how the state expresses the position, as the above research process emphasizes, can provide hints of its motivations.

A final way to address the empirical concern is cross-reference analysis against the broader historical context. Cross-referencing can entail attending to the extent to which states "talk the talk" *and* "walk the walk." Jon Elster, among other scholars, suggests two specific techniques. The first technique is to contemplate the "objective interests" of the state in question and assume that they coincide with the given statement without compelling evidence that suggests the contrary (Elster 2015, 48). The second technique is to focus on the "actual consequences" of the statement and assume that, in the absence of contrary evidence, they match what the state intends to say (Elster 2015, 48). These techniques seem helpful and make their way into the research investigation insofar as "objective interests" and "actual consequences" are available for study. Still, none of these techniques necessarily provide a solution to "take to the bank" and alone count on. My intent in their use is to help stir up further discussion in the case studies, embracing some uncertainty in an account that nevertheless seems most persuasive.

TABLE 1   Historical trajectory of resolutions at the UNGA

Session of the UNGA	UN voting membership	Number of resolutions adopted	Number of resolutions adopted unanimously	Proportion of resolutions adopted unanimously
1st session (1946–1947)	55	141	97	68.8%
2nd session (1947–1948)	57	104	55	53.9%
3rd session (1948–1949)	58	142	54	38.0%
4th session (1949–1950)	59	120	23	19.2%
5th session (1950–1951)	60	162	29	17.9%
6th session (1951–1952)	76	135	19	14.1%
7th session (1952–1953)	76	134	30	22.4%
8th session (1953–1954)	76	118	30	25.4%
9th session (1954–1955)	76	117	29	24.8%
10th session (1955–1956)	76	99	38	38.4%
11th session (1956–1957)	80	137	35	25.5%
12th session (1957–1958)	82	116	42	36.2%
13th session (1958–1959)	82	133	57	42.9%
14th session (1959–1960)	99	135	45	33.3%
15th session (1960–1961)	99	152	67	44.1%
16th session (1961–1962)	104	139	74	53.2%

TABLE 1   Historical trajectory of resolutions at the UNGA (*cont.*)

Session of the UNGA	UN voting membership	Number of resolutions adopted	Number of resolutions adopted unanimously	Proportion of resolutions adopted unanimously
17th session (1962–1963)	110	138	68	49.3%
18th session (1963–1964)	113	134	75	56.0%
19th session (1964–1965)	115	14	14	100%
20th session (1965–1966)	117	165	82	49.7%
21st session (1966–1967)	122	154	64	41.6%
22nd session (1967–1968)	123	144	61	42.4%
23rd session (1968–1969)	126	156	62	39.7%
24th session (1969–1970)	127	176	71	40.3%
25th session (1970–1971)	127	174	61	35.1%
26th session (1971–1972)	132	193	57	29.5%
27th session (1972–1973)	135	199	65	32.7%
28th session (1973–1974)	135	194	76	39.2%
29th session (1974–1975)	138	199	97	48.7%
30th session (1975–1976)	144	236	119	50.4%
31st session (1976–1977)	147	277	167	73.6%
32nd session (1977–1978)	149	289	170	58.8%

TABLE 1   Historical trajectory of resolutions at the UNGA (*cont.*)

Session of the UNGA	UN voting membership	Number of resolutions adopted	Number of resolutions adopted unanimously	Proportion of resolutions adopted unanimously
33rd session (1978–1979)	151	317	171	54.9%
34th session (1979–1980)	152	325	190	58.5%
35th session (1980–1981)	154	368	210	57.1%
36th session (1981–19782)	157	373	211	56.6%
37th session (1982–1983)	158	385	199	51.7%
38th session (1983–1984)	158	356	189	53.1%
39th session (1984–1985)	159	380	210	55.3%
40th session (1985–1986)	159	377	202	53.6%
41st session (1986–1987)	159	345	165	47.8%
42nd session (1987–1988)	159	348	180	51.2%
43rd session (1988–1989)	159	351	190	54.1%
44th session (1989–1990)	159	369	226	61.2%
45th session (1990–1991)	159	367	258	70.3%
46th session (1991–1992)	166	338	240	71.0%
47th session (1992–1993)	179	329	246	74.8%
48th session (1993–1994)	184	367	293	79.8%

TABLE 1 Historical trajectory of resolutions at the UNGA (*cont.*)

Session of the UNGA	UN voting membership	Number of resolutions adopted	Number of resolutions adopted unanimously	Proportion of resolutions adopted unanimously
49th session (1994–1995)	185	351	274	78.1%
50th session (1995–1996)	188	348	244	70.1%
51st session (1996–1997)	188	319	239	74.9%
52nd session (1997–1998)	188	298	229	76.9%
53rd session (1998–1999)	188	303	242	80.0%
54th session (1999–2000)	188	341	271	79.5%
55th session (2000–2001)	189	253	210	83.0%
56th session (2001–2002)	189	360	293	81.4%
57th session (2002–2003)	191	351	278	79.2%
58th session (2003–2004)	191	324	248	76.5%
59th session (2004–2005)	191	325	254	78.1%
60th session (2005–2006)	191	295	219	74.2%
61st session (2006–2007)	191	305	219	71.8%
62nd session (2007–2008)	192	281	201	71.5%
63rd session (2008–2009)	192	317	241	76.0%
64th session (2009–2010)	192	303	232	76.6%

TABLE 1   Historical trajectory of resolutions at the UNGA (*cont.*)

Session of the UNGA	UN voting membership	Number of resolutions adopted	Number of resolutions adopted unanimously	Proportion of resolutions adopted unanimously
65th session (2010–2011)	192	321	248	77.3%
66th session (2011–2012)	193	305	235	77.0%
67th session (2012–2013)	193	310	238	76.7%
68th session (2013–2014)	193	316	252	79.7%
69th session (2014–2015)	193	335	254	75.8%
70th session (2015–2016)	193	312	237	76.0%
71st session (2016–2017)	193	334	251	75.1%
72nd session (2017–2018)	193	321	226	70.4%
73rd session (2018–2019)	193	354	244	68.9%
74th session (2019–2020)	193	315	220	69.8%
75th session (2020–2021)	193	338	238	70.4%
76th session (2021–2022)	193	311	231	74.3%
77th session (2022–2023)	193	345	257	74.5%
78th session (2023–2024)	193	...	...	...
Total	193	19,912	12,291	61.7%

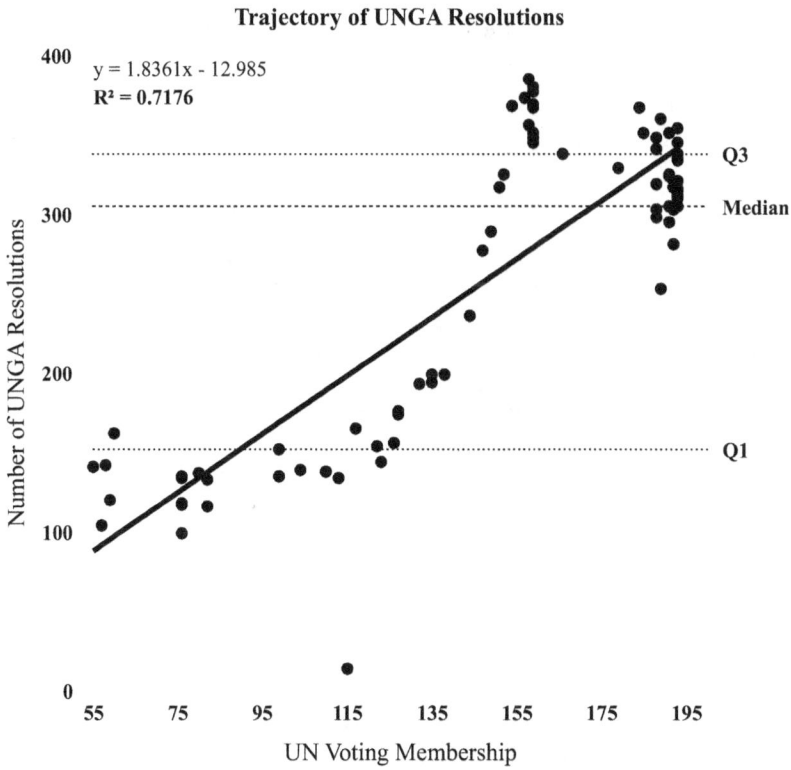

Trajectory of UNGA Resolutions

FIGURE 1   Trajectory of UNGA resolutions

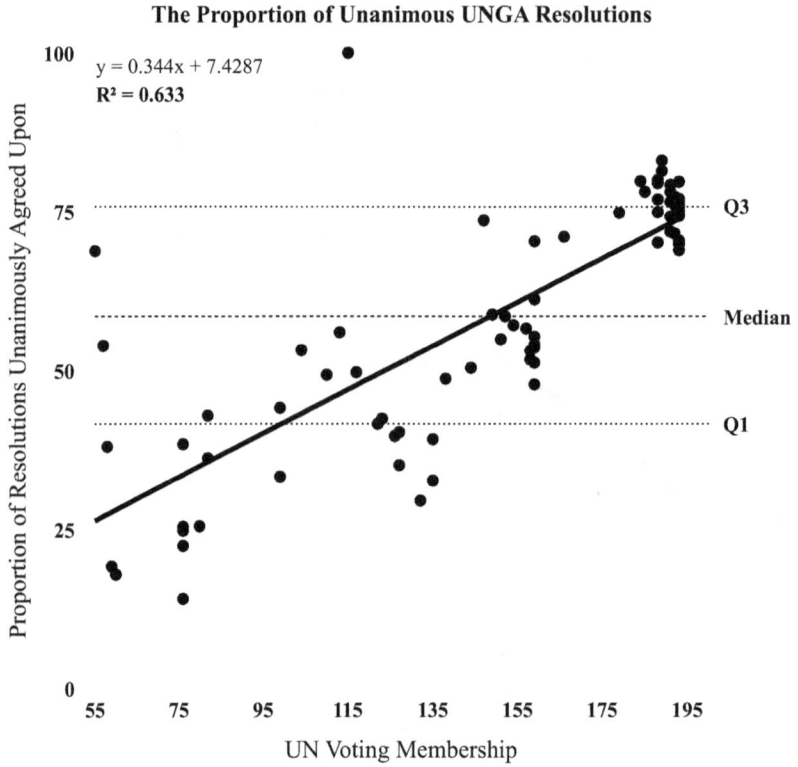

FIGURE 2   The proportion of unanimous UNGA resolutions

Bibliography

Primary Source Works

Declarations

The Non-Aligned Movement. "Declaration of the Heads of State or Government of Non-Aligned Countries." *1st Summit Conference of Heads of State or Government of the Non-Aligned Movement.* September 6, 1961. Available at: https://www.ris.org.in/.

Government Archives

Battle, Lucius. *Memorandum From the Assistant Secretary of State for International Organization Affairs (Cleveland) to Secretary of State.* Kennedy Library, National Security Files, Subjects Series, United Nations (General), 12/61 Box 310. December 22, 1961. Department of State, Office of the Historian, United States of America. Available from: https://history.state.gov/historicaldocuments/frus1961-63v25/d191.

Brown, Sherrod, Klobouchar, Amy, Franken, A. L., Leahy, Patrick, Markey, Edward, Reed, Jack, van Hollen, Chris, and Whitehouse, Sheldon. Letter to President Donald Trump. United States Senate. October 31, 2017.

Bureau of International Organization Affairs for President Kenney. *Memorandum Prepared in the Bureau of Organization Affairs for President Kennedy.* Kennedy Library, National Security Files, Subjects Series, United Nations (General), 1/61–7/61, Box 310. July 24, 1961. Department of State, Office of the Historian, United States of America. Available from: https://history.state.gov/historicaldocuments/frus1961-63v25/d174.

Canada Cabinet Conclusions. *Canada Cabinet Conclusions* (CCC Volume 18–288). *Seventh Session of the General Assembly, First Part, October 14–December 21, 1952. Instructions to the Canadian Delegation. Memorandum from Secretary of state for External Affairs to Cabinet.* Department of External Affairs, Government of Canada. October 9, 1952. Available from: www.international.gc.ca.

Canada Cabinet Conclusions. *Canada Cabinet Conclusions* (CCC Volume 18–289). *Seventh Session of the General Assembly, First Part, October 14–December 21, 1952. Instructions to the Canadian Delegation. South Africa: Race Conflict.* Department of External Affairs, Government of Canada. Available from: www.international.gc.ca.

Canada Cabinet Conclusions. *Canada Cabinet Conclusions* (CCC Volume 2745). *United Nations Resolution on Treatment of Indians in South Africa.* December 12, 1959. Department of External Affairs, Government of Canada. Available from: www.international.gc.ca.

Canada Cabinet Conclusions. *Canada Cabinet Conclusions* (CCC Volume 2746). *Policy Towards South Africa.* November 4, 1960. Department of External Affairs, Government of Canada. Available from: www.international.gc.ca.

Canada Cabinet Conclusions. *Canada Cabinet Conclusions* (CCC Volume 6176). *South Africa, Canadian Policy.* February 11, 1961. Department of External Affairs, Government of Canada Available from: www.international.gc.ca.

Canada Cabinet Conclusions. *Canada Cabinet Conclusions* (CCC Volume 6176). *South Africa, Canadian Policy.* March 2, 1961. Department of External Affairs, Government of Canada. Available from: www.international.gc.ca.

Canada Cabinet Conclusions. *Canada Cabinet Conclusions* (CCC Volume 6176). *South Africa, Canadian Policy.* March 9, 1961. Department of External Affairs, Government of Canada. Available from: www.international.gc.ca.

Canada Cabinet Conclusions. *Canada Cabinet Conclusions* (CCC Volume 2746). *South Africa–Situation in South Africa.* March 31, 1961. Department of External Affairs, Government of Canada. Available from: www.international.gc.ca.

Cleveland, Harlan. *Notes on Discussions: U.S. Strategy in the 16th General Assembly.* Schlesinger Papers, UN Speeches, 8/2/61–8/11/61, Box WH22. August 5, 1961. Department of State, Office of the Historian, United States of America. Available from: https://history.state.gov/historicaldocuments/frus1961-63v25/d177.

Cleveland, Harlan. *Memorandum From the Assistant Secretary of State for International Organization Affairs (Cleveland) to Secretary of State.* Kennedy Library, National Security Files, Subjects Series, United Nations (General), 12/61 Box 310. December 22, 1961. Department of State, Office of the Historian, United States of America. Available from: https://history.state.gov/historicaldocuments/frus1961-63v25/d193.

Cleveland, Harlan. *Memorandum From the Assistant Secretary of State for International Organization Affairs (Cleveland) to Secretary of State Rusk.* National Archives and Records Administration, RG 59, Central Files 1960–63, 320/3–862. March 8, 1962. Department of State, Office of the Historian, United States of America. Available from: https://history.state.gov/historicaldocuments/frus1961-63v25/d197.

Cleveland, Harlan, Wilson, Thomas W., and Sisco Joseph J. *Memorandum Prepared in the Bureau of International Organization Affairs for President Kennedy.* Kennedy Library, National Security Files, Subjects Series, United Nations (General), 1/61–7/61, Box 310. Secret-Confidential Without Tab C. Drafted by Cleveland and Thomas W. Wilson (IO) and Joseph J. Sisco (IO/UNP). July 24, 1961. Department of State, Office of the Historian, United States of America. Available from: https://history.state.gov/historicaldocuments/frus1961-63v25/d174.

Department of External Affairs, Government of Canada. *Memorandum from Permanent Delegation to the United Nations to Secretary of State for External Affairs* (DEA/5475-DW-19-40). *Seventh Session of the General Assembly, First Part, October 14-December 21, 1952. Instructions to the Canadian Delegation. Ad Hoc Committee—Race Conflict in South Africa (Item 66)*. November 27, 1952. Department of External Affairs, Government of Canada. Available from: www.international.gc.ca.

Department of External Affairs, Government of Canada. *Extract from Final Report on the Twelfth Session of the General Assembly, New York, September 17 to December 14, 1957* (DEA/5475-DW-52-D-40). Department of External Affairs, Government of Canada. Available from: www.international.gc.ca.

Department of External Affairs, Government of Canada. *Extract from Final Report on the Fourteenth Session of the General Assembly* (DEA/6-1959/2). *Question of Race Conflict in South Africa Resulting from the Policies of Apartheid of the Government of the Union of South Africa*. October 8, 1959. Department of External Affairs, Government of Canada. Available from: www.international.gc.ca.

Department of External Affairs, Government of Canada. *Memorandum from Under-Secretary of State for External Affairs to Secretary of State for External Affairs. Resumed Fifteenth Session of the General Assembly, March 7 to April 22, 1961*. Apartheid Item at the General Assembly. March 28, 1961. Department of External Affairs, Government of Canada. Available from: www.international.gc.ca.

Diplomatic Security Service from Washington, D.C., United States of America. Public domain. "Hallway of Flags in the United Nations Building in New York City." Wikimedia Commons. Available from: https://commons.wikimedia.org.

Diefenbaker, John. 1960. *Canada, House of Commons Debates*. March 25, 1960. Cols. 2448–2449. *Canada in World Affairs 1959–1961*, R.A. Preston. Cited in Tennyson, Douglas. *Canadian Relations with South Africa: A Diplomatic History*. University Press of America, 1982.

Embassy of the United States of America in Abu Dhabi, the United Arab Emirates. "Démarche Instructions for Cuba Embargo Resolution at the UNGA." Cable from the Embassy of the United States of America in the Abu Dhabi, the United Arab Emirates to the United States Department of State. Reference: ABUDHABI1812_a. October 31, 2007. Available from: wikileaks.org.

Embassy of the United States of America in Amman, Jordan. "Démarche Opposing Cuba's Resolution Against U.S. Embargo: Jordan." Cable from the Embassy of the United States of America in Amman, Jordan to the United States Department of State. Reference: 03AMMAN7088_a. October 30, 2003. Available from: https://wikile aks.org/dnc-emails/emailid/15861.

Embassy of the United States of America in Ashgabat, Turkmenistan. "Démarche on the Cuba's Resolution Condemning the U.S. Economic Embargo Against Cuba." Cable from the Embassy of the United States of America in Ashgabat, Turkmenistan to the United States Department of State. Reference: 07ASHGABAT1162_a. October 26, 2007. Available from: https://wikileaks.org/dnc-emails/emailid/15861.

Embassy of the United States of America in Ankara, Turkey. "Démarche Opposing Cuba's UN Resolution Against the Embargo." Cable from the Embassy of the United

States of America in Ankara, Turkey. 04ANKARA5823_a. October 14, 2004. Available from: wikileaks.org.

Embassy of the United States of America in Bangkok, Thailand. "Démarches Delivered: Cuba Embargo Resolution and Amendment." Cable from the Embassy of the United States of America in Bangkok, Thailand to the United States Department of State. November 8, 2006. Reference: 06BANGKOK6742_a. Available from: wikileaks.org.

Embassy of the United States of America in Belgrade, Serbia. "Serbian Support for EU's Decision to Vote Against Cuba Human Rights Amendment." Cable from the Embassy of the United States of America in Belgrade, Serbia to the United States Department of State. Reference: 06BELGRADE1849_a. November 1, 2007. Available from: wikileaks.org.

Embassy of the United States of America in Beijing, China. "China MFA on Cuba Embargo Resolution." Cable from the Embassy of the United States of America in Beijing, China to the United States Department of State. Reference: 07BEIJING6839_a. October 25, 2007. Available from: wikileaks.org.

Embassy of the United States of America in Bucharest, Romania. "Romania Démarche Delivered on Amending the Cuba Embargo Resolution." Cable from the Embassy of the United States of America in Bucharest, Romania to the United States Department of State. Reference: BUCHAREST001706_a. November 9, 2006. Available from: wikileaks.org.

Embassy of the United States of America in Dili, Timor-Leste. "Timor-Leste Will Vote For Resolution Condemning Cuba Embargo." Cable from the Embassy of the United States of America in Dili, Timor-Leste to the United States Department of State. October 26, 2007. Reference: 07DILI352_a. Available from: wikileaks.org.

Embassy of the United States of America in Amsterdam, the Netherlands. "Netherlands/Cuba: Qualified Support at the EU and UN." Cable from the Embassy of the United States of America in the Hague, the Netherlands to the United States Department of State. Reference: THE HAGUE1957_a. November 1, 2007. Available from: wikileaks.org.

Embassy of the United States of America in Amsterdam, the Netherlands. "Netherlands/Cuba: EU Consensus Position on the Cuba Embargo Resolution." Cable from the Embassy of the United States of America in the Hague, the Netherlands to the United States Department of State. Reference: 06THEHAGUE2385_a. November 6, 2006. Available from: wikileaks.org.

Embassy of the United States of America in the Astana, Kazakhstan. "Kazakhstan Will Support Cuba Embargo Resolution." Cable from the Embassy of the United States of America in the Astana, Kazakhstan to the United States Department of State. Reference: 07ASTANA2958_a. November 1, 2007. Available from: wikileaks.org.

Embassy of the United States of America in the Astana, Kazakhstan. "Kazakhstan to Consider US Position on UNGA Human Rights and Cuba Embargo Resolutions." Cable from the Embassy of the United States of America in the Astana, Kazakhstan to the United States Department of State. Reference: 06ASTANA503_a. November 8, 2006. Available from: wikileaks.org.

Embassy of the United States of America in Athens, Greece. "Greek MFA on June GAERC Issues." Cable from the Embassy of the United States of America in Athens, Greece to the United States Department of State. Reference: 08ATHENS845_a. June 13, 2008. Available from: wikileaks.org.

Embassy of the United States of America in Athens, Greece. "LIBERTAD ACT: Greece and Cuba." Cable from the Embassy of the United States of America in Athens, Greece to the United States Department of State. Reference: 08ATHENS728_a. May 27, 2008. Available from: wikileaks.org.

Embassy of the United States of America in Athens, Greece. "Greece Sticks to EU Line on Cuba." Cable from the Embassy of the United States of America in Athens, Greece to the United States Department of State. Reference: ATHENS2133_a. May 27, 2008. Available from: wikileaks.org.

Embassy of the United States of America in Bandar Seri Begawan, Brunei. "Brunei Likely to Support Cuba Embargo Resolution." Cable from the Embassy of the United States of America in Bandar Seri Begawan, Brunei to the United States Department of State. October 26, 2007. Reference: 07BANDARSERIBEGAWAN321_a. Available from: wikileaks.org.

Embassy of the United States of America in Copenhagen, Denmark. "Danes Welcome Proposals on Cuba, Unmoved on Embargo." Cable from the Embassy of the United States of America in Copenhagen, Denmark to the United States Department of State. Reference: Copenhagen988_a. October 26, 2007. Available from: wikileaks. org.

Embassy of the United States of America in Dar Es Salam, Tanzania. "Tanzania Supports Cuba Embargo Resolution Without Amendment." Cable from the Embassy of the United States of America in Dar Es Salam, Tanzania to the United States Department of State. Reference: 06DARESSALAAM1803_a. Available from: wikileaks.org.

Embassy of the United States of America in Dublin, Ireland. "Irish Likely to Support Cuba's Resolution Against the Embargo." Cable from the Embassy of the United States of America in Dublin, Ireland to the United States Department of State. Reference: 04DUBLIN2610_a. October 22, 2004. Available from: wikileaks.org.

Embassy of the United States of America in Hanoi, Vietnam. "Démarches on Cuba Embargo Resolution Delivered." Cable from the Embassy of the United States of America in Hanoi, Vietnam to the United States Department of State. Reference: 06HANOI2833_a. November 8, 2006. Available from: wikileaks.org.

Embassy of the United States of America in Guatemala City, Guatemala. "Guatemala: Démarche Opposing Cuba's UN Resolution Against the Embargo." Cable from the Embassy of the United States of America in Guatemala City, Guatemala to the United States Department of State. Reference: 04GUATEMALA2636_a. October 18, 2004. Available from: wikileaks.org.

Embassy of the United States of America in Jakarta, Indonesia. "UNGA: Démarches to Indonesia on Cuba Embargo, Country Resolutions." Cable from the Embassy of the United States of America in Jakarta, Indonesia to the United States Department of State. Reference: 06JAKARTA13171_a. October 25, 2007. Available from: wikileaks. org.

Embassy of the United States of America in Kathmandu, Nepal. "Démarche Delivered On Opposing Cuba Embargo Resolution." Cable from the Embassy of the United States of America in Kathmandu, Nepal to the United States Department of State. Reference: KATHMANDU 002960. November 3, 2006.

Embassy of the United States of America in Kigali, Rwanda. "Rwanda Supports Rape Resolution, May Abstain on Cuba Resolution." Cable from the Embassy of the United States of America in Kigali, Rwanda to the United States Department of State. Reference: KIGALI979. October 27, 2007. Available from: wikileaks.org.

Embassy of the United States of America in Kuwait City, Kuwait. "Démarche Delivered: Opposing Cuba's UN Resolution Against the Embargo." Cable from the Embassy of the United States of America in Kuwait City, Kuwait to the United States Department of State. Reference: KUWAIT004964. October 29, 2003. Available from: wikileaks.org.

Embassy of the United States of America in Kuwait City, Kuwait. "Démarche Delivered: Immediate Action Démarche on Amending the Cuba Embargo Resolution." Cable from the Embassy of the United States of America in Kuwait City, Kuwait to the United States Department of State. Reference: 06KUWAIT4421_a. November 8, 2006. Available from: wikileaks.org.

Embassy of the United States of America in Lisbon, Portugal. "Portugal Does not Agree on Cuba Embargo and One Retaliatory Resolution in UN Third Committee." Cable from the Embassy of the United States of America in Lisbon, Portugal to the United States Department of State. Reference: 06LISBON2544_a. November 9, 2006. Available from: wikileaks.org.

Embassy of the United States of America in Lusaka, Zambia. "More on Zambian Preparations for UNGA, UN Human Rights Council and UNESCO Vote." Cable from the Embassy of the United States of America in Lusaka, Zambia to the United States Department of State. Reference: LUSAKA 000649. September 22, 2009. Available from: wikileaks.org.

Embassy of the United States of America in Luxembourg. "Luxembourg to Consider Australian Cuba Embargo Resolution." Cable from the Embassy of the

United States of America in Luxembourg to the United States Department of State. Reference: 06LUXEMBOURG598_a. November 6, 2006. Available from: wikileaks.org.

Embassy of the United States of America in Manila, the Philippines. "Philippines Will Continue its Support for UN Resolution Opposing Cuba Embargo." Cable from the Embassy of the United States of America in Manila, the Philippines to the United States Department of State. Reference: MANILA: 3546_a. October 26, 2007. Available from: wikileaks.org.

Embassy of the United States of America in Manama, Bahrain. "Bahrain Non-Committal on Cuba and China UNCHR Resolutions." Cable from the Embassy of the United States of America in Manama, Bahrain to the United States Department of State. April 6, 2004. Reference: 04MANAMA485_a. Available from: wikileaks.org.

Embassy of the United States of America in Manama, Bahrain. "Bahrain: Opposing Cuba's UN Resolution Against the Embargo." Cable from the Embassy of the United States of America in Manama, Bahrain to the United States Department of State. April 19, 2004. Reference: 04MANAMA1595_a. Available from: wikileaks.org.

Embassy of the United States of America in Manama, Bahrain. "Bahrain: Cuba Embargo Resolution and Australian Amendment." Cable from the Embassy of the United States of America in Manama, Bahrain to the United States Department of State. November 8, 2006. Reference: 06MANAMA1904_a. Available from: wikileaks.org.

Embassy of the United States of America in Ljubljana, Slovenia. "Slovenia on Cuba Embargo Resolution at UNGA." Cable from the Embassy of the United States of America in Ljubljana, Slovenia to the United States Department of State. October 25, 2007. Reference: 07LJUBLJANA672_a. Available from: wikileaks.org.

Embassy of the United States of America in Ljubljana, Slovenia. "Slovenia on Cuba Embargo Resolution at UNGA." Cable from the Embassy of the United States of America in Ljubljana, Slovenia to the United States Department of State. November 3, 2006. Reference: 06LJUBLJANA709_a. Available from: wikileaks.org.

Embassy of the United States of America in Muscat, Oman. "Cuba Embargo and Country Specific Human Rights Resolutions at the UN: Oman." Cable from the Embassy of the United States of America in Muscat, Oman to the United States Department of State. November 6, 2006. Reference: 06MUSCAT1564_a. Available from: wikileaks.org.

Embassy of the United States of America in Muscat, Oman. "Amending the Cuba Embargo Resolution: Oman." Cable from the Embassy of the United States of America in Muscat, Oman to the United States Department of State. November 9, 2006. Reference: 06MUSCAT1572_a. Available from: wikileaks.org.

Embassy of the United States of America in Nassau, the Bahamas. "PM Candid, Unhelpful on UNGA Voting Démarche on Cuba." Cable from the Embassy of the

United States of America in Nassau, the Bahamas to the United States Department of State. Reference: 08NASSAU709_a. October 7, 2008. Available from: wikileaks.org.

Embassy of the United States of America in Nassau, the Bahamas. "Démarche Delivered: Cuba Embargo Resolution." Cable from the Embassy of the United States of America in Nassau, the Bahamas to the United States Department of State. Reference: 06NASSAU1704_a. November 14, 2006. Available from: wikileaks.org.

Embassy of the United States of America in Prague, Czech Republic. "Czech Response to June 13 GAERC Démarche." Cable from the Embassy of the United States of America in Prague, Czech Republic to the United States Department of State. Reference: 05PRAGUE888_a. June 10, 2005. Available from: wikileaks.org.

Embassy of the United States of America in Prague, Czech Republic. "Czechs Plan to Change Style, but not Substance, of their Cuba Policy." Cable from the Embassy of the United States of America in Prague, Czech Republic to the United States Department of State. January 22, 2007. Reference: 07PRAGUE57_a. Available from: wikileaks.org.

Embassy of the United States of America in Prague, Czech Republic. "In-Depth Readout of EU's Cuba Compromise." Cable from the Embassy of the United States of America in Prague, Czech Republic to the United States Department of State. July 1, 2005. Reference: 05PRAGUE1006_a. Available from: wikileaks.org.

Embassy of the United States of America in Prague, Czech Republic. "Czechs Will Support Amendment to Cuba Embargo Resolution." Cable from the Embassy of the United States of America in Prague, Czech Republic to the United States Department of State. November 8, 2006. Reference: 06PRAGUE1386_a. Available from: wikileaks.org.

Embassy of the United States of America in Pretoria, South Africa. "South Africa Unlikely to Push for Democratic Transition in Cuba." Cable from the Embassy of the United States of America in Prague, South Africa to the United States Department of State. August 15, 2006. Reference: 06PRETORIA3342_a. Available from: wikileaks.org.

Embassy of the United States of America in Rome, Italy. "Italy Supports Embargo Resolution, Appreciates Human Rights Proposals." Cable from the Embassy of the United States of America in Rome, Italy to the United States Department of State. October 26, 2007. Reference: ROME2249_a. Available from: wikileaks.org.

Embassy of the United States of America in Rome, Italy. "Italy Voting with the EU on UN Third Committee, Cuba Resolutions." Cable from the Embassy of the United States of America in Rome, Italy to the United States Department of State. November 9, 2006. Reference: 06ROME3051_a. Available from: wikileaks.org.

Embassy of the United States of America in Panama City, Panama. "Panama Will Consider Cuba Resolution and Amendment." Cable from the Embassy of the United

States of America in Panama City, Panama to the United States Department of State. November 8, 2006. Reference: 06PANAMA2189_a. Available from: wikileaks.org.

Embassy of the United States of America in Saana, Yemen. "Démarche Delivered: Cuba's UN Resolution against the Embargo." Cable from the Embassy of the United States of America in Saana, Yemen to the United States Department of State. October 20, 2004. Reference: 04SANAA2723_a. Available from: wikileaks.org.

Embassy of the United States of America in San Jose, Costa Rica. "Costa Rica to vote Against Cuba Embargo Resolution." Cable from the Embassy of the United States of America in San Jose, Costa Rica to the United States Department of State. March 29, 2009. Reference: 07SANJOSE1927_a. Available from: wikileaks.org.

Embassy of the United States of America in San Jose, Costa Rica. "Costa Rica Full Diplomatic Relations with Cuba." Cable from the Embassy of the United States of America in San Jose, Costa Rica to the United States Department of State. October 31, 2007. Reference: 09SANJOSE225_a. Available from: wikileaks.org.

Embassy of the United States of America in San Jose, Costa Rica. "Costa Rica Not Likely to Oppose Cuba Embargo Resolution." Cable from the Embassy of the United States of America in San Jose, Costa Rica to the United States Department of State. March 25, 2009. Reference: 06SANJOSE2543_a. Available from: wikileaks.org.

Embassy of the United States of America in Sofia, Bulgaria. "Cuba Embargo Resolution: Bulgaria Still to Follow EU Line." Cable from the Embassy of the Embassy of the United States of America in Sofia, Bulgaria to the United States Department of State. November 8, 2006. 06SOFIA1541_a. Available from: wikileaks.org.

Embassy of the United States of America in Skopje, Macedonia. "Macedonia Will Follow EU Position on Cuba Embargo Resolution." Cable from the Embassy of the United States of America in Skopje, Macedonia to the United States Department of State. November 4, 2006. Reference: 06SKOPJE1057_a. Available from: wikileaks.org.

Embassy of the United States of America in Suva, Fiji. "Cuba's Jakarta Embassy Reaching out to Nauru." Cable from the Embassy of the United States of America to the United States Department of State. Reference: 07SUVA146_a. March 4, 2007. Available from: wikileaks.org.

Embassy of the United States of America in Warsaw, Poland. "Cuba Embargo Resolution—Poland to Support the Common EU Position." Cable from the Embassy of the United States of America to the United States Department of State. October 26, 2007. Reference: WARSAW2157_a. Available from: wikileaks.org.

Embassy of the United States of America in Warsaw, Poland. "Poland will Follow EU Common Position on Cuba Human Rights Resolution." Cable from the Embassy of the United States of America in Warsaw, Poland to the United States Department of State. November 9, 2006. Reference: 06WARSAW2370_a. Available from: wikileaks.org.

Embassy of the United States of America in Tblisi, Georgia. "Georgia Likely to Support Cuba Embargo Resolution." Cable from the Embassy of the United States of America in Tblisi, Georgia to the United States Department of State. October 26, 2007. Reference: 07TBILISI2660_a. Available from: wikileaks.org.

Embassy of the United States of America in Vienna, Austria. "Démarche to Austria on Amending the Cuba Embargo Resolution—Cubans to Seek No-Action on Amendment." Cable from the Embassy of the United States of America in Vienna, Austria to the United States Department of State. Reference: 06VIENNA3272_a. November 8, 2006. Available from: wikileaks.org.

Embassy of the United States of America in Wellington, New Zealand. "New Zealand Position Unchanged on Cuba's UN Resolution Against the Embargo." Cable from the Embassy of the United States of America in Wellington, New Zealand to the United States Department of State. October 14, 2004. Reference: 04WELLINGTON861_a. Available from: wikileaks.org.

Embassy of the United States of America in Tokyo, Japan. "Japan Will Reconsider its Stance on Cuba Embargo Resolution." Cable from the Embassy of the United States of America in Tokyo, Japan to the United States Department of State. November 8, 2006. Reference: 06TOKYO6434_a. Available from: wikileaks.org.

Embassy of the United States of America in Quito, Ecuador. "Ecuador: Cuba Embargo UN Resolution Démarche." Cable from the Embassy of the United States of America in Quito, Ecuador to the United States Department of State. November 9, 2006. Reference: 06QUITO2736_a. Available from: wikileaks.org.

Fisher, Melia. "Hillary Clinton: The Cuba Embargo Needs To Go, Once And For All." Email received by John Podesta from Melia Fisher, *Hillary Clinton: The Cuba Embargo Needs To Go, Once And For All*, 31 July 2015. Available from: https://wikile aks.org/podesta-emails/emailid/21590.

Fisk, Daniel. "Update on Helms-Burton Implementation." Email received by Marc Thiesen, Bud Nance, Tom Kleine, and Gina Marie Lichacz from Daniel Fisk. May 28, 1996. Available from the Center for Legislative Archives in Washington D.C.

Fisk, Daniel. "Request from Ambassador Stuart Eisenhower Re: WTO Complaint on U.S. Cuba Policy." Email received by Senator Jessie Helms. April 9, 1997. Available from the Center for Legislative Archives in Washington D.C.

Green, Howard. *Memorandum from Secretary of State for External Affairs to Prime Minister* (J.G.D./MG01/XII/C/404). *South Africa and the Commonwealth.* February 24, 1961. Department of External Affairs, Government of Canada. Available from: www.international.gc.ca.

Leger, Jules. *Permanent Representative to North Atlantic Council to Secretary of State for External Affairs* (DEA/50271-M-40). November 22, 1961. Department of External Affairs, Government of Canada. Available from: www.international.gc.ca.

Lloyd, S. "Letter to H. Macmillan." January 2, 1960. *DO 35/10621.* Cited in Hyam, Ronald, and Peter Henshaw. *The Lion and the Springbok: Britain and South Africa Since the Boer War.* Cambridge University Press, 2003.

Macmillan, Harold. *Pointing the Way, 1959–1961.* London: Macmillan, 1972.

Menzies, Robert. "Letter to Dame Pattie." April 6, 1961. *MFP.* Cited in Martin, Allan, and Patsy Hardy. *Robert Menzies: A Life.* Melbourne University Press, 1993. ACLS Humanities E-Book. Available from: http://idiscover.lib.cam.ac.uk.

Murray, G.S. Memorandum from United Nations Division to Commonwealth Division. (DEA/7060–40). Memorandum from United Nations Division to Commonwealth Division. April 4, 1961. Department of External Affairs, Government of Canada. Available from: www.international.gc.ca.

Glazebrook, G. *Memorandum from Head, Commonwealth Division, to Under-Secretary of State for External Affairs.* DEA/50085-H-40. Meeting of Commonwealth Prime Ministers, London, May 3–13, 1960, and Preparations for the 1961 Meeting. Department of External Affairs, Government of Canada. Available from: www .international.gc.ca.

Glazebrook, G. *Memorandum from Under-Secretary of State for External Affairs to Prime Minister* (DEA/7060–40). April 4, 1961. Department of External Affairs, Government of Canada. Available from:www.international.gc.ca.

Green, Howard. *Secretary of State for External Affairs to Permanent Representative to United Nations* (DEA/50189-C-4). September 11, 1961. Department of External Affairs, Government of Canada. Available from: www.international.gc.ca.

Green, Howard. *Memorandum from Secretary of State for External Affairs to Prime Minister* (DEA/50189-C-40). November 16, 1961. Department of External Affairs, Government of Canada. Available from:www.international.gc.ca.

Larin, E.A. *Politicheskaia Istorii Kuba XX Veka.* Moscow, 2007, p. 164. Cited in Bain, Mervyn J. "Russo–Cuban Relations in the 1990s." *Diplomacy & Statecraft* 29.2 (2018): 255–273.

National Intelligence Estimate. *Attitudes of Key World Powers on Disarmament Issues* (NIE 4-2-61). April 6, 1961. President Lyndon B. Johnson Library. Available from: https://history.state.gov/historicaldocuments/frus1961-63v07/pg_35.

Prime Minister's Papers. PREM 11/3073. 1959–1950. The National Archives, UK. *Archives Direct.* Available from: http://www.archivesdirect.amdigital.co.uk/Documents/Deta ils/PREM%2011_3073.

Prime Minister's Papers. PREM 11/3112. 1960. The National Archives, UK. *Archives Direct.* Available from: https://www-archivesdirect-amdigital-co-uk.ezp.lib.cam.ac.uk /Documents/Details/PREM%2011_3112?SessionExpired=True.

Prime Minister's Papers. PREM 11/3598. 1961. The National Archives, UK. *Archives Direct.* Available from: http://www.archivesdirect.amdigital.co.uk/Documents/Deta ils/PREM 11_3598.

Prime Minister's Papers. PREM 11/3109. 1961. The National Archives, UK. *Archives Direct.* Available from: http://www.archivesdirect.amdigital.co.uk/Documents/Details /PREM 11_3109.

Pearson, Lester. "Letter to A.J. Pick." October 7, 1946. DEA Records, File 5600-40C, Vol. 1. Cited in Tennyson, Douglas. *Canadian Relations with South Africa: A Diplomatic History.* University Press of America, 1982, p. 117.

Pearson, Lester. Privy Council Office. *Instructions to the Canadian Delegation. Seventh Session of the General Assembly, First Part, October 14-December 21, 1952. Memorandum from Secretary of State for External Affairs to Cabinet* (PCO 288). October 8, 1952. Department of External Affairs, Government of Canada. Available from: www.international.gc.ca.

Rannenberg, Michael E. "Tittle III Suspension Packet." United States Department of State. The Centre for Legislative Archives, Washington D.C. January 3, 1997.

Robinson, H. B. *Memorandum from Special Assistant to Secretary of State for External Affairs to Secretary of State for External Affairs* (DEA/7060–40). *South African Items at the 1960 General Assembly.* October 14, 1960. Department of External Affairs, Government of Canada. Available from: www.international.gc.ca.

Robinson, H. B. *Memorandum from Special Assistant to Secretary of State for External Affairs to Under-Secretary of State for External Affairs* (DEA/50085-J-40). February 11, 1961. Department of External Affairs, Government of Canada. Available from: www .international.gc.ca.

Robinson, H. B. *Memorandum from Under-Secretary of State for External Affairs to Secretary of State for External Affairs* (DEA/50271-M-40). November 18, 1961. Department of External Affairs, Government of Canada. Available from: www .international.gc.ca.

"State Department Briefing." Copyright 1996 Federal Information Systems Corporation. Federal News Service. May 23, 1996. Available from the Center for Legislative Archives in Washington D.C.

Stevenson, Adlai. *Telegram From the Mission to the United Nations to the Department of State.* National Archives and Records Administration, RG 59, Central Files 1960–63, 230/6–161. Secret; Priority. June 1, 1961. Department of State, Office of the Historian, United States of America. Available from: https://history.state.gov/historicaldo cuments/frus1961-63v25/d171.

The White House. "Press Briefing by Press Secretary Josh Earnest, 4/27/2016." Email received by the Democratic National Convention Press. April 27, 2016. Available from: https://wikileaks.org/dnc-emails/emailid/15861.

Thiessen, Mark. "Statement on US-EU Negotiations on Helms-Burton: Memorandum for Senator Helms." Email received by Bud Nance from Mark Thiessen. April 11, 1997. Available from the Center for Legislative Archives in Washington D.C.

UK Government. "Foreign Secretary Calls for a United Response on the Salisbury Incident." *GOV.UK*. March 13, 2018. www.gov.uk/government/news/foreign-secret ary-calls-for-a-united-response.

UK Government. "Novichok Nerve Agent Use in Salisbury: UK Government Response." *GOV.UK*. March 26, 2018. www.gov.uk/government/news/novichok-nerve-agent-use -in-salisbury-uk-government-response.

United States Mission to the United Nations New York. "Joint Press Statement from the Permanent Representatives to the United Nations of the United States, United Kingdom, and France Following the Adoption." United States Mission to the United Nations New York. July 7, 2017. Available from: https://usun.usmission.gov/joint -press-statement-from-the-permanent-representatives-to-the-united-nations-of -the-united-states-united-kingdom-and-france-following-the-adoption/.

United States Department of State. "Démarching EU States for Human Rights Action on Cuba." Cable from the Department of State to the Embassy/Mission of the United States in Canberra, Ottawa, Brussels, Geneva, and New York. October 23, 2007. Reference: 07STATE147620_a. Available from: wikileaks.org.

United States Department of State. "Cuba/Italy: We Want to But We Can't." Cable from the Embassy of Italy in Havana to the United States Department of State. March 23, 2007. Reference: 07HAVANA298_a. Available from: wikileaks.org.

Media Interviews and Statements

DeLaurentis, Jeffrey. "7 Q's With Jeffrey DeLaurentis." *7 Q's With Jeffrey DeLaurentis | Magazine | The Harvard Crimson*, February 12, 2015, www.thecrimson.com/arti cle/2015/2/12/7-qs-with-jeffrey/.

Earnest, Josh, and Ben Rhodes. "Press Briefing by Press Secretary Josh Earnest and Deputy National Security Adviser Ben Rhodes." *The White House*, February 18, 2016, obamawhitehouse.archives.gov/the-press-office/2016/02/18/ press-briefing-press-secretary-josh-earnest-and-deputy-national-security.

Haley, Nikki. "The UN General Assembly's Shameful Support of Cuba." *The Miami Herald*. November 3, 2018. www.miamiherald.com/opinion/op-ed/article221038 435.html.

Jacobsen, Roberta. "Hearing on U.S.-Cuba Relations." C-Span.org, February 4, 2015, https://www.c-span.org/video/?324144-1/us-cuba-relations.

Pandit, Vijayalakshmi. "Statement by Mrs. Vijayalakshmi Pandit, Leader of the Indian Delegation, at meeting of the Joint Committee of the First and Sixth Committees of the United Nations General Assembly, 26 November 1946." *South Africa History Online* (SAHO). https://www.sahistory.org.za/archive/i-have-written-it-es-reddy-fat ima-meer-international-support-uno-1946.

Power, Samantha. "Remarks at a UN General Assembly Meeting on the Cuba Embargo." *Belfer Center for Science and International Affairs*, October 26, 2016,

www.belfercenter.org/publication/remarks-ambassador-samantha-power-un-gene
ral-assembly-meeting-cuba-embargo.

Rhodes, Ben. "President Obama Is Going to Cuba. Here's Why." Medium, February
18, 2016, medium.com/@rhodes44/president-obama-is-going-to-cuba-here-s-why
-41ecdc0586d8.

Rhodes, Ben. "US-Cuba Thaw: Ben Rhodes on "Frozen" Relations under Trump—
BBC News." Youtube.com, December 20, 2017, https://www.youtube.com/watch?v
=npUGy4EUh-4\.

Rhodes, Ben. "CCTV Exclusive: Ben Rhodes on New US-Cuba Future." CGTN America,
July 20, 2015. https://america.cgtn.com/2015/07/20/cctv-exclusive-ben-rhodes-on
-us-cuba-new-future.

Rice, Susan. "Susan Rice Discusses U.S. Policy Toward Cuba." C-Span, October 14, 2016,
www.c-span.org/video/?416911-1%2Fsusan-rice-discusses-us-policy-cuba.

Sengupta, Kim. "We are Desperate for Money: Pakistan's Imran Khan flies into political
storm in Saudi Arabia." *The Independent,* October 22, 2018, https://www.independ
ent.co.uk/news/world/asia/pakistan-imran-khan-saudi-khashoggi-trump-addr
ess-imf-economy-a8595206.html.

Memoirs

Burns, Eedson Louis Millard. *A Seat at the Table: The Struggle for Disarmament.* Irwin
Publishing, 1972.

Cordier, Andrew and Harrelson, Max. *Public Papers of the Secretaries General of the
United Nations. Volume 6.* Columbia University Press, 2010.

Dean, Arthur H. *Test Ban and Disarmament: The Path of Negotiation.* Vol. 401.
New York: Published for Council on Foreign Relations by Harper & Row, 1966.

Diefenbaker, John G. *One Canada: The Crusading Years 1895–1956.* Vol. 1. Macmillan of
Canada, 1975.

Macmillan, Henry. *Pointing the Way 1959–1961.* Macmillan, 1972.

McCloy, John J. "Balance Sheet on Disarmament." *Foreign Affairs* 40.3 (1962): 339–359.

Meiring, Piet. *Inside Information.* Howard Timmins, 1973.

Menzies, Robert. *Afternoon Light: Some Memories of Men and Events.* Cassell and
Company Ltd., 1968.

Pankin, Boris. The Last Hundred Days of the Soviet Union. Tauris, 1996.

Power, Samantha. *The Education of an Idealist: A Memoir.* HarperLuxe, an Imprint of
HarperCollins Publishers, 2019.

Rhodes, Ben. *The World As It Is: A Memoir of the Obama White House.* Random House
Trade Paperbacks, 2019.

Robinson, Henry. *Diefenbaker's World: A Populist in Foreign Affairs.* University of
Toronto Press, 1989.

Urquhart, Brian. *A Life in Peace and War.* Weidenfeld and Nicolson, 1987.

Seminars

Baird, John. "Canada and the European Crisis with the Hon. John Baird." Forum on Geopolitics. Department of Politics and International Studies. Peterhouse College, University of Cambridge. November 1, 2018.

Official Records of the UNGA Ad Hoc Political Committee

United Nations, General Assembly. *Official Records of the 43rd Meeting of the Ad Hoc Political Committee.* A/AC.38/SR.43 (1950). Available from: UNdocs.org.

United Nations, General Assembly. *Official Records of the 47th Meeting of the Ad Hoc Political Committee.* A/AC.38/SR.47 (1950). Available from: UNdocs.org.

United Nations, General Assembly. *Official Records of the 7th Meeting of the Ad Hoc Political Committee.* A/AC.61/SR.7 (1952). Available from: UNdocs.org.

United Nations, General Assembly. *Official Records of the 32nd Meeting of the Ad Hoc Political Committee.* A/AC.53/SR.32 (1952). Available from: UNdocs.org.

United Nations, General Assembly. *Official Records of the 10th Meeting of the Ad Hoc Political Committee.* A/AC.61/SR.10 (1952). Available from: UNdocs.org.

United Nations, General Assembly. *Official Records of the 11th Meeting of the Ad Hoc Political Committee.* A/AC.61/SR.11 (1952). Available from: UNdocs.org.

United Nations, General Assembly. *Official Records of the 12th Meeting of the Ad Hoc Political Committee.* A/AC.61/SR.12 (1952). Available from: UNdocs.org.

United Nations, General Assembly. *Official Records of the 13th Meeting of the Ad Hoc Political Committee.* A/AC.61/SR.13 (1952). Available from: UNdocs.org.

United Nations, General Assembly. *Official Records of the 14th Meeting of the Ad Hoc Political Committee.* A/AC.61/SR.14 (1952). Available from: UNdocs.org.

United Nations, General Assembly. *Official Records of the 15th Meeting of the Ad Hoc Political Committee.* A/AC.61/SR.15 (1952). Available from: UNdocs.org.

United Nations, General Assembly. *Official Records of the 16th Meeting of the Ad Hoc Political Committee.* A/AC.61/SR.16 (1952). Available from: UNdocs.org.

United Nations, General Assembly. *Official Records of the 17th Meeting of the Ad Hoc Political Committee.* A/AC.61/SR.17 (1952). Available from: UNdocs.org.

United Nations, General Assembly. *Official Records of the 18th Meeting of the Ad Hoc Political Committee.* A/AC.61/SR.18 (1952). Available from: UNdocs.org.

United Nations, General Assembly. *Official Records of the 19th Meeting of the Ad Hoc Political Committee.* A/AC.61/SR.19 (1952). Available from: UNdocs.org.

United Nations, General Assembly. *Official Records of the 20h Meeting of the Ad Hoc Political Committee.* A/AC.61/SR.20 (1952). Available from: UNdocs.org.

United Nations, General Assembly. *Official Records of the 21st Meeting of the Ad Hoc Political Committee.* A/AC.61/SR.21 (1952). Available from: UNdocs.org.

United Nations, General Assembly. *Official Records of the 32nd Meeting of the Ad Hoc Political Committee.* A/AC.53/SR. 32 (1952). Available from: UNdocs.org.

United Nations, General Assembly. *Official Records of the 33rd Meeting of the Ad Hoc Political Committee.* A/AC.53/SR. 33 (1952). Available from: UNdocs.org.

United Nations, General Assembly. *Official Records of the 35th Meeting of the Ad Hoc Political Committee.* A/AC.72/SR. 35 (1953). Available from: UNdocs.org.

United Nations, General Assembly. *Official Records of the 36th Meeting of the Ad Hoc Political Committee.* A/AC.72/SR. 36 (1953). Available from: UNdocs.org.

United Nations, General Assembly. *Official Records of the 39th Meeting of the Ad Hoc Political Committee.* A/AC.72/SR. 39 (1953). Available from: UNdocs.org.

United Nations, General Assembly. *Official Records of the 44th Meeting of the Ad Hoc Political Committee.* A/AC.76/SR.44 (1954). Available from: UNdocs.org.

United Nations, General Assembly. *Official Records of the 45th Meeting of the Ad Hoc Political Committee.* A/AC.76/SR.45 (1954). Available from: UNdocs.org.

United Nations, General Assembly. *Official Records of the 46th Meeting of the Ad Hoc Political Committee.* A/AC.76/SR.46 (1954). Available from: UNdocs.org.

United Nations, General Assembly. *Official Records of the 47th Meeting of the Ad Hoc Political Committee.* A/AC.76/SR.47 (1954). Available from: UNdocs.org.

United Nations, General Assembly. *Official Records of the 90th Meeting of the Ad Hoc Political Committee.* A/AC.76/SR.90 (1954). Available from: UNdocs.org.

United Nations, General Assembly. *Official Records of the 8th Meeting of the Ad Hoc Political Committee.* A/AC.80/SR.8 (1955). Available from: UNdocs.org.

United Nations, General Assembly. *Official Records of the 12th Meeting of the Ad Hoc Political Committee.* A/AC.80/SR.12 (1954). Available from: UNdocs.org.

Official Records of the UNGA Joint Committee of the First and Sixth Committees

United Nations, General Assembly. Official Records of the Second Part of the First Session of the General Assembly: Joint Committee of the First and Sixth Committees. A/C.1&6/SR.1–6 (1946). Available from: UNdocs.org.

Official Records of the UNGA Plenary Meetings

United Nations, General Assembly. *Provisional Record of the 6th Plenary Meeting of the General Assembly.* A/PV.6 (1946). Available from: UNdocs.org.

United Nations, General Assembly. *Provisional Record of the 7th Plenary Meeting of the General Assembly.* A/PV.7 (1946). Available from: UNdocs.org.

United Nations, General Assembly. *Provisional Record of the 8th Plenary Meeting of the General Assembly.* A/PV.8 (1946). Available from: UNdocs.org.

United Nations, General Assembly. *Provisional Record of the 9th Plenary Meeting of the General Assembly.* A/PV.9 (1946). Available from: UNdocs.org.

United Nations, General Assembly. *Summary Record of the 17th Plenary Meeting of the General Assembly.* A/PV.17 (1946). Available from: UNdocs.org.

United Nations, General Assembly. *Provisional Record of the 37th Plenary Meeting of the General Assembly.* A/PV.37 (1946). Available from: UNdocs.org.

United Nations, General Assembly. *Summary Record of the 46th Plenary Meeting of the General Assembly.* A/PV.46 (1946). Available from: UNdocs.org.

United Nations, General Assembly. *Provisional Record of the 47th Plenary Meeting of the General Assembly.* A/PV.47 (1946). Available from: UNdocs.org.

United Nations, General Assembly. *Provisional Record of the 48th Plenary Meeting of the General Assembly.* A/PV.48 (1946). Available from: UNdocs.org.

United Nations, General Assembly. *Provisional Record of the 50th Plenary Meeting of the General Assembly.* A/PV.50 (1946). Available from: UNdocs.org.

United Nations, General Assembly. *Provisional Record of the 51st Plenary Meeting of the General Assembly.* A/PV.51 (1946). Available from: UNdocs.org.

United Nations, General Assembly. *Provisional Record of the 52nd Plenary Meeting of the General Assembly.* A/PV.52 (1946). Available from: UNdocs.org.

United Nations, General Assembly. *Provisional Record of the 85th Plenary Meeting of the General Assembly.* A/PV.85 (1946). Available from: UNdocs.org.

United Nations, General Assembly. *Summary Record of the 101st Plenary Meeting of the General Assembly.* A/PV.101 (1947). Available from: UNdocs.org.

United Nations, General Assembly. *Provisional Record of the 119th Plenary Meeting of the General Assembly.* A/PV.119 (1947). Available from: UNdocs.org.

United Nations, General Assembly. *Provisional Record of the 120th Plenary Meeting of the General Assembly.* A/PV.120 (1947). Available from: UNdocs.org.

United Nations, General Assembly. *Provisional Record of the 121st Plenary Meeting of the General Assembly.* A/PV.121 (1947). Available from: UNdocs.org.

United Nations, General Assembly. *Summary Record of the 157th Plenary Meeting of the General Assembly.* A/PV.157 (1948). Available from: UNdocs.org.

United Nations, General Assembly. *Provisional Record of the 183rd Plenary Meeting of the General Assembly.* A/PV.183 (1948). Available from: UNdocs.org.

United Nations, General Assembly. *Provisional Record of the 213th Plenary Meeting of the General Assembly.* A/PV.213 (1949). Available from: UNdocs.org.

United Nations, General Assembly. *Provisional Record of the 315th Plenary Meeting of the General Assembly.* A/PV.315 (1950). Available from: UNdocs.org.

United Nations, General Assembly. *Provisional Record of the 358th Plenary Meeting of the General Assembly.* A/PV.358 (1952). Available from: UNdocs.org.

United Nations, General Assembly. *Provisional Record of the 360th Plenary Meeting of the 6th Session of the General Assembly.* A/PV.360 (1952). Available from: UNdocs.org.

United Nations, General Assembly. *Provisional Record of the 381st Plenary Meeting of the General Assembly.* A/PV.381 (1952). Available from: UNdocs.org.

United Nations, General Assembly. *Provisional Record of the 401st Plenary Meeting of the 7th Session of the General Assembly.* A/PV.401 (1952). Available from: UNdocs.org.

United Nations, General Assembly. *Provisional Record of the 401st Plenary Meeting of the General Assembly.* A/PV.401 (1952). Available from: UNdocs.org.

United Nations, General Assembly. *Provisional Record of the 497th Plenary Meeting of the General Assembly.* A/PV.497 (1954). Available from: UNdocs.org.

United Nations, General Assembly. *Provisional Record of the 589th Plenary Meeting of the General Assembly.* A/PV.589 (1956). Available from: UNdocs.org.

United Nations, General Assembly. *Provisional Record of the 687th Plenary Meeting of the General Assembly.* A/PV.687 (1957). Available from: UNdocs.org.

United Nations, General Assembly. *Provisional Record of the 693rd Plenary Meeting of the General Assembly.* A/PV.693 (1957). Available from: UNdocs.org.

United Nations, General Assembly. *Provisional Record of the 697th Plenary Meeting of the General Assembly.* A/PV.697 (1957). Available from: UNdocs.org.

United Nations, General Assembly. *Provisional Record of the 723rd Plenary Meeting of the General Assembly.* A/PV.723 (1957). Available from: UNdocs.org.

United Nations, General Assembly. *Provisional Record of the 751st Plenary Meeting of the General Assembly.* A/PV.751 (1958). Available from: UNdocs.org.

United Nations, General Assembly. *Provisional Record of the 755th Plenary Meeting of the General Assembly.* A/PV.755 (1958). Available from: UNdocs.org.

United Nations, General Assembly. *Provisional Record of the 758th Plenary Meeting of the General Assembly.* A/PV.758 (1958). Available from: UNdocs.org.

United Nations, General Assembly. *Provisional Record of the 797th Plenary Meeting of the General Assembly.* A/PV.797 (1959). Available from: UNdocs.org.

United Nations, General Assembly. *Provisional Record of the 871st Plenary Meeting of the General Assembly.* A/PV.871 (1960). Available from: UNdocs.org.

United Nations, General Assembly. *Provisional Record of the 877th Plenary Meeting of the General Assembly.* A/PV.877 (1959). Available from: UNdocs.org.

United Nations, General Assembly. *Provisional Record of the 888th Plenary Meeting of the General Assembly.* A/PV.888 (1960). Available from: UNdocs.org.

United Nations, General Assembly. *Provisional Record of the 981st Plenary Meeting of the General Assembly.* A/PV.981 (1961). Available from: UNdocs.org.

United Nations, General Assembly. *Provisional Record of the 1063rd Plenary Meeting of the General Assembly.* A/PV.1063 (1961). Available from: UNdocs.org.

United Nations, General Assembly. *Provisional Record of the 1192nd Plenary Meeting of the General Assembly.* A/PV.1192 (1963). Available from: UNdocs.org.

United Nations, General Assembly. *Provisional Record of the 1265th Plenary Meeting of the General Assembly.* A/PV.1265 (1964). Available from: UNdocs.org.

United Nations, General Assembly. *Provisional Record of the 1484th Plenary Meeting of the General Assembly.* A/PV.1484 (1966). Available from: UNdocs.org.

United Nations, General Assembly. *Provisional Record of the 84th Plenary Meeting of the 33rd Session of the General Assembly.* A/33/PV.84 (1978). Available from: UNdocs.org.

United Nations, General Assembly. *Provisional Record of the 97th Plenary Meeting of the 34th Session of the General Assembly.* A/34/PV.97 (1979). Available from: UNdocs.org.

United Nations, General Assembly. *Provisional Record of the 94th Plenary Meeting of the 35th Session of the General Assembly.* A/34/PV.97 (1980). Available from: UNdocs.org.

United Nations, General Assembly. *Provisional Record of the 91st Plenary Meeting of the 36th Session of the General Assembly.* A/36/PV.91 (1981). Available from: UNdocs.org.

United Nations, General Assembly. *Provisional Record of the 101st Plenary Meeting of the 37th Session of the General Assembly.* A/37/PV.101 (1982). Available from: UNdocs.org.

United Nations, General Assembly. *Provisional Record of the 1st Plenary Meeting of the 46th Session of the General Assembly.* A/46/PV.1 (1991). Available from: UNdocs.org.

United Nations, General Assembly. *Provisional Record of the 70th Plenary Meeting of the 47th Session of the General Assembly.* A/47/PV.70 (1992). Available from: UNdocs.org.

United Nations, General Assembly. *Provisional Record of the 48th Plenary Meeting of the 48th Session of the General Assembly.* A/48/PV.48 (1993). Available from: UNdocs.org.

United Nations, General Assembly. *Provisional Record of the 45th Plenary Meeting of the 49th Session of the General Assembly.* A/49/PV.45 (1994). Available from: UNdocs.org.

United Nations, General Assembly. *Provisional Record of the 90th Plenary Meeting of the 49th Session of the General Assembly.* A/49/PV.90 (1994). Available from: UNdocs.org.

United Nations, General Assembly. *Provisional Record of the 48th Plenary Meeting of the 50th Session of the General Assembly.* A/50/PV.48 (1995). Available from: UNdocs.org.

United Nations, General Assembly. *Provisional Record of the 57th Plenary Meeting of the 51st Session of the General Assembly.* A/51/PV.57 (1996). Available from: UNdocs.org.

United Nations, General Assembly. *Provisional Record of the 45th Plenary Meeting of the 52nd Session of the General Assembly.* A/52/PV.45 (1997). Available from: UNdocs.org.

United Nations, General Assembly. *Provisional Record of the 37th Plenary Meeting of the 53rd Session of the General Assembly.* A/53/PV.37 (1998). Available from: UNdocs.org.

United Nations, General Assembly. *Provisional Record of the 50th Plenary Meeting of the 54th Session of the General Assembly.* A/54/PV.50 (1999). Available from: UNdocs.org.

United Nations, General Assembly. *Provisional Record of the 56th Plenary Meeting of the 55th Session of the General Assembly.* A/55/PV.56 (2000). Available from: UNdocs.org.

United Nations, General Assembly. *Provisional Record of the 64th Plenary Meeting of the 56th Session of the General Assembly.* A/56/PV.64 (2001). Available from: UNdocs.org.

United Nations, General Assembly. *Provisional Record of the 48th Plenary Meeting of the 57th Session of the General Assembly.* A/57/PV.48 (2002). Available from: UNdocs. org.

United Nations, General Assembly. *Provisional Record of the 54th Plenary Meeting of the 58th Meeting of the General Assembly.* A/58/PV.54 (2003). Available from: UNdocs. org.

United Nations, General Assembly. *Provisional Record of the 44th Plenary Meeting of the 59th Session of the General Assembly.* A/59/PV.44 (2004). Available from: UNdocs. org.

United Nations, General Assembly. *Provisional Record of the 45th Plenary Meeting of the 60th Session of the General Assembly.* A/60/PV.45 (2005). Available from: UNdocs. org.

United Nations, General Assembly. *Provisional Record of the 50th Plenary Meeting of the 61st Session of the General Assembly.* A/61/PV.50 (2006). Available from: UNdocs.org.

United Nations, General Assembly. *Provisional Record of the 38th Plenary Meeting of the 62nd Session of the General Assembly.* A/62/PV.38 (2007). Available from: UNdocs. org.

United Nations, General Assembly. *Provisional Record of the 33rd Plenary Meeting of the 63rd Session of the General Assembly.* A/63/PV.33 (2008). Available from: UNdocs. org.

United Nations, General Assembly. *Provisional Record of the 27th Plenary Meeting of the 64th Session of the General Assembly.* A/64/PV.27 (2009). Available from: UNdocs. org.

United Nations, General Assembly. *Provisional Record of the 36th Plenary Meeting of the 65th Session of the General Assembly.* A/65/PV.36 (2010). Available from: UNdocs. org.

United Nations, General Assembly. *Provisional Record of the 41st Plenary Meeting of the 66th Session of the General Assembly.* A/66/PV.41 (2011). Available from: UNdocs.org.

United Nations, General Assembly. *Provisional Record of the 35th Plenary Meeting of the 67th Session of the General Assembly.* A/67/PV.35 (2012). Available from: UNdocs.org.

United Nations, General Assembly. *Provisional Record of the 38th Plenary Meeting of the 68th Session of the General Assembly.* A/68/PV.38 (2013). Available from: UNdocs.org.

United Nations, General Assembly. *Provisional Record of the 30th Plenary Meeting of the 69th Session of the General Assembly.* A/69/PV.30 (2014). Available from: UNdocs. org.

United Nations, General Assembly. *Provisional Record of the 40th Plenary Meeting of the 70th Session of the General Assembly.* A/70/PV.40 (2015). Available from: UNdocs.org.

United Nations, General Assembly. *Provisional Record of the 32nd Plenary Meeting of the 71st Session of the General Assembly.* A/71/PV.32 (2016). Available from: UNdocs. org.

United Nations, General Assembly. *Provisional Record of the 30th Plenary Meeting of the 72nd Session of the General Assembly.* A/72/PV.30 (2017). Available from: UNdocs. org.

United Nations, General Assembly. *Resumption of the Tenth Emergency Session.* A/ES-10/PV.37 (2017). Available from: UNdocs.org.

United Nations, General Assembly. *Provisional Record of the 38th Plenary Meeting of the 72nd Session of the General Assembly.* A/72/PV.38 (2017). Available from: UNdocs. org.

United Nations, General Assembly. *Provisional Record of the 62nd Plenary Meeting of the 72nd Session of the General Assembly.* A/72/PV.62 (2017). Available from: UNdocs. org.

United Nations, General Assembly. *Provisional Record of the 30th Plenary Meeting of the 73rd Session of the General Assembly.* A/73/PV.30 (2018). Available from: UNdocs.org.

United Nations, General Assembly. *Provisional Record of the 38th Plenary Meeting of the 73rd Session of the General Assembly.* A/73/PV.38 (2018). Available from: UNdocs.org.

United Nations, General Assembly. *Provisional Record of the 30th Plenary Meeting of the 74th Session of the General Assembly.* A/74/PV.28 (2019). Available from: UNdocs.org.

Provisional Records of the UNSC Meetings

United Nations Security Council. Verbatim Record of the 3046th Meeting. A/S/PV.3046 (1992). Available from: UNdocs.org.

United Nations Security Council. *Provisional Record of the 8179th Meeting of the Security Council.* S/PV.8179 (2018). Available from: UNdocs.org.

United Nations Security Council. *Provisional Record of the 8203rd Meeting of the Security Council.* S/PV.8203 (2018). Available from: UNdocs.org.

United Nations Security Council. *Provisional Record of the 8224th Meeting of the Security Council.* S/PV.8224 (2018). Available from: UNdocs.org.

United Nations Security Council. Letter dated 13 March 2018 from the Chargé d'affaires a.i. of the Permanent Mission of the United Kingdom of Great Britain and Northern Ireland to the United Nations addressed to the President of the Security Council. S/2018/218 (2018). Available from: UNdocs.org.

United Nations Security Council. Security Council Press Statement on Security Council Visit to Bangladesh, Myanmar. SC/13331. May 8, 2018. Available from: https://www.un.org/press/en/2018/sc13331.doc.htm.

Official Records of the UNGA Special Political Committee

United Nations, General Assembly. *Official Records of the 7th Meeting of the Special Political Committee.* A/SPC/SR.7 (1957). Available from: UNdocs.org.

United Nations, General Assembly. *Official Records of the 8th Meeting of the Special Political Committee.* A/SPC/SR.8 (1957). Available from: UNdocs.org.

United Nations, General Assembly. *Official Records of the 9th Meeting of the Special Political Committee.* A/SPC/SR.9 (1957). Available from: UNdocs.org.

United Nations, General Assembly. *Official Records of the 10th Meeting of the Special Political Committee.* A/SPC/SR.10 (1957). Available from: UNdocs.org.

United Nations, General Assembly. *Official Records of the 11th Meeting of the Special Political Committee.* A/SPC/SR.11 (1957). Available from: UNdocs.org.

United Nations, General Assembly. *Official Records of the 12th Meeting of the Special Political Committee.* A/SPC/SR.12 (1957). Available from: UNdocs.org.

United Nations, General Assembly. *Official Records of the 13th Meeting of the Special Political Committee.* A/SPC/SR.13 (1957). Available from: UNdocs.org.

United Nations, General Assembly. *Official Records of the 14th Meeting of the Special Political Committee.* A/SPC/SR.14 (1957). Available from: UNdocs.org.

United Nations, General Assembly. *Official Records of the 15th Meeting of the Special Political Committee.* A/SPC/SR.15 (1957). Available from: UNdocs.org.

United Nations, General Assembly. *Official Records of the 16th Meeting of the Special Political Committee.* A/SPC/SR.16 (1957). Available from: UNdocs.org.

United Nations, General Assembly. *Official Records of the 54th Meeting of the Special Political Committee.* A/SPC/SR.54 (1957). Available from: UNdocs.org.

United Nations, General Assembly. *Official Records of the 55th Meeting of the Special Political Committee.* A/SPC/SR.55 (1957). Available from: UNdocs.org.

United Nations, General Assembly. *Official Records of the 56th Meeting of the Special Political Committee.* A/SPC/SR.56 (1957). Available from: UNdocs.org.

United Nations, General Assembly. *Official Records of the 57th Meeting of the Special Political Committee.* A/SPC/SR.57 (1957). Available from: UNdocs.org.

United Nations, General Assembly. *Official Records of the 86th Meeting of the Special Political Committee.* A/SPC/SR.86 (1958). Available from: UNdocs.org.

United Nations, General Assembly. *Official Records of the 87th Meeting of the Special Political Committee.* A/SPC/SR.87 (1958). Available from: UNdocs.org.

United Nations, General Assembly. *Official Records of the 88th Meeting of the Special Political Committee.* A/SPC/SR.88 (1958). Available from: UNdocs.org.

United Nations, General Assembly. *Official Records of the 89th Meeting of the Special Political Committee.* A/SPC/SR.89 (1958). Available from: UNdocs.org.

United Nations, General Assembly. *Official Records of the 90th Meeting of the Special Political Committee.* A/SPC/SR.90 (1958). Available from: UNdocs.org.

United Nations, General Assembly. *Official Records of the 91st Meeting of the Special Political Committee.* A/SPC/SR.91 (1958). Available from: UNdocs.org.

United Nations, General Assembly. *Official Records of the 93rd Meeting of the Special Political Committee.* A/SPC/SR.92 (1958). Available from: UNdocs.org.

United Nations, General Assembly. *Official Records of the 93rd Meeting of the Special Political Committee.* A/SPC/SR.93 (1958). Available from: UNdocs.org.

United Nations, General Assembly. *Official Records of the 94th Meeting of the Special Political Committee.* A/SPC/SR.94 (1958). Available from: UNdocs.org.

United Nations, General Assembly. *Official Records of the 123rd Meeting of the Special Political Committee.* A/SPC/SR.123 (1958). Available from: UNdocs.org.

United Nations, General Assembly. *Official Records of the 142nd Meeting of the Special Political Committee.* A/SPC/SR.140 (1959). Available from: UNdocs.org.

United Nations, General Assembly. *Official Records of the 142nd Meeting of the Special Political Committee.* A/SPC/SR.142 (1959). Available from: UNdocs.org.

United Nations, General Assembly. *Official Records of the 143rd Meeting of the Special Political Committee.* A/SPC/SR.143 (1959). Available from: UNdocs.org.

United Nations, General Assembly. *Official Records of the 144th Meeting of the Special Political Committee.* A/SPC/SR.144 (1959). Available from: UNdocs.org.

United Nations, General Assembly. *Official Records of the 145th Meeting of the Special Political Committee.* A/SPC/SR.145 (1959). Available from: UNdocs.org.

United Nations, General Assembly. *Official Records of the 172nd Meeting of the Special Political Committee.* A/SPC/SR.172 (1959). Available from: UNdocs.org.

United Nations, General Assembly. *Official Records of the 228th Meeting of the Special Political Committee.* A/SPC/SR.228 (1961). Available from: UNdocs.org.

United Nations, General Assembly. *Official Records of the 229th Meeting of the Special Political Committee.* A/SPC/SR.229 (1961). Available from: UNdocs.org.

United Nations, General Assembly. *Official Records of the 230th Meeting of the Special Political Committee.* A/SPC/SR.230 (1961). Available from: UNdocs.org.

United Nations, General Assembly. *Official Records of the 231st Meeting of the Special Political Committee.* A/SPC/SR.231 (1961). Available from: UNdocs.org.

United Nations, General Assembly. *Official Records of the 239th Meeting of the Special Political Committee.* A/SPC/SR.239 (1961). Available from: UNdocs.org.

United Nations, General Assembly. *Official Records of the 240th Meeting of the Special Political Committee.* A/SPC/SR.240 (1961). Available from: UNdocs.org.

United Nations, General Assembly. *Official Records of the 241st Meeting of the Special Political Committee.* A/SPC/SR.241 (1961). Available from: UNdocs.org.

United Nations, General Assembly. *Official Records of the 242nd Meeting of the Special Political Committee.* A/SPC/SR.242 (1961). Available from: UNdocs.org.

United Nations, General Assembly. *Official Records of the 243rd Meeting of the Special Political Committee.* A/SPC/SR.243 (1961). Available from: UNdocs.org.

United Nations, General Assembly. *Official Records of the 244th Meeting of the Special Political Committee.* A/SPC/SR.244 (1961). Available from: UNdocs.org.

United Nations, General Assembly. *Official Records of the 274rd Meeting of the Special Political Committee.* A/SPC/SR.274 (1961). Available from: UNdocs.org.

United Nations, General Assembly. *Official Records of the 339th Meeting of the Special Political Committee.* A/SPC/SR.339 (1962). Available from: UNdocs.org.

Official Records of the First Committee of the General Assembly

United Nations, General Assembly. *Official Records of the 106th Meeting of the 1st Committee of the General Assembly.* A/C.1/SR.106 (1947). Available from: UNdocs.org.

United Nations, General Assembly. *Official Records of the 107th Meeting of the 1st Committee of the General Assembly.* A/C.1/SR.107 (1947). Available from: UNdocs.org.

United Nations, General Assembly. *Official Records of the 108th Meeting of the 1st Committee of the General Assembly.* A/C.1/SR.108 (1947). Available from: UNdocs.org.

United Nations, General Assembly. *Official Records of the 109th Meeting of the 1st Committee of the General Assembly.* A/C.1/SR.109(1947). Available from: UNdocs.org.

United Nations, General Assembly. *Official Records of the 110th Meeting of the 1st Committee of the General Assembly.* A/C.1/SR.110 (1947). Available from: UNdocs.org.

United Nations, General Assembly. *Official Records of the 111th Meeting of the 1st Committee of the General Assembly.* A/C.1/SR.111 (1947). Available from: UNdocs.org.

United Nations, General Assembly. *Official Records of the 112th Meeting of the 1st Committee of the General Assembly.* A/C.1/SR.112 (1947). Available from: UNdocs.org.

United Nations, General Assembly. *Official Records of the 263rd Meeting of the 1st Committee of the General Assembly.* A/C.1/SR.263 (1949). Available from: UNdocs.org.

United Nations, General Assembly. *Official Records of the 265th Meeting of the 1st Committee of the General Assembly.* A/C.1/SR.265 (1949). Available from: UNdocs. org.

United Nations, General Assembly. *Official Records of the 268th Meeting of the 1st Committee of the General Assembly.* A/C.1/SR.268 (1949). Available from: UNdocs. org.

United Nations, General Assembly. *Provisional Record of the 1119th Meeting of the First Committee of the General Assembly.* A/C.1/SR.1119 (1960). Available from: UNdocs. org.

United Nations, General Assembly. *Provisional Record of the 1120th Meeting of the First Committee of the General Assembly.* A/C.1/SR.1120 (1960). Available from: UNdocs. org.

United Nations, General Assembly. *Provisional Record of the 1134th Meeting of the First Committee of the General Assembly.* A/C.1/SR.1134 (1960). Available from: UNdocs. org.

Official Records of the Security Council

United Nations, Security Council. *Official Records of the 853rd Meeting of the Security Council.* S/PV.853 (1960). Available from: UNdocs.org.

United Nations, Security Council. *Official Records of the 856th Meeting of the Security Council.* S/PV.856 (1960). Available from: UNdocs.org.

Treaties

United Nations, General Assembly. *Treaty on the Prohibition of Nuclear Weapons.* A/
CONF.229/2017/8 (2017). Available from: UNdocs.org.

UN Member State Letters/Memorandums

United Nations, Atomic Energy Commission. *Draft international convention to prohibit
the production and employment of weapons based on the use of atomic energy for the
purpose of mass destruction, presented by the Representative of the USSR, Ambassador
A. Gromyko on 19 June 1946.* Draft International Convention: AEC/7 (1946). Available
from: UNdocs.org.

United Nations, General Assembly. *The Delegation of India: Memorandum on the
Position of Indians in the Union of South Africa.* A/68; (1946). Available from: UNdocs.
org.

United Nations, General Assembly. *The Delegation of India: Addendum to the
Memorandum on the Position of Indians in the Union of South Africa.* A/68/Add.1
(1946). Available from: UNdocs.org.

United Nations, General Assembly. *Memorandum by the Government of the Union
of South Africa on the Subject of Indian Legislation.* A/167 (1946). Available
from: UNdocs.org.

United Nations, General Assembly. *Provisional Agenda of the Third Regular Session.
Item Proposed by India. Letter From the Representative of India to the Secretary-
General.* A/577 (1948). Available from: UNdocs.org.

United Nations, General Assembly. *Communication Received by the Secretary-General
From the Representatives of Canada, China, France, the United Kingdom and the
United States of America.* Letter Dated 27 January 1950: A/1253 (1950). Available
from: UNdocs.org.

United Nations, General Assembly. *Communication Received by the Secretary-General
from the Representative of the Union of Soviet Socialist Republics.* Letter Dated 8
February 1950: A/1254 (1950). Available from: UNdocs.org.

United Nations, General Assembly. *Communication dated 27 March 1951 addressed
to the Secretary-General from the Permanent Representative of India to the United
Nations.* A/1794 (1951). Available from: UNdocs.org.

United Nations, General Assembly. *The Question of Race Conflict in the South Africa
Resulting from the Policies of Apartheid of the Government of the Union of South
Africa. Letter dated 1. September 1952 addressed to the Secretary General by the perma-
nent representatives of Afghanistan, Burma, Egypt, India, Indonesia, Iraq, Lebanon,
Pakistan, The Philippines, Saudi Arabia, Syria, and Yemen.* A/2183 (1952). Available
from: UNdocs.org.

United Nations, General Assembly. *Request for the Inclusion of a Supplementary Item in
the Agenda of the Forty-Sixth Session. Necessity of Ending the Economic, Commercial*

and Financial Embargo Imposed by the United States of America Against Cuba. Letter dated 18 August 1991 from the Permanent Representative of Cuba to the United Nations addressed to the Secretary-General. A/46/193 (1991). Available from: UNdocs.org.

United Nations, General Assembly. *Request for the Inclusion of a Supplementary Item in the Agenda of the Forty-Sixth Session. Necessity of Ending the Economic, Commercial and Financial Embargo Imposed by the United States of America Against Cuba. Letter dated 10 September 1991 from the Permanent Representative of Cuba to the United Nations addressed to the Secretary-General.* A/46/193/Add.1 (1991). Available from: UNdocs.org.

United Nations, General Assembly. *Request for the Inclusion of a Supplementary Item in the Agenda of the Forty-Sixth Session. Necessity of Ending the Economic, Commercial and Financial Embargo Imposed by the United States of America Against Cuba. Letter dated 10 September 1991 from the Permanent Representative of Cuba to the United Nations addressed to the Secretary-General.* A/46/193/Add.2 (1991). Available from: UNdocs.org.

United Nations, General Assembly. *Request for the Inclusion of a Supplementary Item in the Agenda of the Forty-Sixth Session. Necessity of Ending the Economic, Commercial and Financial Embargo Imposed by the United States of America Against Cuba. Letter dated 10 September 1991 from the Permanent Representative of Cuba to the United Nations addressed to the Secretary-General.* A/46/193/Add.3 (1991). Available from: UNdocs.org.

United Nations, General Assembly. *Request for the Inclusion of a Supplementary Item in the Agenda of the Forty-Sixth Session. Necessity of Ending the Economic, Commercial and Financial Embargo Imposed by the United States of America Against Cuba. Letter dated 10 September 1991 from the Permanent Representative of Cuba to the United Nations addressed to the Secretary-General.* A/46/193/Add.4 (1991). Available from: UNdocs.org.

United Nations, General Assembly. *Request for the Inclusion of a Supplementary Item in the Agenda of the Forty-Sixth Session. Necessity of Ending the Economic, Commercial and Financial Embargo Imposed by the United States of America Against Cuba. Letter dated 10 September 1991 from the Permanent Representative of Cuba to the United Nations addressed to the Secretary-General.* A/46/193/Add.5 (1991). Available from: UNdocs.org.

United Nations, General Assembly. *Request for the Inclusion of a Supplementary Item in the Agenda of the Forty-Sixth Session. Necessity of Ending the Economic, Commercial and Financial Embargo Imposed by the United States of America Against Cuba. Letter dated 10 September 1991 from the Permanent Representative of Cuba to the United Nations addressed to the Secretary-General.* A/46/193/Add.6 (1991). Available from: UNdocs.org.

United Nations, General Assembly. *Request for the Inclusion of a Supplementary Item in the Agenda of the Forty-Sixth Session. Necessity of Ending the Economic, Commercial and Financial Embargo Imposed by the United States of America Against Cuba. Letter dated 11 September 1991 from the Permanent Representative of Cuba to the United Nations addressed to the Secretary-General.* A/46/193/Add.7 (1991). Available from: UNdocs.org.

United Nations, General Assembly. *Necessity of Ending the Economic, Commercial and Financial Embargo Imposed by the United States of America Against Cuba. Letter dated 11 June 1992 from the Charge d'affairs a.i. of the Permanent Mission of Cuba to the United Nations addressed to the Secretary-General. Note Verbale Dated 7 April 1992 From the Delegation of the Commission of the European Communities and the Embassy of Portugal Addressed to the Department of State of the United States of America.* A/47/273 (1992). Available from: UNdocs.org.

United Nations, General Assembly. *Request for the Inclusion of a Supplementary Item in the Agenda of the Forty-Sixth Session. Necessity of Ending the Economic, Commercial and Financial Embargo Imposed by the United States of America Against Cuba. Letter dated 20 March 1996 from the Permanent Representative of Colombia to the United Nations addressed to the Secretary-General. Statement dated 19 March 1996 issued by the Movement of Non-Aligned Countries.* A/51/85 (1996). Available from: UNdocs.org.

United Nations, General Assembly. *Request for the Inclusion of a Supplementary Suboitem in the Agenda of the Fifty-First Session. International Court of Justice Advisory Opinion on the Legality of the Threat or Use of Nuclear Weapons.* Letter dated 21 August 1996 from the Permanent Representative of Malaysia to the United Nations addressed to the Secretary-General: A/41/194 (1996). Available from: UNdocs.org.

United Nations, General Assembly. *Request for the Inclusion of a Supplementary Item in the Agenda of the Forty-Sixth Session. Necessity of Ending the Economic, Commercial and Financial Embargo Imposed by the United States of America Against Cuba. Letter dated 19 October 1996 from the Permanent Representative of Cuba to the United Nations addressed to the Secretary-General. Juridical analysis of the scope and illegality of the Helms-Burton Act: The viewpoint of an outstanding American law firm.* A/51/531 (1996). Available from: UNdocs.org.

United Nations Reports

United Nations, General Assembly. *Establishment of a commission to deal with the problems raised by the discovery of atomic energy, report of the 1st Committee to the General Assembly.* Report of the 1st Committee: A/12 (1946). Available from: UNdocs. org.

United Nations, General Assembly. *Treatment of Indians in the Union of South Africa. Report of the First and Sixth Joint Committee.* A/205 (1946). Available from: UNdocs. org.

United Nations, General Assembly. *Treatment of Indians in the Union of South Africa. Report of the Ad Hoc Political Committee.* A/1548 (1950). Available from: UNdocs.org.

United Nations, General Assembly. *The Question of Race Conflict in the South Africa Resulting from the Policies of Apartheid of the Government of the Union of South Africa: Report of the Commission Appointed to Study the Racial Situation in the Union of South Africa.* A/2505 (1952). Available from: UNdocs.org.

United Nations, General Assembly. *The Question of Race Conflict in the South Africa Resulting from the Policies of Apartheid of the Government of the Union of South Africa: Report of the Special Political Committee.* A/3722 (1952). Available from: UNdocs.org.

United Nations, General Assembly. *The Question of Race Conflict in the South Africa Resulting from the Policies of Apartheid of the Government of the Union of South Africa: Report of the Commission Appointed to Study the Racial Situation in the Union of South Africa.* A/2610 (1953). Available from: UNdocs.org.

United Nations, General Assembly. *The Question of Race Conflict in the South Africa Resulting from the Policies of Apartheid of the Government of the Union of South Africa: 2nd Report of the Commission Appointed to Study the Racial Situation in the Union of South Africa.* A/2719 (1954). Available from: UNdocs.org.

United Nations, General Assembly. *The Question of Race Conflict in the South Africa Resulting from the Policies of Apartheid of the Government of the Union of South Africa: 3rd Report of the Commission Appointed to Study the Racial Situation in the Union of South Africa.* A/2953 (1955). Available from: UNdocs.org.

United Nations, General Assembly. *Disarmament and the Situation with regard to the fulfillment of General Assembly Resolution 1378 (XIV) of 20 November 1959 on the Question of Disarmament. Suspension of Nuclear and Thermo-Nuclear Tests. Prevention of the Wider Dissemination of Nuclear Weapons. Report of the Disarmament Commission.* Report of the First Committee: A/4680 (1960). Available from: UNdocs.org.

United Nations, General Assembly. *Continuation of Suspension of Nuclear and Thermo-Nuclear Tests and Obligations of States to Refrain from their Renewal. The Urgent Need for a Treaty to Ban Nuclear Weapons Tests Under Effective International Control.* Report of the First Committee: A/4942 (1961). Available from: UNdocs.org.

United Nations, General Assembly. *Continuation of Suspension of Nuclear and Thermo-Nuclear Tests and Obligations of States to Refrain from their Renewal. The Urgent Need for a Treaty to Ban Nuclear Weapons Tests Under Effective International Control.* Report of the First Committee: A/4942/Add.1–3 (1961). Available from: UNdocs.org.

United Nations, General Assembly. *Question of Convening a Conference for the Purpose of Signing a Convention on the Prohibition of the Use of Nuclear and Thermo-nuclear Weapons.* Report of the Secretary-General: A/5174 (1962). Available from: UNdocs. org.

United Nations, General Assembly. *Question of Convening a Conference for the Purpose of Signing a Convention on the Prohibition of the Use of Nuclear and Thermo-nuclear Weapons*. Report of the Secretary-General: A/5174/Add.1–2 (1962). Available from: UNdocs.org.

Office for Disarmament Affairs, United Nations (UNODA). *The United Nations and Disarmament 1945–1970*. Disarmament Affairs Division of the Department of Political and Security Council Affairs. Sales No.: 70.IX.1. June 1970. Available from: UNdocs.org.

Office for Disarmament Affairs, United Nations (UNODA). *General and Complete Disarmament*. Report of the 1st Committee: A/33/435 (1978). Available from: UNdocs. org.

United Nations, Secretary-General. *Necessity of Ending the Economic, Commercial and Financial Embargo Imposed by the United States of America Against Cuba: Report of the Secretary-General*. A/48/448(1993). Available from: UNdocs.org.

United Nations, Secretary-General. *Necessity of Ending the Economic, Commercial and Financial Embargo Imposed by the United States of America Against Cuba: Report of the Secretary-General*. A/49/398(1994). Available from: UNdocs.org.

United Nations, Secretary-General. *General and Complete Disarmament*. Report of the 1st Committee: A/49/699 (1994). Available from: UNdocs.org.

United Nations, Secretary-General. *Necessity of Ending the Economic, Commercial and Financial Embargo Imposed by the United States of America Against Cuba: Report of the Secretary-General*. A/50/401 (1995). Available from: UNdocs.org.

United Nations, Secretary-General. *Necessity of Ending the Economic, Commercial and Financial Embargo Imposed by the United States of America Against Cuba: Report of the Secretary-General*. A/51/335 (1996). Available from: UNdocs.org.

United Nations, Secretary-General. *Necessity of Ending the Economic, Commercial and Financial Embargo Imposed by the United States of America Against Cuba: Report of the Secretary-General*. A/52/342 (1997). Available from: UNdocs.org.

United Nations, Secretary-General. *Necessity of Ending the Economic, Commercial and Financial Embargo Imposed by the United States of America Against Cuba: Report of the Secretary-General*. A/53/320 (1998). Available from: UNdocs.org.

United Nations, Secretary-General. *Necessity of Ending the Economic, Commercial and Financial Embargo Imposed by the United States of America Against Cuba: Report of the Secretary-General*. A/54/259 (1999). Available from: UNdocs.org.

United Nations, Secretary-General. *Necessity of Ending the Economic, Commercial and Financial Embargo Imposed by the United States of America Against Cuba: Report of the Secretary-General*. A/55/172 (2000). Available from: UNdocs.org.

United Nations, Secretary-General. *Necessity of Ending the Economic, Commercial and Financial Embargo Imposed by the United States of America Against Cuba: Report of the Secretary-General*. A/56/276 (2001). Available from: UNdocs.org.

United Nations, Secretary-General. *Necessity of Ending the Economic, Commercial and Financial Embargo Imposed by the United States of America Against Cuba: Report of the Secretary-General.* A/57/264 (2002). Available from: UNdocs.org.

United Nations, Secretary-General. *Necessity of Ending the Economic, Commercial and Financial Embargo Imposed by the United States of America Against Cuba: Report of the Secretary-General.* A/58/287 (2003). Available from: UNdocs.org.

United Nations, Secretary-General. *Necessity of Ending the Economic, Commercial and Financial Embargo Imposed by the United States of America Against Cuba: Report of the Secretary-General.* A/59/448 (2004). Available from: UNdocs.org.

United Nations, Secretary-General. *Necessity of Ending the Economic, Commercial and Financial Embargo Imposed by the United States of America Against Cuba: Report of the Secretary-General.* A/60/213 (2005). Available from: UNdocs.org.

United Nations, Secretary-General. *Necessity of Ending the Economic, Commercial and Financial Embargo Imposed by the United States of America Against Cuba: Report of the Secretary-General.* A/61/132 (2006). Available from: UNdocs.org.

United Nations, Secretary-General. *Necessity of Ending the Economic, Commercial and Financial Embargo Imposed by the United States of America Against Cuba: Report of the Secretary-General.* A/62/92 (2007). Available from: UNdocs.org.

United Nations, Secretary-General. *Necessity of Ending the Economic, Commercial and Financial Embargo Imposed by the United States of America Against Cuba: Report of the Secretary-General.* A/63/93(2008). Available from: UNdocs.org.

United Nations, Secretary-General. *Necessity of Ending the Economic, Commercial and Financial Embargo Imposed by the United States of America Against Cuba: Report of the Secretary-General.* A/64/97 (2009). Available from: UNdocs.org.

United Nations, Secretary-General. *Report of the Ad Hoc Working Group on the Revitalization of the General Assembly.* A/63/959 (2009). Available from: UNdocs.org.

United Nations, Secretary-General. *Necessity of Ending the Economic, Commercial and Financial Embargo Imposed by the United States of America Against Cuba: Report of the Secretary-General.* A/65/83 (2010). Available from: UNdocs.org.

United Nations, Secretary-General. *Necessity of Ending the Economic, Commercial and Financial Embargo Imposed by the United States of America Against Cuba: Report of the Secretary-General.* A/66/114 (2011). Available from: UNdocs.org.

United Nations, Secretary-General. *Necessity of Ending the Economic, Commercial and Financial Embargo Imposed by the United States of America Against Cuba: Report of the Secretary-General.* A/67/118 (2012). Available from: UNdocs.org.

United Nations, Secretary-General. *Necessity of Ending the Economic, Commercial and Financial Embargo Imposed by the United States of America Against Cuba: Report of the Secretary-General.* A/68/116 (2013). Available from: UNdocs.org.

United Nations, Secretary-General. *Report of the Ad Hoc Working Group on the Revitalization of the General Assembly.* A/67/936 (2013). Available from: UNdocs.org.

United Nations, Secretary-General. *Necessity of Ending the Economic, Commercial and Financial Embargo Imposed by the United States of America Against Cuba: Report of the Secretary-General.* A/69/98 (2014). Available from: UNdocs.org.

United Nations, Secretary-General. *Necessity of Ending the Economic, Commercial and Financial Embargo Imposed by the United States of America Against Cuba: Report of the Secretary-General.* A/70/120 (2015). Available from: UNdocs.org.

United Nations, Secretary-General. *Necessity of Ending the Economic, Commercial and Financial Embargo Imposed by the United States of America Against Cuba: Report of the Secretary-General.* A/71/91 (2016). Available from: UNdocs.org.

UNGA *Resolutions and Draft Resolutions*

United Nations, General Assembly. *Establishment of a Commission to Deal with the Problems Raised by the Discovery of Atomic Energy.* Resolution Adopted by the General Assembly: A/RES/1(I) (1946). Available from: UNdocs.org.

United Nations, General Assembly. *Resolutions Adopted Without Reference to a Committee. Persecution and Discrimination.* A/RES/103(I) (1946). Available from: UNdocs.org.

United Nations, General Assembly. *Treatment of People of Indian Origin in the Union of South Africa.* A/RES/44(I) (1946). Available from: UNdocs.org.

United Nations, General Assembly. *Future Status of South West Africa.* A/RES/65(I) (1946). Available from: UNdocs.org.

United Nations, General Assembly. *Consideration of Proposed New Trusteeship Agreements, if Any: Question of South West Africa.* A/RES/141(II) (1947). Available from: UNdocs.org.

United Nations, General Assembly. *Question of South West Africa.* A/RES/227(III) (1948). Available from: UNdocs.org.

United Nations, General Assembly. *Prohibition of the Atomic Weapon and the Reduction by One-Third of the Armaments and Armed Forces of the Permanent Members of the Security Council.* Draft resolution Submitted by Poland: A/C.1/SC.12/4 (1948). Available from: UNdocs.org.

United Nations, General Assembly. *Treatment of People of Indian Origin in the Union of South Africa.* A/RES/265(III) (1949). Available from: UNdocs.org.

United Nations, General Assembly. *Regulation, Limitation and Balanced Reduction of All Armaments; International Control of Atomic Energy.* Resolution Adopted by the General Assembly: A/RES/502(VI) (1952). Available from: UNdocs.org.

United Nations, General Assembly. *Treatment of People of Indian Origin in the Union of South Africa.* A/RES/1248 (XIII) (1958). Available from: UNdocs.org.

United Nations, General Assembly. *The Question of Race Conflict in South Africa Resulting From the Policies of Apartheid of the Government of the Republic of South Africa.* A/RES/1302(XIII) (1958). Available from: UNdocs.org.

United Nations, General Assembly. *The Question of Race Conflict in South Africa Resulting From the Policies of Apartheid of the Government of the Republic of South Africa.* A/RES/1302(XIII) (1959). Available from: UNdocs.org.

United Nations, General Assembly. *Ceylon, Ethiopia, Ghana, Guinea, Liberia, Libya, Nigeria, Somalia, Sudan, Tunisia: draft resolution.* Daft Resolution of the General Assembly: A/C.1/L.254 (1960). Available from: UNdocs.org.

United Nations, General Assembly. *Universal Dissemination of Information on the Consequences of Nuclear War.* Draft Resolution Submitted by Poland: A/C.1/L.260/ REV.1 (1960). Available from: UNdocs.org.

United Nations, General Assembly. *The Question of Race Conflict in South Africa Resulting From the Policies of Apartheid of the Government of the Republic of South Africa.* A/RES/1662(XVI) (1961). Available from: UNdocs.org.

United Nations, General Assembly. *The Question of Race Conflict in South Africa Resulting From the Policies of Apartheid of the Government of the Republic of South Africa.* A/RES/1662(XVI) (1961). Available from: UNdocs.org.

United Nations, General Assembly. *Treatment of People of Indian Origin in the Union of South Africa.* A/RES/1663(XVI) (1961). Available from: UNdocs.org.

United Nations, General Assembly. *Declaration on the Prohibition of the Use of Nuclear and Thermonuclear Weapons.* Resolution Adopted by the General Assembly: A/RES/ 1653(XVI) (1961). Available from: UNdocs.org.

United Nations, General Assembly. *Resolution Adopted by the General Assembly: Manifestations of Racial Prejudice and National and Religious Intolerance.* A/RES/1536(XV) (1962). Available from: UNdocs.org.

United Nations, General Assembly. *Question of Convening a Conference for the Purpose of Signing a Convention on the Prohibition of the Use of Nuclear and Thermo-nuclear Weapons.* Resolution Adopted by the General Assembly: A/RES/1801(XVII) (1963). Available from: UNdocs.org.

United Nations, General Assembly. *Resolution Adopted by the General Assembly at its 1261st Meeting on 20 November 1963.* A/RES/18/1904 (1963). Available from: UNdocs. org.

United Nations, General Assembly. *Question of Convening a Conference for the Purpose of Signing a Convention on the Prohibition of the Use of Nuclear and Thermo-nuclear Weapons.* Resolution Adopted by the General Assembly: A/RES/1909(XVIII) (1964). Available from: UNdocs.org.

United Nations, General Assembly. *Question of Convening a Conference for the Purpose of Signing a Convention on the Prohibition of the Use of Nuclear and Thermo-nuclear*

Weapons. Resolution Adopted by the General Assembly: A/RES/1909(XVIII) (1966). Available from: UNdocs.org.

United Nations, General Assembly. *Question of Convening a Conference for the Purpose of Signing a Convention on the Prohibition of the Use of Nuclear and Thermo-nuclear Weapons*. Resolution Adopted by the General Assembly: A/RES/2164(XXI) (1967). Available from: UNdocs.org.

United Nations, General Assembly. *Comprehensive Study of the Question of Nuclear-weapon-free Zones in All its Aspects*. Resolution Adopted by the General Assembly: A/RES/31/70 (1977). Available from: UNdocs.org.

United Nations, General Assembly. *Non-use of Nuclear Weapons and Prevention of Nuclear War*. Resolution Adopted by the General Assembly: A/RES/37/71B (1978). Available from: UNdocs.org.

United Nations, General Assembly. *Study on Nuclear Weapons*. Resolution Adopted by the General Assembly: A/RES/33/91/D (1978). Available from: UNdocs.org.

United Nations, General Assembly. *Non-use of Nuclear Weapons and Prevention of Nuclear War*. Resolution Adopted by the General Assembly: A/RES/34/83G (1979). Available from: UNdocs.org.

United Nations, General Assembly. *Non-use of Nuclear Weapons and Prevention of Nuclear War*. Resolution Adopted by the General Assembly: A/RES/35/152D (1980). Available from: UNdocs.org.

United Nations, General Assembly. *Non-use of Nuclear Weapons and Prevention of Nuclear War*. Resolution Adopted by the General Assembly: A/RES/36/92I (1981). Available from: UNdocs.org.

United Nations, General Assembly. *Convention on the Prohibition of the Use of Nuclear Weapons*. Resolution Adopted by the General Assembly: A/RES/37/100C (1982). Available from: UNdocs.org.

United Nations, General Assembly. *Convention on the Prohibition of the Use of Nuclear Weapons*. Resolution Adopted by the General Assembly: A/RES/38/73G (1983). Available from: UNdocs.org.

United Nations, General Assembly. *Convention on the Prohibition of the Use of Nuclear Weapons*. Resolution Adopted by the General Assembly: A/RES/39/63H (1984). Available from: UNdocs.org.

United Nations, General Assembly. *Convention on the Prohibition of the Use of Nuclear Weapons*. Resolution Adopted by the General Assembly: A/RES/40/15F (1985). Available from: UNdocs.org.

United Nations, General Assembly. *Resolution Adopted by the General Assembly: Policies of Apartheid of the Government of South Africa*. A/RES/44/27 (1989). Available from: UNdocs.org.

United Nations, General Assembly. *Resolution Adopted by the General Assembly: Policies of Apartheid of the Government of South Africa.* A/RES/44/244 (1990). Available from: UNdocs.org.

United Nations, General Assembly. *Resolution Adopted by the General Assembly: Democratic and Non-racial Elections in South Africa.* A/RES/48/233 (1994). Available from: UNdocs.org.

United Nations, General Assembly. *Request for an Advisory Opinion from the International Court of Justice on the Legality of the Threat or Use of Nuclear Weapons.* Resolution Adopted by the General Assembly: A/RES/49/75 K (1995). Available from: UNdocs.org.

United Nations, General Assembly. *Necessity of Ending the Economic, Commercial and Financial Embargo Imposed by the United States of America Against Cuba: Draft Resolution.* A/47/L.20 (1991). Available from: UNdocs.org.

United Nations, General Assembly. *Necessity of Ending the Economic, Commercial and Financial Embargo Imposed by the United States of America Against Cuba: Revised Draft Resolution.* A/47/L.20/REV.1 (1992). Available from: UNdocs.org.

United Nations, General Assembly. *Necessity of Ending the Economic, Commercial and Financial Embargo Imposed by the United States of America Against Cuba.* Resolution Adopted by the General Assembly: A/RES/47/19 (1993). Available from: UNdocs.org.

United Nations, General Assembly. *Financial Embargo Imposed by the United States of America Against Cuba.* Revised Draft Resolution of the General Assembly: A/RES/L.14/Rev.1 (1993). Available from: UNdocs.org.

United Nations, General Assembly. *Financial Embargo Imposed by the United States of America Against Cuba.* Resolution Adopted by the General Assembly: A/RES/48/16 (1993). Available from: UNdocs.org.

United Nations, General Assembly. *Necessity of Ending the Economic, Commercial and Financial Embargo Imposed by the United States of America Against Cuba.* Resolution Adopted by the General Assembly: A/RES/49/19 (1994). Available from: UNdocs.org.

United Nations, General Assembly. *Necessity of Ending the Economic, Commercial and Financial Embargo Imposed by the United States of America Against Cuba.* Resolution Adopted by the General Assembly: A/RES/50/401 (1995). Available from: UNdocs. org.

United Nations, General Assembly. *Necessity of Ending the Economic, Commercial and Financial Embargo Imposed by the United States of America Against Cuba.* Resolution Adopted by the General Assembly: A/RES/51/335 (1996). Available from: UNdocs. org.

United Nations, General Assembly. *Necessity of Ending the Economic, Commercial and Financial Embargo Imposed by the United States of America Against Cuba.* Resolution Adopted by the General Assembly: A/RES/52/342 (1997). Available from: UNdocs. org.

United Nations, General Assembly. *Necessity of Ending the Economic, Commercial and Financial Embargo Imposed by the United States of America Against Cuba*. Resolution Adopted by the General Assembly: A/RES/53/320 (1998). Available from: UNdocs. org.

United Nations, General Assembly. *Necessity of Ending the Economic, Commercial and Financial Embargo Imposed by the United States of America Against Cuba*. Resolution Adopted by the General Assembly: A/RES/54/259 (1999). Available from: UNdocs. org.

United Nations, General Assembly. *Necessity of Ending the Economic, Commercial and Financial Embargo Imposed by the United States of America Against Cuba*. Resolution Adopted by the General Assembly: A/RES/55/172 (2000). Available from: UNdocs. org.

United Nations, General Assembly. *Necessity of Ending the Economic, Commercial and Financial Embargo Imposed by the United States of America Against Cuba*. Resolution Adopted by the General Assembly: A/RES/56/9 (2001). Available from: UNdocs.org.

United Nations, General Assembly. *Necessity of Ending the Economic, Commercial and Financial Embargo Imposed by the United States of America Against Cuba*. Resolution Adopted by the General Assembly: A/RES/57/11 (2002). Available from: UNdocs.org.

United Nations, General Assembly. *Necessity of Ending the Economic, Commercial and Financial Embargo Imposed by the United States of America Against Cuba*. Resolution Adopted by the General Assembly: A/RES/58/7 (2003). Available from: UNdocs.org.

United Nations, General Assembly. *Necessity of Ending the Economic, Commercial and Financial Embargo Imposed by the United States of America Against Cuba*. Resolution Adopted by the General Assembly: A/RES/59/11 (2004). Available from: UNdocs.org.

United Nations, General Assembly. *Necessity of Ending the Economic, Commercial and Financial Embargo Imposed by the United States of America Against Cuba*. Resolution Adopted by the General Assembly: A/RES/60/12 (2005). Available from: UNdocs.org.

United Nations, General Assembly. *Resolution Adopted by the General Assembly: Nelson Mandela International*. A/RES/64/13 (2005). Available from: UNdocs.org.

United Nations, General Assembly. *Resolution Adopted by the General Assembly: World Summit Outcome*. A/RES/60/1 (2005). Available from: UNdocs.org.

United Nations, General Assembly. *Resolution Adopted by the United Nations General Assembly: 2005 World Outcome Document*. A/RES/60/1 (2005). Available from: UNdocs.org.

United Nations, General Assembly. *Necessity of Ending the Economic, Commercial and Financial Embargo Imposed by the United States of America Against Cuba*. Resolution Adopted by the General Assembly: A/RES/61/11 (2006). Available from: UNdocs.org.

United Nations, General Assembly. *Necessity of Ending the Economic, Commercial and Financial Embargo Imposed by the United States of America Against Cuba*. Resolution Adopted by the General Assembly: A/RES/62/3 (2007). Available from: UNdocs.org.

United Nations, General Assembly. *Necessity of Ending the Economic, Commercial and Financial Embargo Imposed by the United States of America Against Cuba*. Resolution Adopted by the General Assembly: A/RES/63/19 (2008). Available from: UNdocs.org.

United Nations, General Assembly. *Necessity of Ending the Economic, Commercial and Financial Embargo Imposed by the United States of America Against Cuba*. Resolution Adopted by the General Assembly: A/RES/64/97 (2009). Available from: UNdocs.org.

United Nations, General Assembly. *Necessity of Ending the Economic, Commercial and Financial Embargo Imposed by the United States of America Against Cuba*. Resolution Adopted by the General Assembly: A/RES/65/6 (2010). Available from: UNdocs.org.

United Nations, General Assembly. *Necessity of Ending the Economic, Commercial and Financial Embargo Imposed by the United States of America Against Cuba*. Resolution Adopted by the General Assembly: A/RES/66/6 (2011). Available from: UNdocs.org.

United Nations, General Assembly. *Necessity of Ending the Economic, Commercial and Financial Embargo Imposed by the United States of America Against Cuba*. Resolution Adopted by the General Assembly: A/RES/67/118 (2012). Available from: UNdocs.org.

United Nations, General Assembly. *Necessity of Ending the Economic, Commercial and Financial Embargo Imposed by the United States of America Against Cuba*. Resolution Adopted by the General Assembly: A/RES/68/8 (2013). Available from: UNdocs.org.

United Nations, General Assembly. *Necessity of Ending the Economic, Commercial and Financial Embargo Imposed by the United States of America Against Cuba*. Resolution Adopted by the General Assembly: A/RES/69/98 (2014). Available from: UNdocs.org.

United Nations, General Assembly. *Necessity of Ending the Economic, Commercial and Financial Embargo Imposed by the United States of America Against Cuba*. Resolution Adopted by the General Assembly: A/RES/70/120 (2015). Available from: UNdocs.org.

United Nations, General Assembly. *Necessity of Ending the Economic, Commercial and Financial Embargo Imposed by the United States of America Against Cuba*. Resolution Adopted by the General Assembly: A/RES/71/91 (2016). Available from: UNdocs.org.

United Nations, General Assembly. *Combating Intolerance, Negative Stereotyping, Stigmatization, Discrimination, Incitement to Violence and Violence Against Persons, Based on Religion or Belief*. A/RES/1780(XVII) (2016). Available from: UNdocs.org.

United Nations, General Assembly. *Combating Glorification of Nazism, neo-Nazism and other Practices that Contribute to Fueling Contemporary Forms of Racism, Racial Discrimination, Xenophobia and Related Intolerance*. A/RES/70/139 (2016). Available from: UNdocs.org.

United Nations, General Assembly. *The Illicit Trade in Small Arms and Light Weapons in All its Aspects*. Resolution Adopted by the General Assembly: A/RES/72/57 (2017). Available from: UNdocs.org.

United Nations, General Assembly. *Resolution Adopted by the General Assembly on 21 December 2017: Status of Jerusalem.* A/RES/ES-10/19 (2017). Available from: UNdocs. org.

United Nations, General Assembly. *Necessity of Ending the Economic, Commercial and Financial Embargo Imposed by the United States of America Against Cuba.* Resolution Adopted by the General Assembly: A/RES/71/91 (2017). Available from: UNdocs.org.

United Nations, General Assembly. *Necessity of Ending the Economic, Commercial and Financial Embargo Imposed by the United States of America Against Cuba.* Resolution Adopted by the General Assembly: A/RES/71/91 (2018). Available from: UNdocs.org.

UNSC *Resolutions and Draft Resolutions*

United Nations, Security Council. *Resolution Adopted by the Security Council at its 856th Meeting on the 1 April 1960.* S/4300 (1960). Available from: UNdocs.org.

United Nations Yearbooks (UNYB) United Nations, Department of Public Information. *Yearbook of the United Nations.* 1946–1961 and 1991–2016. Available from: https://www.un.org/en/yearbook.

United Nations, Department of Political and Security Council Affairs. *The United Nations and Disarmament 1945–1970.* United Nations Centre for Disarmament Affairs Reference Library. Available from: https://www.un.org/disarmament/publi cations/yearbook/.

Websites

"Apartheid: The National Party's 1947 Manifesto." *Politics Web.* National Party Head Office, May 5, 1947. Available from: www.politicsweb.co.za/news-and-analy sis/apartheid-the-nps-1947-manifesto.

Earnest, Josh. "Press Briefing by Press Secretary Josh Earnest, 12/17/2014." *Obamawhitehouse.archives.gov,* The Obama White House, December 17, 2014, https://obamawhitehouse.archives.gov/the-press-office/2014/12/17/press-brief ing-press-secretary-josh-earnest-12172014.

"General Assembly Demands All States Comply with UN Resolutions Regarding Status of Jerusalem." *UN News Center,* United Nations, December 21, 2017, www.un.org /apps/news/story.asp?NewsID=58330#.WjwqZlSFiqA.

"General Assembly Rules of Procedure." *United Nations,* www.un.org, https://www.un .org/en/ga/about/ropga/.

"Growth in United Nations Membership, 1945-Present." *United Nations,* https://www .un.org/en/about-us/growth-in-un-membership .

"Member States." *United Nations,* http://www.un.org/en/member-states/.

"UN General Assembly Resolutions Tables." Sessions 1–78. *Dag Hammarskjöld Library, United Nations.* https://research.un.org/en/docs/ga/quick/regular.

"UN Charter." *United Nations*, http://www.un.org/en/sections/un-charter/un-char ter-full-text/.

"United Nations Member States." *United Nations*, www.un.org, http://www.un.org/en /member-states/.

"U.S. Public Law 104–114, Statute 814–821." *The Library of Congress*, Congress.gov, March 12, 1996, www.congress.gov/104/plaws/publ114/PLAW-104publ114.pdf.

Secondary Source Work

Academic Publications

Achen, Christopher H., and Duncan Snidal. "Rational Deterrence Theory and Comparative Case Studies." *World politics* 41.2 (1989): 143–169.

Abudula, Abulaiti. "Chinese Foreign Aid and the UNGA Voting Patterns of the Recipients." Dissertation. Sabancı University, 2018.

Adhikari, Bimal. "United Nations General Assembly Voting and Foreign Aid Bypass." *International Politics* 56.4 (2019a): 514–535.

Adhikari, Bimal. "Power Politics and Foreign Aid Delivery Tactics." *Social Science Quarterly* 100.5 (2019b): 1523–1539.

Adler-Nissen, Rebecca. "Stigma Management in International Relations: Transgressive Identities, Norms, and Order in International Society." *International Organization* 68.1 (2014): 143–176.

Alker, Hayward R. "Dimensions of Conflict in the General Assembly." *American Political Science Review* 58.3 (1964): 642–657.

Alker Jr., Hayward R., and M. Bruce. *World Politics in the General Assembly*. New Haven: Yale University Press, 1965.

Al-Mulla, Naif. "International Relations in the United Nations System of Global Governance." Dissertation. Department of Politics and International Studies, University of Cambridge, 2015.

Arangio-Ruiz, Gaetano. "The Normative Role of the General Assembly of the United Nations and the Declaration of Principles of Friendly Relations." Recueil Des Cours, 1972 in Sepúlveda, César. The Reform of the Charter of the Organization of American States. Leiden, the Netherlands: Martinus Nijhoff, 1972.

Ball, M. Margaret. "Bloc Voting in the General Assembly." *International Organization* 5.1 (1951): 3–31.

Bailey, Michael A., Anton Strezhnev, and Erik Voeten. "Estimating Dynamic State Preferences from United Nations Voting Data." *Journal of Conflict Resolution* 61.2 (2017): 430–456.

Bailey, Michael A., and Erik Voeten. "A two-dimensional analysis of seventy years of United Nations voting." *Public Choice* 176.1–2 (2018): 33–55.

Bain, Mervyn J. "Russia and Cuba: "doomed" Comrades?" *Communist and Post-Communist Studies* 44.2 (2011): 111–118.

Bain, Mervyn J. ""Back to the future?" Cuban–Russian relations under Raúl Castro." *Communist and Post-Communist Studies* 48.2–3 (2015): 159–168.

Bain, Mervyn J. "Havana and Moscow, 1959–2009: The Enduring Relationship?" *Cuban Studies* (2010): 126–142.

Bain, Mervyn J. "Havana, Moscow and Washington: A Triangular Relationship at a Time of Change?" *The Latin Americanist* 60.3 (2016a): 323–346.

Bain, Mervyn J. "Moscow, Havana and Asymmetry in International Relations." *Cambridge Review of International Affairs* 29.3 (2016b): 1044–1060.

Bain, Mervyn J. "Havana and Moscow: The Washington Factor." *Fifty Years of Revolution: Perspectives on Cuba, the United States and the World*, 72–89. University Press of Florida, 2012.

Bain, Mervyn J. "Russo–Cuban Relations in the 1990s." *Diplomacy & Statecraft* 29.2 (2018): 255–273.

Barnett, Michael N., and Martha Finnemore. "The Politics, Power, and Pathologies of International Organizations." *International Organization* 53.4 (1999): 699–732.

Bearce, David H., and Stacy Bondanella. "Intergovernmental Organizations, Socialization, and Member-state Interest Convergence." *International Organization* 61.4 (2007): 703–733.

Bennett, Andrew, and Jeffrey T. Checkel. "Process Tracing: From Philosophical Roots to Best Practices." *Simons Papers in Security and Development* 21 (2012): 30.

Bennett, Andrew. *Condemned to Repetition?: The Rise, Fall, and Reprise of Soviet-Russian Military Interventionism, 1973–1996.* MIT Press, 1999.

Bennett, Andrew. "Process Tracing and Causal Inference" (2010). In Harold Brady and David Collier, *Rethinking Social Inquiry.* Rowman and Littlefield, 2010 (second edition).

Beyers, Jan. "Multiple Embeddedness and Socialization in Europe: the Case of Council Officials." *International Organization* 59.4 (2005): 899–936.

Bos, Wilfried, and Christian Tarnai. "Content analysis in Empirical Social Research." *International Journal of Educational Research* 31.8 (1999): 659–671.

Brazys, Samuel, and Diana Panke. "Push and Pull Forces in the UNGA: Analyzing Foreign Policy Change in the Context of International Norms." *International Politics* 54.6 (2017a): 760–774.

Bueno de Mesquita, Bruce. "Measuring Systemic Polarity." *Journal of Conflict Resolution* 19.2 (1975): 187–216.

Burmester, Nicolas, and Michael Jankowski. "One Voice or Different Choice? Vote Defection of European Union Member States in the United Nations General Assembly." *The British Journal of Politics and International Relations* 20.3 (2018): 652–673.

Burmester, Nicolas, and Michael Jankowski. "Reassessing the European Union in the United Nations General Assembly." *Journal of European Public Policy* 21.10 (2014a): 1491–1508.

Burmester, Nicolas, and Michael Jankowski. "The Unsolved Puzzle: Pacific Asia's Voting Cohesion in the United Nations General Assembly—a response to Peter Ferdinand." *The British Journal of Politics and International Relations* 16.4 (2014b): 680–689.

Butler, Larry, and Sarah Stockwell, eds. *The Wind of Change: Harold Macmillan and British Decolonization*. Springer, 2013.

Buzan, Barry. "The English School: an Underexploited Resource in IR." *Review of international Studies* 27.3 (2001): 471–488.

Bull, Hedley. *The Anarchical Society: A Study of Order in World Politics*. Palgrave, 1977.

Bull, Hedley, and Adam Watson. *The Expansion of International Society*. Clarendon Press; Oxford University Press, 1984.

Butterfield, Herbert, Martin Wight, and Hedley Bull. *Diplomatic Investigations: Essays in the Theory of International Politics*. Allen & Unwin, 1966.

Byers, Michael. *Custom, Power and the Power of Rules: International Relations and Customary International Law*. Cambridge University Press, 1999.

Byers, Michael. "Multiple Embeddedness and Socialization in Europe: The Case of Council Officials." *International Organization* 59.4 (2005): 899–936.

Carter, David B., and Randall W. Stone. "Democracy and Multilateralism: The Case of Vote Buying in the UN General Assembly." *International Organization* 69.01 (2015): 1–33.

Chai, Trong R. "Chinese Policy Toward the Third World and the Superpowers in the UN General Assembly 1971–1977: A Voting Analysis." *International Organization* 33.3 (1979): 391–403.

Chayes, Abram, and Antonia Handler Chayes. "On compliance." *International Organization* 47.2 (1993): 175–205.

Checkel, Jeffrey T. "The Constructive Turn in International Relations Theory." *World Politics* 50.2 (1998): 324–348.

Checkel, Jeffrey T. "International Institutions and Socialization in Europe: Introduction and Framework." *International Organization* 59.4 (2005): 801–826.

Checkel, Jeffrey T. "Why Comply? Social Learning and European Identity Change." *International Organization* 55.3 (2001): 553–588.

Clarke, Kevin A. "The Reverend and the Ravens: Comment on Seawright." *Political Analysis* 10.2 (2002): 194–197.

Claude, Inis L. "Collective Legitimization as a Political Function of the United Nations." *International Organization* 20.3 (1966): 367–379.

Claude, Inis L. *Swords Into Plowshares: the Problems and Progress of International Organization*. Random House, 1971.

Collier, David. "Translating Quantitative Methods for Qualitative Researchers: The Case of Selection Bias." *American Political Science Review* 89.2 (1995): 461–466.

Collier, David, and James Mahoney. "Insights and Pitfalls: Selection Bias in Qualitative Research." *World Politics* 49.1 (1996): 56–91.

Cordier, Ander. *Public Papers of the Secretaries General of the United Nations: Volume 7 U Thant 1965–1967.* Columbia University Press, 2010.

Datta, Monti Narayan. "The Decline of America's Soft Power in the United Nations." *International Studies Perspectives* 10.3 (2009): 265–284.

De Lint, George J. *The United Nations: the Abhorrent Misapplication of the Charter in Respect of South Africa.* Kluwer Academic Pub, 1976.

Deitelhoff, Nicole. "The Discursive Process of Legalization: Charting Islands of Persuasion in the ICC case." *International Organization* (2009): 33–65.

Deitelhoff, Nicole, and Linda Wallbott. "Beyond Soft Balancing: Small States and Coalition-Building in the ICC and Climate Negotiations." *Cambridge Review of International Affairs* 25.3 (2012): 345–366.

Deitelhoff, Nicole, and Lisbeth Zimmermann. "Things We Lost in the Fire: How Different Types of Contestation Affect the Robustness of International Norms." *International Studies Review* 22.1 (2020): 51–76.

Devereux, Annemarie. *Australia and the Birth of the International Bill of Human Rights, 1946–1966.* Federation Press, 2005.

Dijkhuizen, Frederieke, and Michal Onderco. "Sponsorship behaviour of the BRICS in the United Nations General Assembly." *Third World Quarterly* 40.11 (2019): 2035–2051.

DiLorenzo, Matthew, and Bryan Rooney. "International Constraints, Political Turnover, and Voting Consistency in the United Nations General Assembly." *Foreign Policy Analysis* (2020).

Dion, Douglas. "Evidence and Inference in the Comparative Case Study." *Comparative Politics* 30.2 (1998): 127–145.

Dixon, William J. "The Emerging Image of U.N. Politics." *World Politics* 34.1 (1981): 47–61.

DeLint, George J. *The United Nations: The Abhorrent Misapplication of the Charter in Respect of South Africa.* Zwolle: Tjeenk Willink, 1976.

Dreher, Axel, Jan-Egbert Sturm, and James Raymond Vreeland. "Global Horse Trading: IMF loans for Votes in the United Nations Security Council." *European Economic Review* 53.7 (2009): 742–757.

Dreher, Axel, Peter Nunnenkamp, and Rainer Thiele. "Does US Aid Buy UN General Assembly Votes? A Disaggregated Analysis." *Public Choice* 136.1–2 (2008): 139–164.

Dreher, Axel, and Jan-Egbert Sturm. "Do the IMF and the World Bank Influence Voting in the UN General Assembly?" *Public Choice* (2012): 363–397.

Dubow, Saul. "Macmillan, Verwoerd, and the 1960 "Wind of Change Speech"." *The Historical Journal* 54.4 (2011): 1087–1114.

Dubow, Saul. "Smuts, the United Nations and the Rhetoric of Race and Rights." *Journal of Contemporary History* 43.1 (2008): 45–74.

Dubow, Saul. "The Commonwealth and South Africa: From Smuts to Mandela." *The Journal of Imperial and Commonwealth History* 45.2 (2017): 284–314.

Dunne, Timothy. *Inventing International Society: A History of the English School.* Springer, 1998.

Eilstrup-Sangiovanni, Mette. *Comments from the Registration Exercise. Department of Politics and International Studies.* University of Cambridge, August 14, 2018.

Elgström, Ole. "Norm Advocacy Networks: Nordic and Like-minded Countries in EU gender and Development policy." *Cooperation and Conflict* 52.2 (2017): 224–240.

Elgström, Ole. "Norm Negotiations. The Construction of New Norms Regarding Gender and Development in EU Foreign Aid Policy." *Journal of European Public Policy* 7.3 (2000): 457–476.

Elo, Satu, and Helvi Kyngäs. "The Qualitative Content Analysis Process." *Journal of Advanced Nursing* 62.1 (2008): 107–115.

Elster, Jon. "Arguing and Bargaining in the Federal Convention and the Assemblée Constituante." In Raino Malnes and Arild Underdal (eds.), *Rationality and Institutions. Essays in Honour of Knut Midgaard*, 13–50. Universitetsforlaget, 1992.

Elster, Jon. *Explaining Social Behavior: More Nuts and Bolts for the Social Scientists.* University of Cambridge Press, 2007.

Elster, Jon. *Explaining Social Behavior: More Nuts and Bolts for the Social Sciences.* Cambridge University Press, 2015.

Ferdinand, Peter. "Rising powers at the UN: an Analysis of the Voting Behaviour of BRICS in the General Assembly." *Third World Quarterly* 35.3 (2014a): 376–391.

Ferdinand, Peter. "Foreign Policy Convergence in Pacific Asia: the Evidence From Voting in the UN General Assembly." *The British Journal of Politics and International Relations* 16.4 (2014b): 662–679.

Finnemore, Martha. "Norms, Culture, and World Politics: Insights from Sociology's Institutionalism." *International Organization* 50.2 (1996): 325–347.

Finnemore, Martha. "Legitimacy, Hypocrisy, and the Social Structure of Unipolarity: Why Being a Unipole Isn't All it's Cracked Up to Be." *World Politics* 61.1 (2009): 58–85.

Finnemore, Martha, and Kathryn Sikkink. "International Norm Dynamics and Political Change." *International organization* 52.4 (1998): 887–917.

Fox, Annette Baker. "The Small States of Western Europe in the United Nations." *International Organization* 19.3 (1965): 774–786.

Freeman, Linda. *The Ambiguous Champion: Canada and South Africa in the Trudeau and Mulroney Years.* University of Toronto Press, 1997.

Foucault, Michel. *The Archaeology of Knowledge: Translated From the French by AM Sheridan Smith.* Pantheon Books, 1972.

Gareau, Frederick H. "Cold-War Cleavages as Seen from the United Nations General Assembly: 1947–1967." *The Journal of Politics* 32.4 (1970): 929–968.

Garfinkel, Alan. *Forms of Explanation*. New Haven: Yale University Press, 1981.

Geddes, Barbara. "How the Cases you Choose Affect the Answers you Get: Selection Bias in Comparative Politics." *Political Analysis,* vol. 2, (1990): 131–150.

Gerring, John. "The Mechanismic Worldview: Thinking Inside the Box." *British Journal of Political Science* 38.1 (2008): 161–179.

Gheciu, Alexandra. "Security Institutions as Agents of Socialization? NATO and the "New Europe"." *International Organization* 59.4 (2005): 973–1012.

Goertz, Gary, and J. Joseph Hewitt. "Concepts and Selection (on) the Dependent Variable." *Goertz (Ibid.)* (2006): 156–179.

Goffman, Erving. *The Presentation of Self in Everyday Life*. Doubleday Anchor Books, 1959.

Goldsworthy, David. "Australian External Policy and the End of Britain's Empire." *Australian Journal of Politics & History* 51.1 (2005): 17–29.

Goldsworthy, David. *Losing the Blanket: Australia and the End of Britain's Empire*. Melbourne University Publishing, 2002.

Goodman, Ryan, and Derek Jinks. "How to Influence States: Socialization and International Human Rights Law." *Duke Law Journal* (2004): 621–703.

Goodman, Ryan, and Derek Jinks. *Socializing States: Promoting Human Rights Through International Law*. Oxford University Press, 2013.

Gong, Gerrit W. *The Standard of Civilization in International Society*. Clarendon Press, 1984.

Guzzini, Stefano. "A Reconstruction of Constructivism in International Relations." *European Journal of International Relations* 6.2 (2000): 147–182.

Hacking, Ian. *The Social Construction of What?* Harvard University Press, 1999.

Hagan, Joe D. "Domestic Political Regime Changes and Third World Voting Realignments in the United Nations, 1946–84." *International Organization* 43.3 (1989): 505–541.

Haydu, Jeffrey. "Making Use of the Past: Time Periods as Cases to Compare and as Sequences of Problem Solving." *American Journal of Sociology* 104.2 (1998): 339–371.

Hayes, Frank. "South Africa's Departure from the Commonwealth, 1960–1961." *The International History Review* 2.3 (1980): 453–484.

Hakimi, Monica. "Constructing an International Community." *American Journal of International Law* 111.2 (2017): 317–356.

Hanrieder, Tine. "The False Promise of the Better Argument." *International Theory* 3.3 (2011): 390–415.

Harbert, Joseph R. "The Behavior of the Ministates in the United Nations, 1971–1972." *International Organization* 30.1 (1976): 109–127.

Haass, Richard. *Economic Sanctions: Too Much of a Bad Thing*. The Brookings Institution. June 1, 1998. Available from: https://www.brookings.edu/research/economic-sancti ons-too-much-of-a-bad-thing/.

Hearder, Jeremy. *Jim Plim: Ambassador Extraordinary: A Biography of Sir James Plimsoll*. Connor Court Publishing, 2015.

Hedström, Peter, and Richard Swedberg, eds. *Social Mechanisms: An Analytical Approach to Social Theory*. Cambridge University Press, 1998.

Hehir, Aidan, and Hillel Neuer. "Help or Hindrance? International Organizations & Human Rights." *Cambridge Middle East and North Africa Forum*. Gonville and Caius College, University of Cambridge. 25 Jan. 2018.

Henshaw, Peter. "Canada and the "South African Disputes" at the United Nations, 1946–1961." *Canadian Journal of African Studies* 33.1 (1999): 1–52.

Hilliker, John, and Donald Barry. *Canada's Department of External Affairs, Volume 2: Coming of Age, 1946–1968*. Vol. 20. McGill-Queen's Press-MQUP, 1995.

Holsti, O. (1968). "Content Analysis." Chapter 16 in G. Lindzey and E. Aronson, (eds.), *The Handbook of Social Psychology*, 2nd edition. Reading, MA: Addison-Wesley.

Hooghe, Liesbet. "Several Roads Lead to International Norms, but Few via International Socialization: A Case Study of the European Commission." *International Organization* 59.4 (2005): 861–898.

Hooijmaaijers, Bas, and Stephan Keukeleire. "Voting cohesion of the BRICS countries in the UN General Assembly, 2006–2014: A BRICS too Far?" *Global Governance: A Review of Multilateralism and International Organizations* 22.3 (2016): 389–408.

Holloway, Steven. "Forty Years of United Nations General Assembly Voting." *Canadian Journal of Political Science* 23.02 (1990): 279–296.

Holloway, Steven. "US Unilateralism at the UN: Why Great Powers Do Not Make Great Multilateralists." *Global Governance* (2000): 361.

Holloway, Steven K., and Rodney Tomlinson. "The New World Order and the General Assembly: Bloc Realignment at the UN in the Post-Cold War World." *Canadian Journal of Political Science* 28.02 (1995): 227–254.

Hovet, Thomas. *Bloc Voting at the United Nations*. Harvard University Press, 1960.

Hsieh, Hsiu-Fang, and Sarah E. Shannon. "Three Approaches to Qualitative Content Analysis." *Qualitative Health Research* 15.9 (2005): 1277–1288.

Hurd, Ian. *After Anarchy: Legitimacy and Power in the United Nations Security Council*. Princeton University Press, 2008.

Hurd, Ian. "Legitimacy and Authority in International Politics." *International Organization* 53.2 (1999): 379–408.

Hurd, Ian. "Legitimacy at the United Nations." Northwestern University, 2011.

Hurd, Ian. "Legitimacy, Power, and the Symbolic Life of the UN Security Council." *Global Governance* 8.1 (2002): 35–51.

Hurd, Ian F. "International Law and the Politics of Diplomacy." *Diplomacy and the Making of World Politics*. Cambridge University Press, 2015,pp. 31–54.

Hurd, Ian. "The Strategic Use of Liberal Internationalism: Libya and the UN sanctions, 1992–2003." *International Organization* 59.3 (2005): 495–526.

Hurd, Ian. "Constructivism." *The Oxford Handbook of International Relations*. Oxford University Press, 2009.

Hurd, Ian. "The UN Security Council and the International Rule of Law." *The Chinese Journal of International Politics* 7.3 (2014): 361–379.

Hyam, Ronald, and Peter Henshaw. *The Lion and the Springbok: Britain and South Africa Since the Boer War*. Cambridge University Press, 2003.

Huldt, Bo. *Sweden, the United Nations and Decolonization*. Esselte Studium, 1974.

Jackson, Richard L. *The Non-aligned, the UN, and the Superpowers*. Praeger Publishers, 1983.

Jin, Xi, and Madeleine O. Hosli. "Pre-and post-Lisbon: European Union voting in the United Nations general assembly." *West European Politics* 36.6 (2013): 1274–1291.

Joachim, Jutta. "Framing Issues and Seizing Opportunities: The UN, NGOs, and Women's rights." *International Studies Quarterly* 47.2 (2003): 247–274.

Johnston, Alastair Iain. "Treating International Institutions as Social Environments." *International Studies Quarterly* 45.4 (2001): 487–515.

Johnston, Alastair Iain. "Conclusions and Extensions: Toward Mid-range Theorizing and Beyond Europe." *International Organization* 59.4 (2005): 1013–1044.

Johnstone, Ian. "Security Council Deliberations: The Power of the Better Argument." *European Journal of International Law* 14.3 (2003): 437–480.

Johnstone, Ian. "Legislation and Adjudication in the UN Security Council: Bringing Down the Deliberative Deficit." *American Journal of International Law* 102.2 (2008): 275–308.

Kim, Soo Yeon, and Bruce Russett. "The New Politics of Voting Alignments in the United Nations General Assembly." *International Organization* 50.4 (1996): 629–652.

Klotz, Audie. Norms in International Relations: The Struggle Against Apartheid. Cornell University Press, 1995.

Ikenberry, G. John, and Charles A. Kupchan. "Socialization and Hegemonic Power." *International Organization* 44.3 (1990): 283–315.

Karnad, Bharat. *India's Nuclear Policy*. Westport, CT: Praeger Security International, 2008.

Karnad, Bharat. "Walking Back Delusional Nuclear Policies." *Strategic Analysis* 42.3 (2018): 181–193.

Keck, Margaret E., and Kathryn Sikkink. "Transnational Advocacy Networks in International and Regional Politics." *International Social Science Journal* 51.159 (1999): 89–101.

Keohane, Robert. *After Hegemony. Cooperation and Discord in the World Political Economy*. Princeton University Press, 1984.

Keohane, Robert. "Political Influence in the General Assembly." *International Conciliation* 36 (1966): 1.

Klotz, Audie. *Norms in International Relations: The Struggle Against Apartheid*. Cornell University Press, 1995.

Klotz, Audie. "Norms and Sanctions: lessons from the Socialization of South Africa." *Review of International Studies* 22.2 (1996): 173–190.

Klotz, Audie. "Norms Reconstituting Interests: Global Racial Equality and US Sanctions Against South Africa." *International Organization* 49.3 (1995): 451–478.

King, Gary, Robert O. Keohane, and Sidney Verba. *Designing Social Inquiry: Scientific Inference in Qualitative Research*. Princeton University Press, 1994.

Krebs, Ronald R., and Patrick Thaddeus Jackson. "Twisting Tongues and Twisting Arms: The Power of Political Rhetoric." *European Journal of International Relations* 13.1 (2007): 35–66.

Krippendorff, Klaus. *Content Analysis: An Introduction to its Methodology*. Sage, 2004.

Koremenos, Barbara, Lipson, Charles, and Snidal, Duncan. *The Rational Design of International Institutions*. Cambridge University Press, 2003.

Kuziemko, Ilyana, and Eric Werker. "How Much is a Seat on the Security Council Worth? Foreign Aid and Bribery at the United Nations." *Journal of Political Economy* 114.5 (2006): 905–930.

Laffey, Mark, and Jutta Weldes. "Beyond Belief: Ideas and Symbolic Technologies in the Study of International Relations." *European Journal of International Relations* 3.2 (1997): 193–237.

Lantis, Jeffrey S. "Agentic Constructivism and the Proliferation Security Initiative: Modeling Norm change." *Cooperation and Conflict* 51.3 (2016): 384–400.

Landler, Mark. "Trump Threatens to End American Aid: 'we're Watching Those Votes' at the U.N." *The New York Times*, 20 Dec. 2017, www.nytimes.com/2017/12/20/world /middleeast/trump-threatens-to-end-american-aid-were-watching-those-votes-at -the-un.html.

Legro, Jeffrey W. "Which Norms Matter? Revisiting the Failure of Internationalism." *International Organization* (1997): 31–63.

LeoGrande, William M. "Normalizing US—Cuba Relations: Escaping the Shackles of the Past." *International Affairs* 91.3 (2015): 473–488.

Lloyd, Lorna. "'A Most Auspicious Beginning': The 1946 United Nations General Assembly and the Question of the Treatment of Indians in South Africa." *Review of International Studies* 16.2 (1990): 131–153.

Lieberson, Stanley. "Small N's and Big Conclusions: An Examination of the Reasoning in Comparative Studies Based on a Small Number of Cases." *Social Forces* 70.2 (1991): 307–320.

Lewis, Jeffrey. "The Janus Face of Brussels: Socialization and Everyday Decision Making in the European Union." *International Organization* 59.4 (2005): 937–971.

Iida, Keisuke. "Third World Solidarity: The Group of 77 in the UN General Assembly." *International Organization* 42.02 (1988): 375–395.

Lijphart, Arend. "The Analysis of Bloc Voting in the General Assembly: A Critique and a Proposal." *The American Political Science Review* 57.4 (1963): 902–917.

Luif, Paul. *EU Cohesion in the UN General Assembly.* Vol. 49. Paris: European Union Institute for Security Studies, 2003.

Lundborg, Per. "Foreign Aid and International Support as a Gift Exchange." *Economics & Politics* 10.2 (1998): 127–142.

Mahoney, James, and Gary Goertz. "The Possibility Principle: Choosing Negative Cases in Comparative Research." *American Political Science Review* 98.4 (2004): 653–669.

Mahoney, James. "The Logic of Process Tracing Tests in the Social Sciences." *Sociological Methods & Research* 41.4 (2012): 570–597.

Mantilla, Giovanni. *Dr Giovanni Mantilla: "We should never take international law at face value".* Interview with Sonaj Hansen. Cambridge Journal of Political Affairs. April 13, 2021. https://www.cambridgepoliticalaffairs.co.uk/interviews/giovanni-mantilla.

Mantilla, Giovanni. "Forum Isolation: Social Opprobrium and the Origins of the International Law of Internal Conflict." *International Organization* 72.2 (2018): 317.

Mantilla, Giovanni. *Lawmaking Under Pressure: International Humanitarian Law and Internal Armed Conflict.* Cornell University Press, 2020b.

Mantilla, Giovanni. "Social Pressure and the Making of Wartime Civilian Protection Rules." Forthcoming article in the *European Journal of International Relations* 26.2 (2020a). Available from: https://www.repository.cam.ac.uk/handle/1810/295034.

Mantilla, Giovanni. "The Protagonism of the USSR and Socialist States in the Revision of International Humanitarian Law." *Journal of the History of International Law/ Revue d'histoire du droit international* 21.2 (2019): 181–211.

Mantilla, Giovanni. "Independent Report by Giovanni Mantilla." Examination for the PhD Degree. Department of Politics and International Studies. University of Cambridge. Cambridge. October 15, 2021.

Marin-Bosch, Miguel. "How Nations Vote in the General Assembly of the United Nations." *International Organization* 41.4 (1987): 705–724.

Martin, Allan and Hardy, Patsy. *Robert Menzies a Life* (ACLS Humanities E-Book). Melbourne University Press, 1993. Available from: http://idiscover.lib.cam.ac.uk.

McAdam, Doug, John D. McCarthy, and Mayer N. Zald, eds. *Comparative Perspectives on Social Movements: Political Opportunities, Mobilizing Structures, and Cultural Framings.* Cambridge University Press, 1996.

McGillion, Chris. "Inter-Alliance Conflict: Cuba, Europe, and America's Global Reach." In *Cuba, the United States, and the Post-Cold War World: The International Dimensions of the Washington-Havana Relationship,* edited by Morris Morley and Chris McGillion, 2005, pp. 97–147.

McNamara, Kathleen. "Rational Fictions: Central Bank Independence and the Social Logic of Delegation." *West European Politics* 25.1 (2002): 47–76.

Mearsheimer, John. "Anarchy and the Struggle for Power" (2001). In Colin Elman and Michael Jenson, *The Realism Reader*. Routledge, 2014.

Mearsheimer, John. "The False Promise of International Institutions." *International Security* 19.3 (1994): 5–49.

Meyers, Benjamin D. "African Voting in the United Nations General Assembly." *The Journal of Modern African Studies* 4.02 (1966): 213–227.

Meyer, John W., and Brian Rowan. "Institutionalized Organizations: Formal Structure as Myth and Ceremony." *American Journal of Sociology* 83.2 (1977): 340–363.

Miller, N.A. "Trying to Stay Friends: Cuba's Relations with Russia and Eastern Europe in the Age of US Supremacy." University Press of Florida, 2005, pp. 59–96.

Milliken, Jennifer. "The Study of Discourse in International Relations: A Critique of Research and Methods." *European Journal of International Relations* 5.2 (1999): 225–254.

Morley, Morris H., and McGillion, Chris. *Unfinished Business: America and Cuba after the Cold War, 1989–2001*. Cambridge: Cambridge University Press.

Morley, Morris H., and McGillion, Chris. *Cuba, the United States, and the Post-Cold War World: The International Dimensions of the Washington-Havana Relationship*. University Press of Florida, 2005.

Mosler, Martin, and Niklas Potrafke. "International Political Alignment during the Trump Presidency: Voting at the UN general Assembly." *International Interactions* (2020): 1–17.

Most, Benjamin A., and Harvey Starr. "Case Selection, Conceptualizations and Basic Logic in the Study of War." *American Journal of Political Science* 26.4 (1982): 834–856.

Murphy, Philip. *Party Politics and Decolonization: The Conservative Party and British Colonial Policy in Tropical Africa 1951–1964*. Oxford University Press, 1995.

Nathanson, Nathaniel L. "Constitutional Crisis at the United Nations: The Price of Peace-Keeping." *The University of Chicago Law Review* 32.4 (1965): 621–658.

Neuendorf, Kimberly A. *The Content Analysis Guidebook*. Sage, 2016.

Obydenkova, Anastassia V., and Vinícius G. Rodrigues Vieira. "The Limits of Collective Financial Statecraft: Regional Development Banks and Voting Alignment with the United States at the United Nations General Assembly." *International Studies Quarterly* 64.1 (2020): 13–25.

O'Malley, Alanna. "India, Apartheid and the New World Order at the UN, 1946–1962." *Journal of World History* 31.1 (2020): 195–223.

Onuf, Nicholas Greenwood. *World of Our Making: Rules and Rule in Social Theory and International Relations*. Routledge, 2012.

Ovendale, Ritchie. "Macmillan and the Wind of Change in Africa, 1957–1960." *The Historical Journal* 38.2 (1995): 455–477.

Ovendale, Ritchie. "The South African Policy of the British Labour Government, 1947–51." *International Affairs (Royal Institute of International Affairs 1944-)* 59.1 (1982): 41–58.

Panke, Diana. "The UNGA—A Talking Shop? Exploring Rationales For the Repetition of Resolutions in Subsequent Negotiations." *Cambridge Review of International Affairs* 27.3 (2014): 442–458.

Panke, Diana, and Brazys, Samuel. "Why Do States Change Positions in the United Nations General Assembly?." *International Political Science Review* 38.1 (2017b): 70–84.

Panke, Diana, and Ulrich Petersohn. "Why International Norms Disappear Sometimes." *European Journal of International Relations* 18.4 (2012): 719–742.

Parsons, Talcott. *Structure and Process in Modern Societies*. Free Press, 1960.

Pollack, Mark A. "Principal-Agent Analysis and International Delegation: Red Herrings, Theoretical Clarifications and Empirical Disputes." *Bruges Political Research Paper No. 2* (2007).

Powers, Richard J. "United Nations Voting Alignments: A New Equilibrium." *The Western Political Quarterly* 33.2 (1980): 167–184.

Potrafke, Niklas. "Does Government Ideology Influence Political Alignment with the US? An Empirical Analysis of Voting in the UN General Assembly." *The Review of International Organizations* 4.3 (2009): 245–268.

Perkovich, George. *India's Nuclear Bomb: the Impact on Global Proliferation*. University of California Press, 1999.

Petrova, Margarita H. "Rhetorical Entrapment and Normative Enticement: How the United Kingdom Turned from Spoiler into Champion of the Cluster Munition Ban." *International Studies Quarterly* 60.3 (2016): 387–399.

Petrova, Margarita H. "Naming and Praising in Humanitarian Norm Development." *World Politics* 71.3 (2019): 586–630.

Petrova, Margarita H. "Independent Report by Margarita H. Petrova." Examination for the PhD Degree. Department of Politics and International Studies. University of Cambridge. Cambridge. October 14, 2021.

Price, Richard. "Reversing the Gun Sights: Transnational Civil Society Target Land Mines." *International Organization* 52.3 (1998): 613–644.

Ragin, Charles C. *Fuzzy-set Social Science*. University of Chicago Press, 2000.

Rai, Kul B. "Foreign policy and voting in the UN General Assembly." *International Organization* 26.3 (1972): 589–594.

Rapport, Aaron. *Comments from the Registration Exercise*. Department of Politics and International Studies. University of Cambridge. August 14, 2018.

Resende-Santos, João. *Neorealism, States, and the Modern Mass Army*. Cambridge University Press, 2007.

Risse, Thomas. ""Let's Argue!": Communicative Action in World Politics." *International Organization* 54.1 (2000): 1–39.

Rogowski, Ronald. "The Role of Theory and Anomaly in Social Scientific Inference." *American Political Science Review* 89.2 (1995): 467–470.

Rosert, Elvira. "Norm Emergence as Agenda Diffusion: Failure and Success in the Regulation of Cluster Munitions." *European Journal of International Relations* 25.4 (2019): 1103–1131.

Rowe, Edward T. "Changing Patterns in the Voting Success of Member States in the United Nations General Assembly: 1945–1966." *International Organization* 23.02 (1969): 231–253.

Ruggie, John Gerard. "What Makes the World Hang Together? Neo-utilitarianism and the Social Constructivist Challenge." *International organization* 52.4 (1998): 855–885.

Schimmelfennig, Frank. "Strategic Calculation and International Socialization: Membership Incentives, Party Constellations, and Sustained Compliance in Central and Eastern Europe." *International Organization* (2005): 827–860.

Schimmelfennig, Frank. "The Community Trap: Liberal norms, Rhetorical Action, and the Eastern Enlargement of the European Union." *International organization* (2001): 47–80.

Schimmelfennig, Frank. The EU, NATO and the Integration of Europe: Rules and Rhetoric. Cambridge University Press, 2003.

Schwebel, Stephen M. "The Effect of Resolutions of the UN General Assembly on Customary International Law." *Proceedings of the Annual Meeting (American Society of International Law)*. The American Society of International Law, 1979.

Seabra, Pedro, and Edalina Rodrigues Sanches. "South–South Cohesiveness Versus South–South Rhetoric: Brazil and Africa at the UN General Assembly." *International Politics* 56.5 (2018): 585–604.

Seawright, Jason, and John Gerring. "Case Selection Techniques in Case Study Research: A Menu of Qualitative and Quantitative Options." *Political Research Quarterly* 61.2 (2008): 294–308.

Schaefer, Brett, and Anthony Kim. "The U.S. Should Link Foreign Aid and U.N. General Assembly Voting." *The Heritage Foundation* (2011).

Schaefer, Brett, and Anthony Kim. "UN General Assembly: Foreign Aid Recipients Vote Against the US." *The Heritage Foundation* (2013a).

Schaefer, Brett, and Anthony Kim. "Thirty Years of Voting in the U.N. General Assembly: The U.S. Is Nearly Always in the Minority." *The Heritage Foundation* (2013b).

Schaefer, Brett, and Anthony Kim. "The U.S. Should Employ Foreign Aid in Support of U.S. Policy at the U.N." *The Heritage Foundation* (2018).

Schatzki, Theodore R. "Peripheral Vision: The Sites of Organizations." *Organization Studies* 26.3 (2005): 465–484.

Schegloff, Emanuel A. "Naivete vs. Sophistication or Discipline vs. Self-indulgence: A Rejoinder to Billig." *Discourse & Society* 10.4 (1999): 577–582.

Skocpol, Theda, ed. *Vision and Method in Historical Sociology*. Cambridge University Press, 1984.

Searle, John R. *The Construction of Social Reality*. Simon and Schuster, 1995.

Sharman, Jason. *Consultation. Kings College*, University of Cambridge. December 4, 2019.

Sharman, Jason. Email Consultation. University of Cambridge, December 17, 2019.

Smith, Karen Elizabeth, and Katie Verlin Laatikainen, eds. *Group Politics in UN Multilateralism*. Brill | Nijhoff, 2020.

Sosnovsky, Alexandr. "On the Benefit of Routine Professionalism." *Moskovskiye Novosti*, no. 21, 26 May–2 June 1996, p. 5. Cited in Bain, Mervyn J. "Havana, Moscow and Washington: A Triangular Relationship at a Time of Change?" *The Latin Americanist* 60.3 (2016a): 323–346.

Sparti, Davide. *Se un leone potesse parlare: Indagine sul comprendere e lo spiegare*. Firenze: Sansoni, 1992. Cited in Guzzini, Stefano. "A Reconstruction of Constructivism in International Relations." *European Journal of International Relations* 6.2 (June 2000); 147–182.

Stinchcombe, Arthur L. *Constructing Social Theories*. University of Chicago Press, 1987.

Stockman, Frans. *Roll Calls and Sponsorship: A Methodological Analysis of Third World Group Formation in the United Nations*. Sijthoff International Publishing Company, 1977.

Strüver, Georg. "What Friends are Made of: Bilateral Linkages and Domestic Drivers of Foreign Policy Alignment with China." *Foreign Policy Analysis* 12.2 (2016): 170–191.

Stultz, Newell M. "Evolution of the United Nations Anti-Apartheid Regime." *Human Rights. Quarterly* 13 (1991): 1.

Suchman, Mark C. "Managing legitimacy: Strategic and Institutional Approaches." *Academy of Management Review* 20.3 (1995): 571–610.

Suzuki, S. Japan's Socialization into Janus-Faced European International Society. *European Journal of International Relations* 11.1 (2005): 137–164.

Swidler, Ann. "Culture in Action." *American Sociological Review* 51.2 (1986): 273–286.

Tannenwald, Nina. "How Strong Is the Nuclear Taboo Today?" *The Washington Quarterly* 41.3 (2018a): 89–109.

Tannenwald, Nina. "Stigmatizing the Bomb: Origins of the Nuclear Taboo." *International Security* 29.4 (2005): 5–49.

Tannenwald, Nina. "The Nuclear Taboo: The United States and the Normative Basis of Nuclear Non-use." *International organization* 53.3 (1999): 433–468.

Tannenwald, Nina. *The Nuclear Taboo: The United States and the Non-Use of Nuclear Weapons Since 1945*. Cambridge University Press, 2007.

Tannenwald, Nina. "The Vanishing Nuclear Taboo." *Foreign Affairs.* 97 (2018b): 16.

Tennyson, Douglas. *Canadian Relations with South Africa: A Diplomatic History*. University Press of America, 1982.

Teune, Henry, and Adam Przeworski. *The Logic of Comparative Social Inquiry.* New York: Wiley-Interscience, 1970.

Thompson, Alexander. "Coercion Through IOs: The Security Council and the Logic of Information Transmission." *International Organization* 60.1 (2006): 1–34.

Thompson, Alexander. Channels of Power: *The UN Security Council and US Statecraft in Iraq.* Cornell University Press, 2015.

Tocci, Nathalie. "Academia and Practice in European Foreign Policy: What Can we Learn From Each Other? The Hinsley Memorial Lecture." Department of Politics and International Studies. St. Johns College, University of Cambridge. November 6, 2018.

Tocci, Nathalie. *Who is a Normative Foreign Policy Actor?* Brussels: Centre for European Policy Studies, 2008a.

Tocci, Nathalie. "The European Union as a Normative Foreign Policy Actor." In *Who is a Normative Foreign Policy Actor. The European Union and Its Global Partners. Centre for European Policy Studies* (2008b): 24.

Voeten, Erik. "Clashes in the Assembly." *International Organization* 54.2 (2000): 185–215.

Voeten, Erik. "Resisting the Lonely Superpower: Responses of States in the United Nations to US Dominance." *Journal of Politics* 66.3 (2004): 729–754.

Voeten, Erik. "Data and Analyses of Voting in the UN General Assembly" (July 17, 2012). Available at SSRN: http://ssrn.com/abstract=2111149 or http://dx.doi.org/10.2139/ssrn.2111149.

Wang, Te-Yu. "US foreign Aid and UN Voting: An Analysis of Important Issues." *International Studies Quarterly* 43.1 (1999): 199–210.

Waltz, Kenneth N. *Theory of International Politics.* Addison-Wesley Publishing Company Inc., 1979.

Weber, Max. *Gesammelte Aufsätze zur Wissenschaftslehre.* 1988 [1922]. Tübingen: J.C.B. Mohr (Paul Siebeck). Cited in Guzzini, Stefano. "A Reconstruction of Constructivism in International Relations." *European Journal of International Relations* 6.2 (June 2000): 147–182.

Weber, Robert. (1990). *Quantitative Applications in the Social Sciences: Basic Content Analysis.* Thousand Oaks, CA: SAGE Publications Ltd.

Weinberg, Darren. "The Epistemological Foundations of Qualitative Social Research I." Social Science Research Methods Centre, University of Cambridge. October 16, 2017.

Weinberg, Darren. "The Epistemological Foundations of Qualitative Social Research II." Social Science Research Methods Centre, University of Cambridge. October 18, 2017.

Weinberg, Darren. "Language and Social Practice: An Introduction to Conversation Analysis." Social Science Research Methods Centre, University of Cambridge. January 23, 2018.

Weinberg, Darren. "Ordinary Talk." Social Science Research Methods Centre, University of Cambridge. January 30, 2018.

Weinberg, Darren. "Institutional Talk." Social Science Research Methods Centre, University of Cambridge. February 5, 2018.

Wendt, Alexander. "Anarchy is What States Make of It: The Social Construction of Power Politics (1992)." *International Theory*, 129–177. London: Palgrave Macmillan, 1995.

Wendt, Alexander. *Social Theory of International Politics*. Cambridge University Press, 1999.

Wang, Te-Yu. "US foreign Aid and UN Voting: An Analysis of Important Issues." *International Studies Quarterly* 43.1 (1999): 199–210.

Wittkopf, Eugene R. "Foreign Aid and United Nations Votes: A Comparative Study." *American Political Science Review* 67.03 (1973): 868–888.

Woo, Byungwon, and Eunbin Chung. "Aid for Vote? United Nations General Assembly Voting and American Aid Allocation." *Political Studies* (2017): 0032321717739144.

Xun, Pang, and Wang Shuai. "The International Political Significance of Chinese and US Foreign Aid: As Seen in United Nations General Assembly Voting." *Social Sciences in China* 39.1 (2018): 5–33.

Zakaria, Fareed. "The Rise of Illiberal Democracy." *Foreign Affairs* 76 (1997): 22.

Zarakol, Ayşe. "Ontological (in) Security and State Denial of Historical Crimes: Turkey and Japan." *International relations* 24.1 (2010): 3–23.

Zarakol, Ayşe. "What Made the Modern World Hang Together: Socialisation or Stigmatisation?" *International Theory* 6.2 (2014): 311–332.

Zimbalist, Andrew. "Teetering on the Brink: Cuba's Current Economic and Political Crisis." *Journal of Latin American Studies* 24.2 (1992): 407–418.

Zinnes, Dina A. "Three Puzzles in Search of a Researcher: Presidential Address." *International Studies Quarterly* 24.3 (1980): 315–342.

Zürn, Michael, and Jeffrey T. Checkel. "Getting Socialized to Build Bridges: Constructivism an Rationalism, Europe and the nation-state." *International Organization* 59.4 (2005): 1045–1079.

News

Adams, Frank. "Indians Supported in African Dispute: U.N. Committee Votes to Ask Governments to Talk It Over and Make Their Reports." *The New York Times*. ProQuest Historical Newspapers. November 18, 1947. Available from: https://idiscover.lib.cam .ac.uk.

Ahren, Ralph. "Austrian Far-right Leader Sympathetic to Israel on Jerusalem Recognition." *TimesofIsrael.com*, The Times of Israel. December 11, 2017, https://www.timesofisrael.com/austrian-far-right-leader-backs-moving-embassy-to -jerusalem-in-sentiment/.

Anderson, David. "U.N. Soft in Plea to South Africa: Motion, Voted 43 to 0. Urges Parley with New Delhi on Indians' Status in Union." *The New York Times*. ProQuest Historical Newspapers. December 10, 1955. Available from: https://idiscover.lib.cam .ac.uk.

"Apartheid 'Doomed': Strong Words by Mr. Menzies." *The Guardian*. ProQuest Historical Newspapers. April 11, 1961. Available from: https://idiscover.lib.cam.ac.uk.

"Assembly Stalled on Discrimination: India Sees Moral Victory After 2 Proposals Fail of Majority in South African Case." *The New York Times*. ProQuest Historical Newspapers. November 21, 1947. Available from: https://idiscover.lib.cam.ac.uk.

Barrett, George. "South Africa Hits Indian 'Slaughter': U.N. Delegate Turns on His Attacker on Trustee Row—Gets Reprimand From Chair." *The New York Times*. ProQuest Historical Newspapers. November 12, 1948. Available from: https://idisco ver.lib.cam.ac.uk.

Brewer, Sam. "U.N. Will Debate Atomic Arms Ban: Political Group to Discuss African-Asian Plea Today." *New York Times*. November 8, 1961. ProQuest Historical Newspapers. Available from: https://idiscover.lib.cam.ac.uk.

Brewer, Sam. "U.N. Adopts Bans on Nuclear Arms Over U.S. Protest." *New York Times*. November 25, 1961. ProQuest Historical Newspapers. Available from: https://idisco ver.lib.cam.ac.uk.

Brewer, Sam. "U.S. and Britain, in Shift at U.N. Support Appeal to South Africa." *The New York Times*. ProQuest Historical Newspapers. October 12, 1963. Available from: https://idiscover.lib.cam.ac.uk.

"Britain Off The Fence." *The Guardian*. ProQuest Historical Newspapers. April 6, 1961. Available from: https://idiscover.lib.cam.ac.uk.

"British Decision 'Not Unexpected'." Support for Antiapartheid move in U.N. *The Guardian*. ProQuest Historical Newspapers. April 7, 1961. Available from: https: //idiscover.lib.cam.ac.uk.

Beaumont, Peter. "US Will "Take Names of Those Who Vote to Reject Jerusalem Recognition"." *Theguardian.com*, The Guardian. December 21, 2017. https://www .theguardian.com/us-news/2017/dec/20/us-take-names-united-nations-vote-to-rej ect-jerusalem-recognition

"Bush Renews Waiver of Helms-Burton Provision." *PBS NewsHour*. July 17, 2001. www .pbs.org/newshour/politics/politics-july-dec01-cuba_07-17.

"Canadian Criticism of South Africa: But no Commonwealth Expulsion Move." *The Guardian*. ProQuest Historical Newspapers. February 6, 1960. Available from: https: //idiscover.lib.cam.ac.uk.

"Cuba: President's Title III Decision on Helms-Burton Act." *U.S. Department of State Archive*. July 16, 1999. https://1997-2001.state.gov/regions/wha/fs_990716_cuba_title III.html.

Dewan, Angela, Jordan, Carol, and Veselinovic, Milena. "These Are the Countries Expelling Russian Diplomats." *CNN*. October 22, 2018. edition.cnn.com/2018/03/26/europe/full-list-of-russian-diplomats-expelled-over-s-intl/index.html.

Dyer, Evan. "UN Vote Today on Jerusalem Presents Dilemma for Trudeau Government." *CBCnews*, CBC/Radio Canada. December 21, 2017. www.cbc.ca/news/politics/un-vote-us-jerusalem-canada-1.4459354.

"FAE: Trends." USID. *FAE: Dashboard*. https://2012-2017.usaid.gov/data/dataset/54687 edc-5876-45c3-84a0-9c0aa509c8fe.

"General Assembly Overwhelmingly Adopts Resolution Asking Nations Not to Locate Diplomatic Missions in Jerusalem | Meetings Coverage and Press Releases." *United Nations*, United Nations. December 21, 2017. www.un.org/press/en/2017/ga11 995.doc.htm.

Green, David B. "Fact Check: Why Israeli UN Envoy's Speech on Jerusalem Missed the Mark." *Haaretz.com*. December 22, 2017. https://www.haaretz.com/israel-news /2017-12-22/ty-article/fact-check-why-israeli-un-envoys-speech-on-jerusalem-mis sed-the-mark/0000017f-f504-d460-afff-ff66c4230000.

Hayman, F. H. "White Supremacy." *The Guardian*. June 6, 1960. Available from: https://idiscover.lib.cam.ac.uk.

Landau, Noa. "Haley Warns UN Members: Trump "Will Be Watching" Vote on U.S. Recognition of Jerusalem." *Haaretz.com*, Haaretz News. December 20, 2017. https://www.haaretz.com/israel-news/2017-12-20/ty-article/haley-warns-un-memb ers-trump-will-be-watching-un-vote-on-jerusalem/0000017f-f45a-d044-adff-f7fb8 3830000

Lewis, Ori. "Netanyahu Hosts U.S. Embassy Celebrations in Jerusalem, But Most Diplomats Absent." *Global News*, Global News. May 13, 2018. globalnews.ca/news/ 4205924/us-embassy-jerusalem-celebrations-netanyahu/.

Lynch, Colum. "Haley Warns Diplomats on Jerusalem: Trump Is Watching You." *Foreign Policy*. December 19, 2017. https://foreignpolicy.com/2017/12/19/haley-warns-dip-lomats-on-jerusalem-trump-is-watching-you/.

"India Denounces Apartheid to U.N.: Warns South African Racial Policy May Cause Conflict—Says Only Reds Gain." *The New York Times*. ProQuest Historical Newspapers. December 7, 1954. Available from: https://idiscover.lib.cam.ac.uk.

"India Firm on South Africa Issue: Delegates Prepare For Stiff Fight In U. N. Assembly." *The Times of India*. ProQuest Historical Newspapers. October 3, 1948. Available from: https://idiscover.lib.cam.ac.uk.

"India Groups Bids U.N. Outlaw South Africa." *The New York Times*. ProQuest Historical Newspapers. May 29, 1950. Available from: https://idiscover.lib.cam.ac.uk.

"Indian in UN Hits South Africa Act: Mme. Pandit, Envoy to the U.S. Condemns the Segregation of Her 300,000 Countrymen." *The New York Times*. ProQuest Historical Newspapers. November 15, 1950. Available from: https://idiscover.lib.cam.ac.uk.

"India's Move On South-West Africa Fails: Sensation Caused by Cuban Withdrawal of Amendment." *The Times of India.* ProQuest Historical Newspapers. November 21, 1948. Available from: https://idiscover.lib.cam.ac.uk.

"India Renews Charges: Asks U.N. Assembly Action on Conditions in South Africa." *The New York Times.* ProQuest Historical Newspapers. July 18, 1948. Available from: https://idiscover.lib.cam.ac.uk.

"India Resists Controls on Atom Station: Dispute with UN Agency." *The Guardian.* August 10, 1962. ProQuest Historical Newspapers. Available from: https://idisco ver.lib.cam.ac.uk.

"Informal Talks on Racial Issue." *The Guardian.* ProQuest Historical Newspapers. May 4, 1960. Available from: https://idiscover.lib.cam.ac.uk.

Jamali, Fadhil. 1950. Quoted in *The New York Times.* "Indian in UN Hits South Africa Act: Mme. Pandit, Envoy to the U.S. Condemns the Segregation of Her 300,000 Countrymen." November 15. Accessed via ProQuest Historical Newspapers. Available from: https://idiscover.lib.cam.ac.uk.

Hamilton, Thomas. "U.N. on South Africa. Hammerskjold Faces Difficult Task in Mission to Ease Segregation." *The New York Times.* ProQuest Historical Newspapers. April 3, 1960. Available from: https://idiscover.lib.cam.ac.uk.

"Hillary Clinton Urges Congress to Lift to Embargo on Cuba." *Bloomberg.Com*, Bloomberg. July 31, 2015. www.bloomberg.com/news/videos/2015-07-31/hillary-clin ton-calls-for-lifting-of-cuba-trade-embargo.

Klapper, Bradley, and Matthew Lee. "U.S. Weighs Abstention on Cuba Embargo Vote at U.N." *Orange County Register*, Orange County Register. September, 21, 2015. www.ocr egister.com/2015/09/21/us-weighs-abstention-on-cuba-embargo-vote-at-un/.

"Labour Motion of Censure." *The Guardian.* ProQuest Historical Newspapers. March 23, 1961. Available from: https://idiscover.lib.cam.ac.uk.

Lippman, Thomas. "Clinton Suspends Provision of Law That Targets Cuba." *Washingtonpost.com.* January 4, 1997. https://www.washingtonpost.com/arch ive/politics/1997/01/04/clinton-suspends-provision-of-law-that-targets-cuba/34c72 745-e0d4-4076-850f-ddde1bfa7959/.

Maclellan, Nancy. "India, South Africa seek Settlement: Delegates of Two Dominions Discuss Minority Question Amicably in U.N. Lounge." *The New York Times.* ProQuest Historical Newspapers. September 20, 1947. Available from: https://idiscover.lib .cam.ac.uk.

"Malan Calls U.N. Cancer: Says Organization is Eating at Peace of the World." *The New York Times.* ProQuest Historical Newspapers. October 22, 1953. Available from: https://idiscover.lib.cam.ac.uk.

Marsh, Sarah. "Exclusive: U.S. House Democrats urge Biden to revert to Obama-era Cuba detente." Reuters News. March 3, 2021. https://www.reuters.com/article/us -cuba-usa-exclusive-idUSKBN2AV1HS.

Mclaughlin, Kathleen. "U.S. Eases Stand on South Africa: Bid to End Attacks on Race Policy." *New York Times*. ProQuest Historical Newspapers. January 17, 1957. Available from: https://idiscover.lib.cam.ac.uk.

"Menzies Opposed Verwoerd's Step. But Australian Premier Says South African Race Policy Will Prove Unworkable." *The New York Times*. ProQuest Historical Newspapers. March 20, 1960. Available from: https://idiscover.lib.cam.ac.uk.

Middleton, Drew. "Britain's Problem. Officials See South Africa's Decision Raising More Issues Than It." *The New York Times*. ProQuest Historical Newspapers. March 17, 1961. Available from: https://idiscover.lib.cam.ac.uk.

Mogherini, Frederica. "Remarks by HR/VP Mogherini on the announcement by U.S. President Donald Trump on Jerusalem." December 7, 2017. https://eeas.eur opa.eu/headquarters/headquarters-homepage/36962/remarks-hrvp-mogher ini-announcement-us-president-donald-trump-jerusalem_en.

Nair, Ajay, and Greg Heffer. "Who's Standing with the UK? World Leaders React to Tensions with Russia Over Salisbury Spy Poisoning." *Sky News*. March 15, 2018. www .sky.com/story/whos-standing-with-the-uk-world-leaders-react-to-tensions-with -russia-over-salisbury-spy-poisoning-11290160.

"Nehru Will Raise Apartheid Issue." *The New York Times*. May 2, 1960. Available from: https://idiscover.lib.cam.ac.uk.

Netanyahu, Benjamin. "PM Netanyahu's Response to UN General Assembly Vote." Israel Ministry of Foreign Affairs, December 21, 2017. https://mfa.gov.il/MFA/PressR oom/2017/Pages/PM-Netanyahus-response-to-UN-General-Assembly-vote-21 -December-2017.aspx.

News, CBC. ""Canada Calls for Calm" While Abstaining from UN Vote to Nullify U.S. Move on Jerusalem." *CBCnews*, CBC/Radio Canada. December 21, 2017. www.cbc.ca /news/politics/canada-jerusalem-un-1.4460257.

"Nigeria Assails Apartheid." *The New York Times*. ProQuest Historical Newspapers. May 3, 1960. Available from: https://idiscover.lib.cam.ac.uk.

"Parley Step Urged Upon South Africa: Human Rights Angle of India's Case Pressed by Pakistan, Supporting U.S. Appeal." *The New York Times*. ProQuest Historical Newspapers. November 16, 1947. Available from: https://idiscover.lib.cam.ac.uk.

Pick, Hella. ""Ban-the-Bomb" UN Motion: UK Opposition." *The Guardian*. ProQuest Historical Newspapers. November 10, 1961. Available from: https://idiscover.lib.cam .ac.uk.

"Risk of "Big Disaster": Mr Nehru on Apartheid." *The Guardian*. May 7, 1960. ProQuest Historical Newspapers. Available from: https://idiscover.lib.cam.ac.uk.

Teltsch, Kathleen. "Stevenson Chides Critics of U.S. Stand on Africa." *New York Times*. ProQuest Historical Newspapers. July 23, 1963. Available from: https://idiscover.lib .cam.ac.uk.

Teltsch, Kathleen. "U.S. Asks U.N. to Condemn South Africa's Race Policy: Plimpton Says Americans Have Color Problems But Act on Them." *New York Times*. ProQuest Historical Newspapers. October 20, 1962. Available from: https://idiscover.lib.cam .ac.uk.

"'The Final Year': An Inside Account of Diplomacy in the Obama Administration." *The Institute of Politics at Harvard University*. April 26, 2018. iop.harvard.edu/ forum/%E2%80%9C-final-year%E2%80%9D-inside-account-diplomacy-obama-administration.

Trumbull, Robert. "Nehru is Hopeful on Peace Outlook: Says India Will Not Be Aligned With Any 'Bloc'—His Tone on Indonesia More Moderate." *The New York Times*. ProQuest Historical Newspapers. March 24, 1949. Available from: https://idisco ver.lib.cam.ac.uk.

"Rebuff for Mr. Menzies Failure to condemn South Africa." *The Guardian*. ProQuest Historical Newspapers. April 11, 1960. Available from: https://idiscover.lib.cam.ac.uk.

Ronan, Thomas P. "South Africa's Apartheid Policy Stirs Debate on Commonwealth." *The New York Times*. ProQuest Historical Newspapers. March 5, 1961. Available from: https://idiscover.lib.cam.ac.uk.

"Slav Countries Attack South Africa In U. N.: Racial Policy Against Natives Condemned." *The Times of India*. ProQuest Historical Newspapers. November 14, 1948. Available from: https://idiscover.lib.cam.ac.uk.

"South Africa's Dilemma." *The New York Times*. ProQuest Historical Newspapers. October 25, 1962. Available from: https://idiscover.lib.cam.ac.uk.

"South Africa Held in Peril of Riots: U.N. Is Told by India, Urging Inquiry, That Racial Hatred is Growing in Durban." *The New York Times*. ProQuest Historical Newspapers. May 10, 1949. Available from: https://idiscover.lib.cam.ac.uk.

"South Africa Fails in Final U.N. Vote: Assembly Approves Creation of Board on Race Issue—India Hails Decision." *The New York Times*. *ProQuest Historical Newspapers*. December 6, 1952. Available from: https://idiscover.lib.cam.ac.uk.

"Tory Attack on PM Over South Africa. "Share of Blame for Breach."" *The Guardian*. ProQuest Historical Newspaper. April 25, 1961. Available from: https://idiscover.lib .cam.ac.uk.

Udayakumar, Geeta, Mohan, Ganesh, and Kumar, Radha. "Pakistan's Shameful Lie at UN: Ambassador Lodhi Tries to Pass off Palestinian as Pellet Gun Victim from Kashmir." *India Today*. September 23, 2017. indiatoday.intoday.in/story/pakistan-lie-at-un-general-assembly-sushma-swaraj-maleeha-lodhi-rawya-abu-joma-palestine-kashmir/1/1054896.html.

"U.N. Votes to Scan South Africa Bias: Committee Approves Renewal of Committee Despite Warning Nation Won't Cooperate." *The New York Times*. ProQuest Historical Newspapers. December 9, 1954. Available from: https://idiscover.lib.cam.ac.uk.

"U.S. Bars Blanket Pledge." *The New York Times*. ProQuest Historical Newspapers. November 11, 1961. Available from: https://idiscover.lib.cam.ac.uk.

"U.S. Denounces Apartheid." *The Guardian*. ProQuest Historical Newspapers. October 25, 1961. Available from: https://idiscover.lib.cam.ac.uk.

"U.S. Favors Board in African Dispute: 3 More Nations in Accord, but France and 2 Others Oppose Arab-Asian Bloc's Plan." *The New York Times*. ProQuest Historical Newspapers. November 6, 1952. Available from: https://idiscover.lib.cam.ac.uk.

"U.S. leads boycott of UN talks on nuclear weapons ban." *Aljazeera*. November 27, 2017. https://www.aljazeera.com/news/2017/03/leads-boycott-talks-nuclear-weap ons-ban-170327191952287.html.

Voeten, Erik. "For the First Time Ever, the U.S. Will Abstain When the U.N. Votes against Its Embargo on Cuba. That's a Big Deal." *The Washington Post*, WP Company. April 18, 2019. www.washingtonpost.com/news/monkey-cage/wp/2016/10/26/the-u-n -will-vote-against-the-u-s-embargo-on-cuba-for-the-first-time-ever-the-u-s-will -abstain-and-thats-a-big-deal/.

Vinograd, Samantha. "US vs. UN: Who's Taking Sides over Jerusalem and Why?" *CNN*. December 22, 2017. https://edition.cnn.com/2017/12/22/opinions/jerusalem-un -vote-us-bullying-vinograd-opinion/index.html.

"Volte-Face by Mr. Menzies policy on S. Africa at UN." *The Guardian*. ProQuest Historical Newspapers. April 10, 1961. Available from: https://idiscover.lib.cam.ac.uk.

Waggoner, Walter. "Nehru Criticizes Soviet on Testing: Agrees with Stevenson that Atom Blasts are 'Evil'." *New York Times*. ProQuest Historical Newspapers. November 13, 1961. Available from: https://idiscover.lib.cam.ac.uk.

Wilkie, Douglas. ""Australians" Censure of Mr. Menzies. Overdoing Things on S. Africa." *The Guardian*. ProQuest Historical Newspapers. March 23, 1961. Available from: https://idiscover.lib.cam.ac.uk.

Wilkie, Douglas. "Few Regrets in Australia. An Eye on Asian Neighbors." *The Guardian*. ProQuest Historical Newspapers. March 17, 1961. Available from: https://idiscover.lib .cam.ac.uk.

Wilkie, Douglas. "Liberal Critics of Mr. Menzies Conduct of Foreign Policy." *The Guardian*. ProQuest Historical Newspapers. March 30, 1961. Available from: https: //idiscover.lib.cam.ac.uk.

"6 States Back India in South Africa Case." *The New York Times*. ProQuest Historical Newspapers. November 15, 1947. May 10, 1949. Available from: https://idiscover.lib .cam.ac.uk.

Index

www.ingramcontent.com/pod-product-compliance
Lightning Source LLC
Chambersburg PA
CBHW030732280326
41926CB00086B/1183